THAT'S SO GAY!

Perspectives on Sexual Orientation and Gender Diversity Series

HIV+ Sex: The Psychological and Interpersonal Dynamics of HIV-Seropositive Gay and Bisexual Men's Relationships
Edited by Perry N. Halkitis, Cynthia A. Gómez, and Richard J. Wolitski

Sexual Orientation and Mental Health: Examining Identity and Development in Lesbian, Gay, and Bisexual People
Edited by Allen M. Omoto and Howard S. Kurtzman

Lesbian and Gay Parents and Their Children: Research on the Family Life Cycle
Abbie E. Goldberg

That's So Gay! Microaggressions and the Lesbian, Gay, Bisexual, and Transgender Community
Kevin L. Nadal

THAT'S SO GAY!

MICROAGGRESSIONS AND THE LESBIAN, GAY, BISEXUAL, AND TRANSGENDER COMMUNITY

KEVIN L. NADAL

AMERICAN PSYCHOLOGICAL ASSOCIATION • WASHINGTON, DC

Published by
American Psychological Association
750 First Street, NE
Washington, DC 20002
www.apa.org

To order
APA Order Department
P.O. Box 92984
Washington, DC 20090-2984
Tel: (800) 374-2721; Direct: (202) 336-5510
Fax: (202) 336-5502; TDD/TTY: (202) 336-6123
Online: www.apa.org/pubs/books
E-mail: order@apa.org

In the U.K., Europe, Africa, and the Middle East, copies may be ordered from
American Psychological Association
3 Henrietta Street
Covent Garden, London
WC2E 8LU England

Typeset in Meridien by Circle Graphics, Inc., Columbia, MD

Printer: Maple Press, York, PA
Cover Designer: Mercury Publishing Services, Inc., Rockville, MD

The opinions and statements published are the responsibility of the authors, and such opinions and statements do not necessarily represent the policies of the American Psychological Association.

Library of Congress Cataloging-in-Publication Data

Nadal, Kevin L.
  That's so gay! microaggressions and the lesbian, gay, bisexual, and transgender community /
Kevin L. Nadal. — 1st ed.
    p. cm. — (Contemporary perspectives on lesbian, gay, and bisexual psychology.)
  Includes bibliographical references and index.
  ISBN 978-1-4338-1280-4 — ISBN 1-4338-1280-0 1. Sexual minorities—Civil rights.
2. Discrimination. 3. Homophobia. 4. Transphobia. I. Title.

  HQ73.N24 2013
  306.76—dc23
                                            2012033272

British Library Cataloguing-in-Publication Data
A CIP record is available from the British Library.

Printed in the United States of America
First Edition

DOI: 10.1037/14093-000

*This book is dedicated to all children and adolescents
who have ever been bullied for being who they are.
I hope they realize that they are not alone.*

*This book is also dedicated to the little ones in my life,
especially Noah Cruz, Seneca, Mikah, Malcolm,
Jamielyn, Jessiemae, Julianna, Faith, Emmaline,
Danielle, Jordan, Gavin, Noah Zachary, Delaney, Darcy,
Thalia, Bubby, Cammy, Umahon, Ryley, Lani, Elijah,
Tristan, Tyler, Alexander, Angelica, Isabelle, Nelia, Emma,
and Grace. I hope they learn that regardless of how they
identify in the future and regardless of with whom they
fall in love, they were born this way.*

Contents

Foreword
Derald Wing Sue

That's So Gay! Microaggressions and the Lesbian, Gay, Bisexual, and Transgender Community by Professor Kevin Nadal is an exceptional book; it is scholarly, insightful, practical, and destined to change the multicultural landscape of the field. No other text in the field has attempted to apply the conceptual and empirical framework of microaggression research to lesbian, gay, bisexual, and transgender (LGBT) populations; has done it in such a successful and meaningful fashion; or has provided such concrete and practical solutions for individuals, institutions, and our society. Nadal should be commended for this groundbreaking work that will enrich graduate and undergraduate courses in gender studies, LGBT studies, mental health practice, prejudice and discrimination, law and training, social justice, and multiculturalism. The book is written in such a clear and understandable fashion that even the general population will find it enlightening and valuable to their roles as parents, teachers, employers, employees, friends, families, and neighbors.

This book traces how new research on the manifestation, dynamics, and harmful impact of microaggressions on socially devalued groups has become highly relevant to the field of psychology, to education, and to the broader society. *Microaggressions* are the everyday verbal, nonverbal, and environmental slights, snubs, or insults—whether intentional or unintentional—that communicate hostile, derogatory, or negative messages to target persons, based solely on their marginalized group status. Nadal artfully reveals how these hidden messages may invalidate the group identities or experiential reality of target persons, demean them on a personal or group level, communicate that they are lesser human beings, suggest that they do not belong with the majority group, and/or relegate them to inferior status and treatment.

Microaggressions generally are discussed from the perspective of race and racism, but any marginalized group in our society may become a target: LGBT populations, women, individuals with disabilities, members of religious minorities, and so on. Nadal's thesis is that the most detrimental forms of microaggressions are usually delivered by well-intentioned individuals who are unaware that they have engaged in harmful conduct toward a socially devalued group. These everyday occurrences may, on the surface, appear quite harmless, trivial, or be described as "small slights," but research indicates that they have a powerful impact on the psychological well-being of LGBT populations and affect their standard of living by creating inequities in health care, education, and employment.

Seven riveting chapters immediately pull readers into the "storyline" while making the research and concepts understandable even to laypersons. Each chapter is introduced with vignettes that illustrate Nadal's assertions and findings. Readers embark on a journey from the historical evolution of perceptions of LGBT people in the United States and around the world, to defining important terms and concepts related to heterosexism.

Where his book shines, however, is in his unique application of the microaggression model to understanding the life experience of LGBT populations. Here Nadal defines microaggressions, provides concrete examples of their manifestations, and summarizes research (including his own) on their harmful impact on LGBT identity development, mental health, physical health, and quality of life. Because Nadal is at the forefront of microaggression research, he is uniquely qualified to provide a new and innovative model for understanding the microaggressive experiences of LGBT persons. His process model is multidimensional and holistic in nature in that he includes the concept of *intersectionality*, whereby other social group identities (e.g., race, gender, social class) intersect with one another as they influence the perception of microaggressions and mediate or moderate their impact.

Finally, this is not simply an academic treatise that points out problems without providing solutions. Although Nadal provides suggestions throughout each chapter about what can be done to combat microaggressions, his final chapter ("Conclusion: What Can You Do?") provides recommendations for how a variety of institutions, including families, educational settings, workplaces, neighborhoods, and governmental agencies, can prevent or ameliorate microaggressions toward LGBT people.

In summary, kudos to Kevin Nadal for providing a much-needed and valuable resource to our field. This book should be required reading for all who believe in bettering the human condition.

Preface

As I reflect upon my life, I realize that this book is so meaningful to me for many reasons. Perhaps the main reason is because I do consider myself to be one of the lucky ones. When I was 7 years old and struggling with my gay identity, I often wondered if I could ever be happy. Here I was—the only gay person I knew in my family and community. As a child of immigrants who grew up in a huge Filipino American and Catholic family, I had no idea that LGBT—that is, lesbian, gay, bisexual, and transgender—people existed. Sure, I had seen some on TV, but they were often portrayed negatively, and my family definitely did not seem to like them. So when I started to feel that I was different—that I liked "girly" things (e.g., musical theater, beauty pageants, figure skating) and that I was attracted to boys—I felt lost and hopeless. I felt like God was punishing me for something. I felt like I was bad, dirty, and deficient. I felt like my family could never love me and that they would disown me. Worst of all, I felt like I was the only one.

When I was 14, I was bullied, which definitely made things worse. Some kids at my high school must have thought that I was too effeminate or that my voice was too high-pitched. Or maybe they were just jealous that I went to all of the school dances with pretty girls (as friends, of course). I heard the word *faggot* at least once a day, but usually three or four times. Some of the boys made weird high-pitched noises as I walked down the hall, which I discovered was their way of mocking my voice. On a daily basis, these boys asked my female friends if I was gay, why I was gay, and why I just didn't tell everyone. My female friends would tell me, and I would just laugh it off. If I couldn't even admit to myself that I was gay, how would I ever admit it to anyone else? And if I couldn't admit to being gay, how would I ever be able to tell the teachers that I was being harassed? I'd have to tell them that the boys called me a *faggot,* which, in my head, meant that I would be admitting to being something I wasn't ready to face.

There were times when I didn't think I could go on. I had no one to turn to. I had no LGBT role models. Everyone just assumed that because I was a smart Filipino kid, I was fine. No one knew that a part of me was dying inside every single day. No one knew that each day I had to convince myself that it would be worth it to make it to the next. No one knew that I easily could have been an LGBT teen suicide statistic.

I honestly can't tell you how I got through this dark part of my life. The bullying eventually stopped, and the rest of my high school years actually ended up being quite pleasant. But perhaps I went through this daily experience of physically and psychologically feeling the immense pain and sorrow of being victimized so that I would have the opportunity to gain my passion for social justice and equal rights. Perhaps I needed to endure this so that, as an adult, I could feel compassion and empathy for the kids whose reality is daily bullying. Perhaps this needed to be part of my history so that I could help to change the future.

I share this part of my life with you because I hope to personally convey how hurtful it is to be the victim of discrimination. Sadly, childhood bullying was the first of many experiences I have had with being mistreated for who I am. While in my adult life, I react in different ways when I am the victim of prejudice, I always reflect back on how I felt as that 14-year-old boy: hopeless, isolated, and alone. And I wonder what I can do to ensure that no one else ever feels that same way.

These next seven chapters paint a picture of the various ways in which LGBT people can be victimized in their everyday lives. Sometimes the bias behind these incidents will be overt and obvious; other times these experiences can be subtle. Regardless, they have a profound effect on the lives of the people who encounter them. Throughout the text, you will read about a spectrum of experiences of LGBT people. There are case studies, which are composites of experiences of multiple individuals, that describe the complexities of being LGBT, as well as the struggle in dealing with discrimination. There are also quotes and narratives from real LGBT people who have shared their personal stories through literature and in the media. As you read about all of these experiences, I hope you find it in your heart to acknowledge that, even at the time of this writing, discrimination is still a problem that affects all of us. Most important, if we all truly care about the future of our society, I hope that you will do your part to prevent others from perpetuating hate and prejudice so that we can prevent innocent victims from feeling hopeless, isolated, and alone.

Acknowledgments

T
his book holds a special place in my heart for the people who have done so much to enrich my life. First, I'd like to thank the American Psychological Association (APA), particularly Division 44: Society for the Psychological Study of Lesbian, Gay, Bisexual, and Transgender Issues and Y. Barry Chung, for believing in the purpose of this text. I am eternally grateful to my mentor, Derald Wing Sue, not only for his kind Foreword for this book but also for introducing me to the concept of microaggressions and for supporting me over the past decade. I thank all of my mentors for believing in me throughout all of these years, in particular, Jeannett Castellanos, Elizabeth Fraga, Alfiee Breland, and Maureen O'Connor. Thanks to classmates and colleagues who have watched me transform from a young doctoral student to a professor and scholar, while forming meaningful friendships with me along the way. I extend special thanks to Silvia Mazzula, Sidney Smith, David Rivera, Bryant Williams, Munyi Shea, and Melissa J. H. Corpus. I am thankful to my colleagues at John Jay College of Criminal Justice for their support of my research and my life, especially Maureen All-wood, Preeti Chauhan, and Deryn Strange. To my students and former students who have been instrumental in helping me to conduct microaggression research: I hope you realize how grateful I am for you all and how proud I am that you are all becoming the future leaders of psychology. I especially thank Kristin Davidoff, Lindsey Davis, Alexis Forbes, Whitney Fujii-Doe, Katie Griffin, Sahran Hamit, Marie-Anne Issa, Alexis Johnson, Jayleen Leon, David Marshall, Victoria McKenzie, Vanessa Meterko, Amalia Quintanilla, Avy Skolnik, Julie Sriken, Michelle Wideman, Yinglee Wong, and everyone else who has been part of our research team along the way. I thank, too, Vivian Lu and David Wei Zhou, the editors and

creators of *The Microaggressions Project*, not only for providing me with so many real and rich examples of microaggressions for this book but also for creating a forum in which individuals across the world can express themselves and feel validated. Finally, I thank the leaders of the APA's Committee on Lesbian, Gay, Bisexual, and Transgender Concerns, in particular, Michael Mobley, Vic Muñoz, Ellyn Kaschak, and Helen Hsu, for being supportive of my research and allowing me a platform to showcase my work more greatly in the field of psychology.

I have been lucky enough to have family members who have become my friends as well as friends who have become my family. Whether you are one of my LGBT sisters or brothers, or one of our needed allies, you have changed my life. Many thanks, especially to my parents and brothers, who may not have understood at first what it meant to have a gay son or sibling but who I know now wish me nothing but happiness. I also thank other family members: Christiano Tomas Nadal, Ryan Abugan, Jackie Chan, Agnes Fajutagana, Althea Zabal Fiorani, Dana Prado, Gail Prado, Jed Prado, Ryan Punzalan, Terri Rino, Mateo Rynne, Stephanie Rynne, Debbie Rino Santos, Leah Suansing, Julian Tamayo, Pamela Tamayo, Joni Yabut, Glenn Zabal, and Juliet Zabal.

I am grateful to my friends for their never-ending laughs, hugs, and support. Thank you, Andrea Lozada and Jonathan Stefiuk, for the extra words of encouragement and much-needed work breaks, and Tracy Barlow Meyer and Risë Nelson, for the unconditional cheerleading and support. Much love also to James Alba, Laila Alchaar, Clarissa Aljentera, Dalene Alojipan, Jason Barrios, Annalisa Burgos, Michelle Camaya, Ryan Cantorna, Melissa Cariño, Sharon Chia Claros, Hanna Crespo, Lorial Crowder, E. J. David, Mathilda De Dios, Ben de Guzman, Aubrey Deperio, Mimi Docena, Lauren Fisher, Beverly Fontillas, JoAnn Garcia, Debbie Green, Thea Green, Kathleen Claire Guiang, Claudia Huerta, Cara Jacobson, Angela Kim, Cara Koerber, Sophia Kong, Jennifer Kuwabara, Kelsey Lebrun, Lilian Liu, Marcia Liu, Kristine Magat, Bernadette Manzano, Dina Maramba, Daniel Mercado, Jeff Myers, Yael Nitkin-Kaner, Marie Obaña, John Pasquarello, Laura Romo, Melissa Lara Valdez, Nicole Watkins, and Yeun Mi Yim.

To the past and present leaders and organizers of the LGBT community, thank you for your conviction, perseverance, and passion, and especially for your willingness to advocate for all our voices to be heard. To the various LGBT people who have participated in my research studies, thank you for sharing your stories and representing our greater community. To my students, professors, peers, and colleagues who have voiced their opinions and perspectives on a number of LGBT topics in the classroom, workshops, and conferences, thank you for always pushing me to learn, reflect, and think critically about different worldviews. Last but not least, to all LGBT people who I have ever encountered: Thank you for existing.

Maraming salamat (many thanks) from the bottom of my heart.

THAT'S SO GAY!

Introduction

Ryan is a 32-year-old gay, White, Jewish American man who has been working as a college administrator at a large university in a rural area for the past 5 years. Although he loves his current job as an administrator on campus, he sometimes feels uncomfortable with the types of homophobic language and behaviors that he notices in the office. Sometimes coworkers will say things like "That's so gay" when talking about something that is embarrassing or appalling. Other times coworkers will assume that Ryan is heterosexual and ask him whether he has a girlfriend or if they can set him up on a date with their female friend or family member.

Ryan is upset with this entire situation and decides that he wants to address this issue. He schedules an appointment with the provost of the university (a White American heterosexual woman) to discuss his concerns about the heterosexism he experiences. When talking with the provost, Ryan is told that he "shouldn't let things like that bother him" and that he "should try not to be so sensitive." Ryan feels misunderstood

DOI: 10.1037/14093-001
That's So Gay! Microaggressions and the Lesbian, Gay, Bisexual, and Transgender Community, by K. L. Nadal

and invalidated. He leaves the office feeling lost, hopeless, and angry all at the same time.

Stephanie is a 28-year-old Asian American woman who is currently in a romantic relationship with a 27-year-old African American lesbian named Debbie. Stephanie identifies as bisexual and has done so since she was 18 years old. Over the past 10 years, Stephanie has had relationships with both women and men; however, for the past 4 years, she has dated women almost exclusively. She had two other romantic relationships with women before Debbie, with whom she has been exclusive for the past year. Both women accept the other's sexual identity and are currently in a happy monogamous relationship.

Stephanie decides to bring Debbie to her 10-year high school reunion. Although some of Stephanie's current friends know she is bisexual, many of her classmates had not heard. At the reunion, Stephanie sees one of her old classmates, Thomas (with whom she was friends during most of her adolescence), and she decides to approach him. After they greet each other, Stephanie introduces Debbie as her girlfriend. Thomas astonishingly replies with "What? Are you a lesbian?", to which Stephanie replies, "Well, no; I'm actually bisexual, but I don't think that really matters, does it?" Thomas laughs and says, "Well, I guess not . . . So— I'm single, and you two are very beautiful women. What are you both doing later?" Stephanie and Debbie look at each other and roll their eyes; they say goodbye politely, feeling belittled and upset.

Agnes is a 20-year-old Latina transgender woman who is visiting her local metropolitan university for the first time. After attending a community college for the past 2 years, she is interested in transferring to a local 4-year university to pursue a career in fashion design. Thus, she is visiting several campuses within a 50-mile radius that offer her major. Agnes makes an appointment to see the local admissions counselor, so that she can discuss requirements, financial aid, and other logistical information.

When Agnes first arrives on campus, she realizes that she has to first check in with a security guard. When she reaches the front desk, the security guard looks at her, snickers, and asks to see her identification. Without hesitation, she pulls out her driver's license and hands it to him. Because Agnes's photo on the ID is one of her before her gender reassignment surgery, the man says to her, "This isn't you. This is a man!" Agnes replies with "I know . . . I'm transgender—but that *is* me." The security guard hesitates, looks her up and down, and says, "Wait, so do you have a penis?" Agnes, embarrassed, tries to politely answer his question by replying, "I really don't think that's any of your business."

However, because she knows he has the authority to let her into the building, she refrains from yelling at him or getting visibly upset. He eventually lets her check in, smiling condescendingly as she walks through the turnstile. Agnes leaves feeling dehumanized, furious, puzzled, and hurt.

Microaggressions: The New Face of Discrimination

Each of these opening vignettes represents a *microaggression* (sometimes, a series of microaggressions). In recent years, there has been an increase in literature that describes this subtle, unconscious, and unintentional discrimination that is experienced by people of color; women; lesbian, gay, bisexual, and transgender (LGBT) people; religious minorities; people with disabilities; and people of other marginalized groups. In contrast to outright assaults and other crimes, or prejudicial treatment motivated by fear or dislike of "the other," microaggressions are "brief and common-place daily verbal, behavioral, or environmental indignities, whether intentional or unintentional, that communicate hostile, derogatory, or negative slights and insults toward members of oppressed groups" (Nadal, 2008, p. 23). Research has found that microaggressions can occur in various settings and have detrimental impacts on the individuals who experience them (see Sue, 2010, for a review).

Although there are myriad ways that racism, sexism, heterosexism, and genderism manifest differently, many authors in the fields of psychology and education have described a new trend in discrimination. Because of changes in public opinion and policy in the United States, it has become unacceptable and offensive for Americans to express blatant discriminatory thoughts, statements, or behaviors toward minority groups, in particular, in public settings. People of majority backgrounds (e.g., White Americans, men, heterosexuals) may believe that they are good people who believe in equality and may choose not to associate with those who are blatantly racist, sexist, or heterosexist. For example, because most White Americans associate the term *racism* with White supremacist groups, they may view themselves as nonracist and fail to recognize the biases and stereotypes that they hold about people of color (Dovidio, Gaertner, Kawakami, & Hodson, 2002). Similarly, many heterosexual people may consider themselves to be good and open-minded people because they do not engage in hate crimes or blatant discrimination toward LGBT people; however, they still "may be oblivious to the ways that they harass or insult LGBT individuals (or allow others to)"

(Nadal, Rivera, & Corpus, 2010, p. 219). So, although political correctness may seem positive in that it may lead to fewer instances of blatant discrimination (e.g., hate crimes; racial, sexist, and homophobic slurs), it may also result in the lack of awareness of one's unconscious or subconscious biases and unintentional behaviors.

According to Sue et al. (2007), three forms of microaggressions are proposed to exist. The first kind, *microassaults,* are defined as the use of explicit derogations either verbally or nonverbally, as demonstrated through name-calling, avoidant behavior, or discriminatory actions toward the intended victim. For example, maliciously calling a person of Asian descent "Oriental" or telling a Latino person to "go back where you came from" are both forms of a microassault. The second type, *microinsults,* are often unconscious and are described as verbal or nonverbal communications that convey rudeness and insensitivity and demean a person's heritage or identity. For instance, when a person with a disability is spoken to in a condescending tone, or when a woman is told she is not capable of something, a subtle message is sent that these individuals are inferior to the dominant group (i.e., able-bodied persons or men). The last type of microaggressions, called *microinvalidations,* are also often unconscious and include communications that exclude, negate, or nullify the realities of individuals of oppressed groups. An example may include a White professor telling a student of color that she or he complains about racism too much. Such a message, although seemingly innocuous, indirectly invalidates the racial realities that a person of color faces on a regular basis.

These same three microaggression categories can be applied to the experiences of LGBT people (Nadal, Rivera, & Corpus, 2010). Perhaps the most common forms of microassaults are the homophobic slurs that LGBT people hear on a regular basis. Overhearing words like *faggot* or *dyke*—which are commonplace phrases heard by LGBT youth in their school systems (Gay, Lesbian, and Straight Education Network, 2010)—can be hurtful to LGBT individuals, regardless of whether the term is used jokingly or is directed at them. Microinsults, which are often unconscious and unintentional, can affect LGBT people in myriad ways. For example, a subtle glare of disgust or shock when an LGBT couple is displaying affection to each other conveys that person's feelings of discomfort or disapproval toward LGBT people. Similarly, if a coworker or family member consistently refers to a transgender person by the wrong pronoun (particularly when it had already been addressed or corrected), a message is sent that the enactor does not see the importance of such language, does not accept the transgender person's identity, or both. Finally, an example of a microinvalidation (or a statement that excludes, negates, or nullifies LGBT experiences) would include, for example, a heterosexual person vehemently denying that she or he is homophobic after an LGBT person confronts her or him about a biased statement or behavior.

Previous studies that have examined microaggressions have investigated the impacts of racial microaggressions on people of color (e.g., Nadal, 2011; Nadal, Escobar, Prado, David, & Haynes, 2012; Pierce, Carew, Pierce-Gonzalez, & Willis, 1978; Sue, Bucceri, et al., 2009; Sue, Capodilupo, & Holder, 2008; Sue, Lin, et al., 2009; Sue, Nadal, et al., 2008) and multiracial people (Nadal, Wong, Griffin, et al., 2011). Researchers have also examined gender microaggressions and women (Capodilupo et al., 2010; Nadal, 2010a; Nadal, Hamit, Lyons, Weinberg, & Corman, in press), religious microaggressions and religious minorities (Nadal, Griffin, Hamit, Leon, Tobio, & Rivera, 2012; Nadal, Issa, Griffin, Hamit, & Lyons, 2010), and ability microaggressions and persons with disabilities (Keller & Galgay, 2010). Finally, in recent years, there has also been an increase in the literature involving sexual orientation and transgender microaggressions toward LGBT people (Balsam, Molina, Beadnell, Simoni, & Walters, 2011; Nadal, Issa, et al., 2011; Nadal, Rivera, & Corpus, 2010; Nadal, Skolnik, & Wong, 2012; Nadal, Wong, Issa, et al., 2011; Shelton & Delgado-Romero, 2011; L. C. Smith, Shin, & Officer, 2012; Wright & Wegner, 2012).

What This Book Covers and Whom It Is For

The purpose of this book is to highlight the microaggressions that LGBT people experience on an everyday basis and to examine the impacts that such experiences have on mental health. In Chapter 1, I review the historical currents of acceptance and rejection of LGBT people in society and trace the research literature on discrimination and microaggressions and their psychological effects through their roots in race and gender studies. In Chapter 2, I comb through a finer level of race, gender, and LGBT research to reveal a taxonomy of microaggressions that I use as a lens to focus the research review and examples in Chapters 3, 4, and 5.

In Chapters 3, 4, and 5, I provide an overview of the current theoretical and empirical literature involving microaggressions toward various subgroups within the LGBT community. Because LGBT people may experience microaggressions differently on the basis of an array of unique identities, Chapter 3 is focused on sexual orientation microaggressions (which are experienced by lesbian, gay, and bisexual people), and Chapter 4 focuses on gender identity microaggressions (which are experienced by transgender and *gender nonconforming* people). In Chapter 5, I discuss how *intersectional identities* influence the types of microaggressions experienced by LGBT people of color, as well as *intersectional microaggressions* based on gender, age, social class, ability, and religion. Furthermore, in Chapters 6 and 7 I offer practical guidance on how to identify and deal with microaggressions as they occur, and I discuss implications for policy and clinical practice.

In this book, my aim is to provide readers with some initial insight into the different types of microaggressions that exist by sharing various examples of all kinds of people within the LGBT community. Vignettes are presented throughout; they describe microaggressions that may be conscious (i.e., the perpetrator may be conscious of her or his actions but might not recognize any negative consequences), unconscious (i.e., the perpetrator may be completely oblivious to her or his statements or behaviors), intentional (i.e., the perpetrator may have been purposeful in hurting or offending another but may not view the behavior as problematic), and unintentional (i.e., the perpetrator did not mean to hurt or offend another person).

For people who have encountered microaggressions, it may be validating to read that others have shared common experiences and have had similar responses. One of the purposes of this book is to normalize these reactions and perhaps provide recommendations for how to deal with these types of microaggressions in the future. For individuals who have committed microaggressions (consciously, intentionally, or not), it may be difficult to recognize that your behaviors may have had a negative impact on others. The purpose of this book is not to shame you or guilt you about some of these past behaviors; instead, I hope that by highlighting how these actions may hurt others, you may become more aware of your unconscious biases, challenge yourself to change behaviors that may negatively affect others, and educate and confront others about microaggressions in order to prevent such instances from occurring in the future.

What You Will Get From This Book

Readers of all backgrounds can benefit from this book. First, it can serve as a resource for researchers who are interested in further understanding how microaggressions may influence LGBT people's everyday lives. By means of the thorough literature review that is presented, researchers will gain a sense of what empirical work has already been done, so that they can brainstorm what future research questions they may want to initiate or build upon. Furthermore, practitioners in the helping professions (e.g., psychotherapists, physicians, social workers) may use the book to attain an understanding of the types of experiences that may negatively affect their clients' or patients' lives. This knowledge can potentially guide their work with their clients or patients, by helping them to build stronger therapeutic relationships and to conceptualize treatment plans that may be effective for them. Educators, trainers, and professors may use this book as a resource for educating their constituents (e.g., students, trainees) about microaggressions in order to advance their work and professional relationships. In addition, managers, consultants, and company presidents may find this book to be a helpful source for understanding the types of dynamics that may affect their work environments.

The book can also be extremely useful to laypeople of all professional and educational backgrounds. I bold key terms and include a glossary in every chapter, as a way of educating others about the varied terminology that has been used in describing the LGBT community. Perhaps people who have a friend or family member who has just "come out of the closet" can find this text beneficial in helping to gaining some basic knowledge about LGBT experiences while learning about the various elements that either strengthen or hurt a relationship. Moreover, in addition to the vignettes, I try to include anecdotal examples from the media, from qualitative research, from nonfiction narratives, and even from the website The Microaggressions Project (http://www.microaggressions.com). In doing so, I hope that people will see how microaggressions may manifest in every element of life and affect the spectrum of LGBT-identified people.

Finally, I include discussion questions throughout each chapter as a way for readers to gain some insight into their own beliefs, opinions, or biases. Because personal attitudes, values, and worldviews may have an impact on the ways that people interact with others, it is important for everyone to critically reflect upon these ideas and how they may influence behaviors. It may be helpful for readers to examine these discussion questions on their own first, before discussing them with peers. For example, perhaps readers can journal about some of their responses to these questions independently before engaging in discussions with classmates or colleagues. This way, individuals will have the opportunity to have thought about their opinions and personal experiences thoroughly before sharing them with others. Educators and instructors may use these discussion questions as a way of eliciting thought-provoking questions from their students and allow honest dialogues to occur. As with any discussion, facilitators must assess participants' sense of personal safety and willingness to share and make decisions accordingly.

For instance, perhaps deeper and emotionally provocative questions can be reserved for groups in which trust and rapport has already been established.

Can You Accidentally Commit a Microaggression?

Think back to the vignettes about Ryan, Stephanie and Debbie, and Agnes. Why did they feel hurt? In the first vignette, Ryan is distressed about the subtle heterosexism that he experiences in the workplace. His coworkers use language that is likely unconscious. When people say "That's so gay," they may not necessarily be thinking about gay people but may have just become accustomed to equating "gay" with "bad" or "weird." And when his coworkers assume that Ryan is heterosexual, they may not be conscious or intentional in conveying their views of heterosexuality as the norm, but they indirectly communicate this in their assumption. When Ryan discusses this issue with the provost at his university, he is met with another microaggression, in which he is essentially told that he is overreacting and that his feelings are invalid. This leads Ryan to feel further alienated, causing him more distress and anxiety. Perhaps Ryan may give up and not complain about these microaggressions to anyone else; however, in doing so, he may repress his emotions, which may cause more anguish and even lead to physiological symptoms. Perhaps Ryan may choose to confront his coworkers (as well as his provost), but perhaps doing so would put his job at risk, creating a tense and hostile work environment that he would not want to work in. Ryan's situation is exemplary of the types of difficult decisions people have to make when they encounter microaggressions in the workplace.

The vignette of Stephanie and Debbie demonstrates the types of microaggressions that can occur in an instant. When Stephanie encounters her old classmate, Thomas, and she introduces Debbie as her girlfriend, two microaggressions occur sequentially. First, he assumes that she is a lesbian and does so in a way that makes Stephanie feel like she has to justify her sexual orientation. Second, Thomas objectifies both women by presuming that they would want to engage in a "three-way" with him. In these types of quick microaggressions, both Stephanie and Debbie have to decide immediately how they want to react. They can choose to get angry and vocalize their disgust to Thomas, or they can choose to smile and pretend that nothing that Thomas had said was wrong or disrespectful. In this case, the couple chose to be polite as possible (albeit rolling their eyes in disapproval). Perhaps they believed that this passive–aggressive behavior would be enough for him to take the hint that they were not pleased with his comment, or perhaps they just wanted the interaction to be over with so that they could continue to have a pleasant evening.

In the third vignette, Agnes faces some difficulty in dealing with a campus security guard. Because her driver's license does not match her current gender presentation, the security guard gives her trouble and asks her an evasive question. He is rude throughout the interaction, often laughing and smiling at her in a condescending and disparaging way. Similar to the case of Stephanie and Debbie, Agnes chooses to remain as calm as possible, primarily because she knows that she needs to cooperate with him in order to arrive at her appointment on time. However, perhaps she begins to wonder whether this is the type of institution that she would want to attend; perhaps other people on campus would be disrespectful toward her and would not be accepting of transgender people in general.

In all three vignettes, the perpetrators of the microaggressions may actually have no idea that they committed a microaggression. Ryan's coworkers who make heterosexist and *heteronormative* comments may not recognize that their actions and statements convey their belief that heterosexuality is the norm while LGBT people and experiences are abnormal. If they were to be confronted regarding their behavior, they may simply say that asking whether someone is married with children is a common question to ask everyone and that phrases such as "That's so gay" are harmless because they aren't actually referring to gay people. Ryan's provost may not realize that by telling him to "not be so sensitive," she invalidated his feelings about his experiences. If challenged regarding her behavior, she might respond that she was trying to empower him and that she would tell anyone who complained about an office conflict to overcome it. Perhaps she might even become defensive and rationalize that she is not heterosexist and views everyone equally. She might even draw from her own experience as a woman, claiming that there is no way that she could be heterosexist or homophobic because she encounters sexism on a regular basis.

Stephanie's old classmate, Thomas, may not recognize that his comment was offensive. Many times, individuals may make hurtful statements and declare, "I was just joking." Perhaps Thomas genuinely thought he was being funny and did not really expect that the two women would take him up on his offer. It is possible that Thomas would say that his statement was a nice one because his intention was to compliment two women whom he thought were attractive. It is also conceivable that Thomas could react with another microaggression by telling the two women that they were both overreacting or that they needed to stop being "angry lesbians"—both which are common experiences for lesbian and bisexual women who confront their microaggressors.

Similarly, the security guard in Agnes's case may simply be unaware of the way he treated her. Like Thomas, he might also say that he was "just joking" with her and that he was simply following standard university procedures because her driver's license photo did not correspond to her real-life physical appearance. On the other hand, perhaps he is aware of his transphobic attitudes and biases and mistreated Agnes intentionally. If this were the case, then perhaps the microaggression was blatant, conscious, and deliberate. However, because Agnes does not know the security guard's exact intention, she simply walks away with a spectrum of feelings, not knowing whether she handled the situation correctly or whether she should take further action. Perhaps if the guard had simply refused to let her into the building and explicitly told her it was because of her gender presentation, she would be better able to label his comments as overt discrimination. If that were the case, she might then report it to someone from the university or seek other appropriate measures. Instead, she leaves feeling confused and agitated, among other emotions.

Furthermore, the vignette of Agnes reflects a common experience for transgender people, in particular, those who have more difficulty in *passing* (i.e., the ability to be regarded as a member of the sex or gender with which one identifies). Many transgender people who do not take hormones or do not go through gender reassignment surgery (often referred to as *pre-operation* or *pre-op* transgender people) may physically appear as their birth sex, which does not match the gender they feel internally and psychologically. Some transgender people who do take hormones and decide to undergo medical procedures (often referred to as *post-operation* or *post-op* transgender people) still do not fully "pass" and experience discrimination accordingly. On the contrary, transgender people who pass may still encounter microaggressions because people may not know of their transgender identity. For instance, if someone who identifies as a transgender man (i.e., female-to-male) underwent surgery and is taking hormones, he may be treated as any cisgender (i.e., non-transgender) man would. In those instances, however, perhaps people may make transphobic or heterosexist remarks to him, or around him, which may then be classified as microaggressions.

Why did the people who hurt Ryan, Stephanie, and Agnes say what they said and act as they did? Microaggressions can be, and often are, unintentional. In addition, people who have been victims of microaggressions in certain situations can perpetrate microaggressions on others unknowingly in other situations. For these reasons, I have aspired to present many scenarios throughout the book featuring people who embrace a diverse set of identities. Do you find yourself in any of these scenarios, either as a victim or as a well-intentioned person who hurts another without meaning to? In either case, it is my hope that the research-based data you find in this book will help you discover new paths of scientific inquiry and that the tools provided for LGBT advocacy can help you identify practical steps to take in furthering equality for all people.

A Brief History of Lesbian, Gay, Bisexual, and Transgender People and Civil Rights

1

D espite the strides toward equality and diversity in the United States with regard to race, gender, religion, and disability, serious disparities still exist and encompass all areas of life, from earning and institutional leadership to basic health and safety. For example, a recent examination of the Fortune 500 list—a report of the top 500 companies in the United States with the largest revenues—revealed that only five of the top CEOs in the country are African American, only seven are Asian American, and only seven are Latino/a (Alliance for Board Diversity, 2008). Similarly, the U.S. Census Bureau (2008) reported that although 40.7% of White Americans earn $50,000 or more annually, only 24.9% of people color earn as much. People of color tend to graduate from college at rates much lower than White Americans (Orfield, Marin, & Horn, 2005), and these groups tend to have higher rates of cardiovascular disease, diabetes, and other health problems (Barr, 2008). In terms of disparities based on **gender**, there has still never been a female president of the United States; only four women have been U.S. Supreme Court justices

DOI: 10.1037/14093-002
That's So Gay! Microaggressions and the Lesbian, Gay, Bisexual, and Transgender Community, by K. L. Nadal

throughout history; and, according to Catalyst (2011a), there are only 15 female CEOs of the Fortune 500 companies. Furthermore, in 2011, women's average salaries were still significantly lower than those of men—women, on average, earned approximately three fourths of what men earned for the same type of work (Catalyst, 2011b). People of various religious minority groups, in particular, Jewish and Muslim people, are still victims of religious-based **hate crimes** in the United States (Nadal, Issa, Griffin, Hamit, & Lyons, 2010), and many institutional barriers continue to block people with disabilities from equal access to employment and other opportunities (Keller & Galgay, 2010).

When it comes to understanding discrimination toward **lesbian, gay, bisexual, and transgender (LGBT)** people, it may appear at first glance that **heterosexism, homophobia, genderism,** and **transphobia** have decreased in U.S. society. One could cite many examples, across the fields of mental health, academia, public safety, the military, and the media. For instance, in 1973, *homosexuality* was officially removed as a psychological diagnosis from the *Diagnostic and Statistical Manual of Mental Disorders,* signifying that a nonheterosexual sexual orientation was no longer viewed as psychologically abnormal (Chernin & Johnson, 2003). In the 1970s, the field of **queer studies** emerged across the United States, legitimizing the history and experiences of LGBT and **queer** people in academia. In 2009, President Barack Obama signed the Matthew Shepard and James Byrd Jr. Hate Crimes Prevention Act, which made it a federal crime to assault an individual because of his or her **sexual orientation** or **gender identity** (Weiner, 2009). In 2010, Obama signed the Don't Ask Don't Tell Repeal Act, reversing the prohibition on serving in the military for gays and lesbians who were *out,* or open about their identity (Bumiller, 2011). Finally, in 2010, the Gay & Lesbian Alliance Against Defamation reported a significant increase in the number of LGBT characters in broadcast television, as well as the highest percentage of LGBT-identified characters in television history (at almost 4%), signifying the shift in American culture toward greater awareness and acceptance of LGBT people (Gay & Lesbian Alliance Against Defamation, 2011).

Although these examples of LGBT equality are viewed as huge gains for the LGBT community, there are many ways that **institutional discrimination** toward LGBT people may be much more blatant than racism and sexism. First, there are still many laws at the federal, state, and local levels that discriminate against LGBT people. For instance, as of 2012, only nine states in the United States allowed same-sex marriage, with an abundance of states that banned it altogether and even more that banned adoption by LGBT individuals and couples. Only 21 out of 50 states outlaw workplace discrimination on the basis of sexual orientation, and only 15 states outlaw workplace discrimination on the basis of gender identity. According to a report by the U.S. General

Accounting Office in 2004, same-sex couples are denied 1,138 benefits, rights, and protections, which negatively influences policies concerning Social Security, taxes, employee benefits, and medical care (Levitt et al., 2009). Furthermore, Title VII of the Civil Rights Act of 1964 prohibits workplace discrimination based on sex, race, color, religion, and national origin, but it does not directly cover sexual orientation or gender identity (Berkley & Watt, 2006). Finally, despite the recent federal legislation protecting LGBT people against hate crimes, only 24 out of 50 states have passed legislation that punishes hate crimes based on sexual orientation (Anti-Defamation League, 2001; Gay, Lesbian, and Straight Education Network, 2010). As a result, equal employment opportunities and other civil rights are not guaranteed for LGBT people in the majority of the states in this country.

One of the other ways in which heterosexism and transphobia may differ vastly from other forms of discrimination is the notion that **interpersonal discrimination** may still be blatant and overt toward LGBT people. Although some literature supports the fact that old-fashioned racism and sexism have become much more subtle in everyday life (Nadal, 2010a, 2011b; Sue et al., 2007), LGBT people may be victims of various forms of overt discrimination, harassment, and **bullying** on a regular basis. One study with 450 participants found that 94% of lesbian, gay, and bisexual participants reported that they had been victimized by a crime at least once in their lifetime, and about one third of those participants reported that the victimization was due to their sexual orientation (Herek, Cogan, & Gillis, 2002). Another study revealed that 20% of lesbian, gay, and bisexual respondents had experienced a personal or property crime because of their sexual orientation, about half had encountered verbal harassment because of their sexual orientation, and one tenth reported having experienced employment or housing discrimination (Herek, 2008). Similarly, the 2009 National School Climate Survey found that nearly nine out of 10 LGBT students experienced harassment at school and that nearly two thirds felt unsafe because of their sexual orientation (Gay, Lesbian, and Straight Education Network, 2010). The same survey reported that nearly one third of LGBT students had skipped at least 1 day of school in the past month to avoid being harassed and that those who were harassed regularly had lower grade-point averages than those who were not harassed as frequently. Although all of these statistics are already significant, they may be even higher because LGBT people tend not to report instances of discrimination when they occur. For example, several studies have found that LGBT people are less likely to report hate crimes than other groups (Bernstein & Kostelac, 2002; Dunbar, 2006; Herek et al., 2002; Peel, 1999), signifying that the number of hate crimes toward LGBT people is likely much higher than what is on record.

Furthermore, many studies have indicated that LGBT individuals experience high levels of psychological distress (or minority stress) because of their sexual orientation or gender identity, which may then lead to various mental health disparities (I. H. Meyer, 1995, 2003). Many studies have suggested that LGBT persons are at higher risk of mental health problems (e.g., depression, substance abuse disorders) and physical health problems (e.g., high blood pressure; Cochran, 2001; Cochran, Mays, Alegria, Ortega, & Takeuchi, 2007; I. H. Meyer, 2003; I. H. Meyer & Northridge, 2007). One study found that LGBT youth had a high prevalence of suicide attempts; 42% of an urban sample and 32% of a rural sample, had attempted suicide at least once in their lifetime (Waldo, Hesson-McInnis, & D'Augelli, 1998). Another study revealed that gay and lesbian individuals were 2.5 times more likely to have a mental health problem in their lifetime compared with their heterosexual counterparts (I. H. Meyer, 2003), whereas another study reported that LGBT youth were more likely to be depressed than their heterosexual counterparts (Almeida, Johnson, Corliss, Molnar, & Azrael, 2009). Thus, it is evident that a large number of LGBT adults and youth are victims of hate crimes and harassment; it is also clear that when individuals do experience such discrimination, their mental health, physical health, and overall well-being are affected significantly.

In the sections that follow, I provide a brief history of LGBT people across the world. I then present a basic introduction to the LGBT civil rights movement in the United States, as a way of providing a context in which to view discrimination throughout the history of our country. I describe the current state of LGBT rights in the United States, discussing the impact of contemporary issues (e.g., bullying, prohibitions of same-sex marriage) and how such issues affect the entire LGBT community. Finally, I share a comprehensive review of the previous psychological literature on LGBT discrimination, including hate crimes, antigay harassment, **modern heterosexism**, transphobia, and genderism, as well as the ways that each of these variables can negatively influence LGBT mental health.

A Brief History of LGBT People and Civil Rights

Although most elementary books documenting the history of world may not state so, LGBT people have existed since the dawn of time. Egyptian hieroglyphics depict the tomb of the royal servants Khnumhotep and Ninkhkhum (who lived in the 25th century BCE); they are credited as being the first same-sex couple identified by name (Dowson, 2006).

In Ancient Greece, same-sex relationships between males were documented as early as the 7th century BCE (Dover, 1978). During this time, a female poet named Sapphos of Lesbos wrote about her relationships with women, which is where the term *lesbian* is believed to have originated (Stern, 2009; Wilhelm, 1995). Famous leaders such as Alexander the Great and Julius Caesar are documented as being bisexual or having had same-sex sexual and romantic relationships, and same-sex marriages in both Rome and Greece are now thought to have been legal and acceptable during their reigns (Stern, 2009). In the Western hemisphere, various Native American tribes are said to have accepted two-spirited, transgender, or **gender nonconforming** people as early as the 1700s (Bronski, 2011; Gilley, 2006). Thus, it is clear that homosexuality, bisexuality, and gender nonconformity are not new concepts but have existed in various parts of the world for centuries.

Although many religious group leaders and members may view homosexuality as an "abomination," it is important to notice that even the Bible describes several same-sex romantic relationships. For example, in the book of Solomon, the characters of David and Jonathan are introduced. David, often known as the underdog who slayed Goliath, was also involved in an intimate relationship with a man named Jonathan:

> The soul of Jonathan was knit to the soul of David, and Jonathan loved him as himself. Saul took him that day and did not let him return to his father's house. Then Jonathan made a covenant with David because he loved him as himself. Jonathan stripped himself of the robe that was on him and gave it to David, with his armor, including his sword and his bow and his belt. So David went out wherever Saul sent him, and prospered; and Saul set him over the men of war. (1 Samuel 18:1–4)

Some people may argue that David and Jonathan's relationship was platonic, whereas others advocate that they did indeed have a romantic relationship, given that their relationship was described in the same ways that other bible passages referred to heterosexual couples (Boswell, 1994).

Furthermore, in the Book of Ruth, a letter is written from Ruth to a woman named Naomi:

> Where you go, I will go; where you lodge, I will lodge; your people shall be my people, and your God my God. Where you die, I will die—there I will be buried. May the Lord do thus and so to me, and more as well, if even death parts me from you. (Ruth 1: 16–17)

Because the passage describes the love of two people, it is often read at many heterosexual Christian wedding ceremonies. Although there may be arguments as to whether Ruth and Naomi did indeed have a romantic relationship, many laypeople assume that the passage describes a heterosexual relationship, when it actually describes a relationship between two women.

Despite these many instances of LGBT people in the history of the world, it became common during the Middle Ages for many countries (including the United States) to criminalize homosexuality and convict LGBT people, in particular, gay men, of **sodomy** (Bronski, 2011). The act of punishing sodomy was common in many European countries (especially those with strong Christian influences). For example, the Buggery Act of 1533, which was enacted by King Henry VIII of England, was an antisodomy law that lasted for 3 centuries and made "buggery" (or sex between two men or sex between a man and a beast) punishable by hanging (Aggrawal, 2008).

In the 19th and 20th centuries, Brazil, France, Indonesia, the Netherlands, and other countries began to decriminalize homosexuality or lessen the punishments for engaging in homosexual acts. However, in most countries (including the United States), LGBT people were still being punished during this time (Bronski, 2011). One notable example occurred in 1895, when famous writer Oscar Wilde was convicted in England for "gross indecency" (i.e., lewd public acts) and sentenced to 2 years of hard labor in prison (Stern, 2009; Wilpers, 2010). Meanwhile, in the United States, the New York Police Department in 1903 raided a gay bathhouse for the first time and arrested 12 men on sodomy charges (Chauncey, 1995). Such instances were commonplace for the next 60 or 70 years. In fact, in the United States, it was not until 1961 that a state (Illinois) removed a sodomy law from its criminal code (Eskridge, 2008). Also, although 20 states in total had repealed their sodomy laws by 1979, many of these repeals came only after long legal battles (Bronski, 2011).

In addition to being punished for sodomy, LGBT people were also criminalized throughout the history of the United States, even if they were not involved in any same-sex sexual behavior. For example, in 1953, President Dwight Eisenhower issued an executive order dismissing all homosexuals from federal employment—which included both civilian and military positions (D'Emilio, 1983). This presidential order only reinforced the notion that LGBT people were not to be trusted, could be treated as second-class citizens, or both.

Furthermore, it was during this time that homosexuality was first believed to be a mental illness, which eventually shaped the stigmas and perceptions of LGBT people today (Institute of Medicine [IOM], 2011). Sigmund Freud is usually credited with first defining sexual orientation as one's attractions toward men or women and defining people as "heterosexuals" and "homosexuals." He also believed that homosexuality represented a less-than-optimal outcome for psychosexual behavior but should not be considered an illness (IOM, 2011). However, in the early 1900s, physicians, sexologists, and psychologists began to view homosexuality as a pathological disorder, in contrast to heterosexuality, which was viewed as normal behavior (IOM, 2011). In the 1950s, the *Diagnostic and Statistical Manual of Mental Disorders* listed homosexuality as a "sociopathic personality disturbance" (American Psychiatric Association, 1952); as a result, for decades psychiatrists and psychologists attempted to "cure" homosexual people of their "disorder" through electroshock therapy, lobotomy, hormone and drug treatments, and even castration (American Psychological Association, 2009; IOM, 2011). None of these treatments were viewed as effective, which eventually led both the American Psychiatric Association and American Psychological Association to discontinue viewing homosexuality as a mental disorder.

While antigay sentiment continued throughout the United States, the Stonewall riots in New York City in 1969 marked the birth of the LGBT rights movement. When New York Police Department police officers raided the Stonewall Inn, a local bar in Greenwich Village, bar patrons (most of who were transgender) fought back, and a riot ensued (Bronski, 2011; Chauncey, 1995). The following year, communities in New York, Los Angeles, and San Francisco began the tradition of holding LGBT pride parades in their local cities, leading to more visibility of LGBT people in major metropolitan areas. In the next few years, several strides toward LGBT rights occurred, including the first out lesbian and gay Americans elected to public office: Kathy Kozachenko in Ann Arbor, Michigan, in 1974; Elaine Noble in Massachusetts in 1975; Allan Separs in Minnesota in 1976; and Harvey Milk in San Francisco in 1977 (Schlitter, 2008).

Contemporary LGBT Issues in the United States

Many issues have emerged over the past 40 years that demonstrate that the fight for LGBT equality is still ongoing. These include the antigay sentiment that initially emerged from the HIV/AIDS crisis in the 1980s and still continues today; the increase in media attention regarding hate crimes after the murder of Matthew Shepard in 1998; the fight for same-sex marriage in the United States, which became more visible at the brink of the 21st century; and the focus on anti-LGBT teen bullying that occurred in 2010.

In the early 1980s, the HIV/AIDS virus was first discovered in New York and San Francisco. Because it was found mostly in gay men, it was initially labeled the "gay disease," which eventually led to a national antigay sentiment, in particular, from religious groups (Bronski, 2011). During this time, gay and bisexual men who were diagnosed with HIV/AIDS began to experience a dual discrimination because of their sexual orientation and their HIV status; many were fired from their jobs, evicted from their homes, and shunned by their family members and friends (Jonsen & Stryker, 1993). In 1988, more than 7,200 incidents of antigay harassment or victimization cases were reported to the National Gay and Lesbian Task Force; out of these, 17% were HIV/AIDS related (Berrill, 1992). This anti-LGBT sentiment is still pervasive in present times, as demonstrated by the members of fundamentalist Christian groups, the most outspoken of which may be the Westboro Baptist Church, based in Topeka, Kansas, whose members have continually and publicly denounced LGBT people, often protesting LGBT events, as well as funerals of LGBT individuals, with signs like "God Hates Fags" or "AIDS Kills Fags."

In 1998, hate crimes against LGBT people came to the forefront when Matthew Shepard, a young gay White man, was killed in Laramie, Wyoming, because of his sexual orientation (Noelle, 2002). Shepard's murder eventually led to changes in hate crime legislation at local, state, and eventually federal levels (Weiner, 2009); however, in the 10 years that followed, hate crimes were still prevalent for lesbian, gay, and bisexual people (Federal Bureau of Investigation, 2008), and were particularly prevalent toward transgender people (Nadal, Skolnik, & Wong, 2012). The first International Transgender Day of Remembrance was held in November 2009 to remember the 200 or more transgender people across the globe who had been killed within that past year and the 600 murders of transgender people throughout U.S. history (International Transgender Day of Remembrance, 2009). Finally, hate crimes against LGBT people of color have also been pervasive over the past decade, but many not have received as much media attention as Shepard's case. For example, in 2003, a 15-year-old lesbian Black American woman named Sakia Gunn was murdered as a result of a hate crime in New Jersey (S. D. Smith, 2004). Although several thousand local individuals (mostly LGBT people of color) attended her funeral services, the event is one that is relatively unknown in public discourse, suggesting that hate crimes committed against individuals who are both racial and sexual minorities may not be nationally publicized, as compared with those against White LGBT individuals.

The fight for same-sex marriage remains a pressing issue for LGBT people in the United States. In 2004, Massachusetts became the first state to legalize same-sex marriage. Over the next several years, five other states and Washington, DC, followed suit, including New York, which in 2011 became the largest state to allow same-sex couples to marry.

In 2012, propositions that allowed same-sex marriage were passed by popular vote in the states of Maryland, Maine, and Washington; it was the first time a proposition in support of same-sex marriage had won. Despite these victories, there have also been setbacks. For example, after the state of California legalized same-sex marriage in June 2008, Proposition 8, which banned same-sex marriage, was passed by voters, although in 2012 the U.S. Circuit of Appeals proclaimed the proposition to be unconstitutional. In 2008, same-sex marriage was banned in two other states, and adoption of children by LGBT people was banned in Arkansas. During this time, many LGBT community members and allies responded with national campaigns like "No H8" (a photo campaign in opposition to Proposition 8) and American Apparel's "Legalize Gay" t-shirt line (which became popularized by LGBT people and allies around the country). The well-known LGBT magazine *The Advocate* proclaimed on its November 16, 2008, cover: "Gay is the New Black," claiming that the struggles of LGBT people are similar to those of African Americans before and after the civil rights movement. At the time of this writing, in 2012, the issue of same-sex marriage is still being debated by political leaders and others.

Bullying has also become an issue in the LGBT community. In fall 2010, six LGBT youth committed suicide in the span of mere weeks. Although teen suicide in itself may not be viewed as a new phenomenon, these six individuals gained national attention because they were all reported to have committed suicide as a result of their peers bullying them because they identified, or were perceived as, LGBT. One of these young people was Seth Walsh, a 13-year-old from California who was bullied every day by his peers at school because he was gay. After being taunted on a regular basis, he finally could not handle the agony and hung himself from a tree in his backyard (Alexander, 2010). At the other end of the country was Tyler Clementi, an 18-year-old college freshman at Rutgers University in New Jersey, whose roommate, without Clementi's knowledge, posted a streaming video of him on the Internet kissing another man. Afterward Clementi, who was allegedly a closeted gay man, reportedly feeling humiliated, posted a suicide note on Facebook, jumped off of the George Washington Bridge, and died (Schwartz, 2010).

After these events, nationally syndicated sex columnist Dan Savage initiated the national "It Gets Better" Campaign (http://www.itgetsbetter.org), which aims to increase awareness about LGBT bullying and discourage LGBT youth from viewing suicide as a viable option. Celebrities and everyday people made videos sharing personal messages and stories of triumph, including members of the LGBT community (e.g., Ellen DeGeneres, Adam Lambert, Neil Patrick Harris) and LGBT allies (e.g., Kathy Griffin, Lady Gaga, President Obama, and Secretary of State Hillary Clinton). During this time, many individuals in the media (e.g., through news programs such as *Anderson Cooper 360* on CNN) began to hypothesize reasons why bullying existed and why bullying toward LGBT youth, specifically, has led to a trend in suicide. Some people explained that school systems were not protecting these LGBT young people or creating a safe space for them, whereas others hypothesized that parents and educators were not teaching their children or students that bullying was wrong and could have severe consequences (Nadal & Griffin, 2011). Regardless of the cause, the surge in teen suicides has led to an increase in media awareness of LGBT bullying, documenting it as a contemporary problem for LGBT people today.

Review of Research on LGBT Discrimination

It is clear that discrimination toward LGBT people has existed in the United States and across the world for a long time and that it has taken both overt and subtle forms. Over the past several decades, a vast amount of literature has described the ways that discrimination has negatively influenced people's mental health. In this section, I explore the previous research regarding the forms of discrimination, focusing in particular on hate crimes toward LGBT people, heterosexism and antigay harassment, and transphobia and genderism. I define each of these terms and describe how each type of discrimination has influenced the lives of LGBT people, as well as how each may lead to mild to severe psychological consequences.

HATE CRIMES

A *hate crime* can be defined as a criminal act in which the victim is targeted because of actual or perceived race, color, religion, national origin, ethnicity, disability, or sexual orientation (Anti-Defamation League, 2001). Examples of various hate crimes include physical assaults, hate mail, threatening phone calls, vandalism, fires, and bombings. As previously noted, hate crimes have been pervasive in the history of LGBT people across the world; however, they may not have been recognized that way until more recent years. It was not until 1990 that the term *hate crime* was officially identified by the U.S. judicial system (Willis, 2008). Although hate crime legislation for LGBT people was first recognized by the federal government in 2009, several state and local jurisdictions still do not recognize hate crimes based on sexual orientation and gender identity (Anti-Defamation League, 2001; Gay, Lesbian, and Straight Education Network, 2010).

Previous authors have described an array of reasons why individuals may perpetrate hate crimes toward LGBT individuals; these include their discomfort with LGBT people, their own discomfort with themselves, and/or their desire to possess power over another individual (Nadal, Rivera, & Corpus, 2010). Although a few studies have examined hate crime bias and motivation, some of the research on individuals' and bystanders' perceptions of hate crimes demonstrates the influence of prejudice against LGBT people. For instance, one study found that antigay attitudes may lead to increased anger toward, and disapproval of, gay hate crime victims, as well as support and empathy for the hate crime perpetrator (Rayburn & Davison, 2002). Another study revealed that individuals with antigay biases often blame gay hate crime victims (Lyons, 2006). Finally, one study found that individuals revealed more empathy for victims of hate crimes based on religion, ethnicity/national origin, and disability than they did for victims of hate crimes based on sexual orientation or race (Griffin, 2010). Thus, it is evident that biases toward LGBT people still exist and may even negatively affect the ways that individuals view LGBT people who have been victimized.

Many types of hate crimes affect LGBT people, including being harassed or physically assaulted at school or a workplace, or in public, for one's sexual orientation or gender identity; having one's home or property vandalized because of one's sexual orientation or gender identity; or being threatened verbally because of one's sexual orientation or gender identity. As mentioned earlier, previous studies have found that a sizable number of LGBT people have been victimized by a hate crime in their lifetime (Herek, 2008; Herek, Cogan, & Gillis, 2002), signifying a high prevalence of such discrimination toward LGBT people. Other studies have found that hate crimes toward gay men are particularly brutal, with patterns of harm such as overkill, brutality, excessive mutilation, and aggravated assault, as well as the use of weapons such as guns, baseball bats, knives, clubs, blunt objects, chains, vehicles, ropes, and restraints (Bell & Vila, 1996; Comstock, 1991; Willis, 2004). One study found that gay and bisexual men were more likely to experience a hate-related sexual assault than gay and bisexual women (Rothman, Exner, & Baughman, 2011). Another study revealed that sexual assaults occurred for both gay men and lesbians, resulted in significantly more posttraumatic stress disorder symptoms than other types of assaults, and had a long-term effect of more than 2 years (Rose & Mechanic, 2002). Finally, one of the few studies that examined the topic found that hate crimes toward transgender and gender nonconforming people is especially violent and that transgender victims are targeted for violence for more complex reasons than simply their **gender variance** (Stotzer, 2008).

As noted earlier, it is necessary to recognize that when examining hate crimes—in particular, hate crimes based on sexual orientation and gender identity—actual statistics are likely incorrect, for a few major reasons. First, hate crimes toward LGBT people tend to go underreported for a number of reasons, in particular, fear of retaliation by their attackers (Dunbar, 2006) and victims' perceived or actual view of homophobia of police officers and the criminal justice system (Bernstein & Kostelac, 2002; Peel, 1999). Furthermore, LGBT people who are still "in the closet" may not want to report hate crimes as a way of avoiding admittance of their sexual identity, whereas others may blame themselves for being victimized. Sometimes, LGBT people who are victimized by hate crimes may experience emotions like shame, guilt, embarrassment, and fear, which then prevents them from reporting hate crimes when they occur (Garnets, Herek, & Levy, 1990; Herek, 2000). Furthermore, because of the heterosexism and transphobia that are often pervasive within the criminal justice system, hate crimes toward LGBT people may not be labeled as such. As a result, it is common for perpetrators to be convicted of less punishable charges and serve shorter sentences because their criminal act was not determined to be a hate crime.

Finally, because hate crimes toward LGBT people are assumed to be based on sexual orientation, they do not fully capture the true experiences of those who identify as transgender. According to the Federal Bureau of Investigation (2008), there were 1,265 reported antibias incidents toward individuals on the basis of sexual orientation in 2007. The breakdown of these hate crimes is as follows: anti-male homosexual (772 incidents), anti-female homosexual (145 incidents), antihomosexual (304 incidents), antiheterosexual (22 incidents), and antibisexual (22 incidents). On the basis of these statistics it is unclear whether hate crimes committed against transgender individuals are ignored or are categorized incorrectly into one of the previous categories. Thus, it is likely that hate crimes toward transgender people are not being accounted for by the FBI or any other institution.

Some research has examined how LGBT individuals experience and cope with hate crimes. Although victims of any crime may experience significant psychological distress, previous research has found that hate crimes toward LGBT victims may also result in more severe psychological consequences than nonbias crimes; these include depression, anxiety, posttraumatic stress disorder, and other mental health disparities in victims (Cheng, 2004; Herek & Capitanio, 1999; McDevitt, Balboni, Garcia, & Gu, 2001). Some research has suggested that gay male victims of hate crimes in particular experience both immediate and long-term physical and psychological consequences (Garnets et al., 1990). First, because of physical injuries that are sustained as a result of violent hate crimes, victims may experience physical symptoms, such as sleep disturbance, headaches, and restlessness; second, they may concurrently experience psychological distress, based on their inability to feel secure, to view the world as orderly and meaningful, and to gain a sense of self-worth (Garnets et al., 1990). Hate crime victims may blame themselves and develop an internalized heterosexism, and they may learn to believe that being gay is bad, deficient, a punishment (Garnets et al., 1990). Furthermore, previous research has suggested that some victims of hate crimes experience psychological distress for long periods of time after their incidents; for example, one study found no significant differences in the amount of anxiety between recent hate crime victims and victims of crimes from more than 5 years earlier (Herek, Gillis, & Cogan, 1999).

Intersectional identities may also play a factor in one's experience of hate crimes. One major study reported that 70% of anti-LGBT murder victims are people of color but only 55% of the total number of reported hate crimes involve LGBT people of color (Dixon, Frazer, Mitchell-Brody, Mirzayi, & Slopen, 2010). Another study found that whereas LGBT people of color from poor and working-class backgrounds may experience more physically violent hate crimes than middle-class LGBT White people, middle-class LGBT White people were more likely to perceive their violent experiences as severe (D. Meyer, 2010). Trans-gender women of color and of lower socioeconomic status may be particularly prone to hate crimes because of their multiple oppressed identities (Stotzer, 2008). Given all of these factors, when examining hate crimes, people must recognize that other social identities may influence the type of hate crime, its severity, the intention of the perpetrator, and the coping mechanisms and psychological outcomes of the victims.

Finally, research has supported the fact that when a hate crime occurs, LGBT people may experience a **vicarious traumatization**. This means that even though LGBT individuals were in no way involved in the hate crime (i.e., they were not present, they do not know the victim personally, and/or they do not live anywhere near the scene of the crime), their fundamental assumptions of benevolence and meaningfulness of the world (and of other people) were challenged (Noelle, 2002). Often, experiencing this vicarious traumatization could negatively affect one's own mental health and self-worth, regardless of any personal connection to the victim (Noelle, 2002). For example, when Steven Lopez Mercado, a 19-year-old teen in Puerto Rico, was found decapitated, dismembered, and partially burned as a result of a hate crime in 2009 (Brice & Sebazco, 2009), it is possible that many LGBT individuals may have been vicariously traumatized. Although they may not have ever met the young Mercado (who some say identified as a gay man but was dressed in **drag** when he was killed), the event may have had negative consequences on their **worldviews** or their mental health. Thus, it is crucial to recognize that hate crimes not only nega-tively influence the victims (or the families of victims) but also can have a detrimental impact on the entire LGBT community.

HETEROSEXISM AND ANTIGAY HARASSMENT

Although it may be less acceptable for hate crimes to occur and more acceptable for people to become tolerant of LGBT people in many parts of the country, a significant level of anti-LGBT sentiment still exists. Earlier in this chapter, I highlighted some of the ways that anti-LGBT sentiment has manifested institutionally (e.g., past sodomy laws, current laws that prevent same-sex marriage). However, in the next sections, I examine the many ways in which LGBT people are discriminated against interpersonally. Although parents today may be more likely to teach their children about equality and diversity, some research suggests that anti-LGBT bias begins as early as childhood and adolescence. For example, one study found that anti-LGBT prejudice increased during one's middle school or junior high school years for both boys and girls and increased even more in the high school years for boys (Baker & Fishbein, 1998). When such prejudice is conscious, it may lead to direct and overt discrimination. However, when such prejudice is unconscious, it may lead to unintentional behaviors that may still signify discrimination.

There are a few ways that researchers have defined biases that individuals may develop about LGBT people at an early age. *Sexual prejudice* has been described as "all negative attitudes based on sexual orientation, whether the target is homosexual, bisexual, or heterosexual" (Herek, 2000, p. 19). However, given the history of heterosexism in the United States, it is more likely that the term would apply to the negative attitudes held by heterosexuals about nonheterosexual people. Some of these prejudices may include negative views about homosexual behavior; people with a homosexual or bisexual orientation; and communities of gay, lesbian, and bisexual people. I assert that *sexual prejudice* is preferable to the term *homophobia*, because *homophobia* implies that one has a fear of homosexuals. *Sexual prejudice*, however, implies not fear but instead a bias toward, aversion to, or negative perception of LGBT people (Herek, 2000).

Antigay harassment has been defined as "verbal or physical behavior that injures, interferes with, or intimidates lesbian women, gay men, and bisexual individuals" (Burn, Kadlec, & Rexer, 2005, p. 24). Antigay harassment may not intentionally be used to be hurtful to LGBT people. For example, when adolescents (in particular, heterosexual young men) use words like *faggot* or *homo* as a way of insulting or hurting others, they may not necessarily be accusing someone of being a homosexual but of being weak or less masculine (Burn, 2000). Similarly, when adolescents (and adults) use the word *gay* as a synonym for bad, undesirable, or weird, individuals may not necessarily be using the term to insult gay people (Burn et al., 2005). However, even though the intention may not be malicious or overtly homophobic in nature, such behavior may indicate one's heterosexist biases. Perhaps someone who uses such terms unconsciously believes that LGBT people are inferior or bad. Although some people may view such language as harmless, anti-LGBT statements should be avoided because they have the potential to cause distress and hurt in the LGBT people who overhear them.

Another term that has been described in the literature is *heterosexist harassment,* or "insensitive verbal and symbolic (but non-assaultive) behaviors that convey animosity toward non-heterosexuality" (Silverschanz, Cortina, Konik, & Magley, 2008, p. 179). The authors conceptualized heterosexist harassment as having two forms: (a) personal (or direct) experiences and (b) ambient (or indirect) experiences. *Personal* experiences are situations in which an individual is directly targeted because of her or his sexual orientation (i.e., being called a "dyke" or "queer" as an insult), whereas *ambient* experiences include situations in which the LGBT individual is indirectly targeted (e.g., someone making offensive jokes about LGBT persons in front of an LGBT individual). In many ways, direct heterosexism aligns with overt sexual prejudice and anti-gay harassment in that all three involve discriminatory behavior that is aimed at LGBT individuals; however, ambient (or indirect heterosexism) is unique in that it describes instances in which an enactor may reveal heterosexual biases without being conscious of any wrongdoing on her or his part. For example, if an individual were to ask a male coworker if he has a wife and kids (in particular, when one does not know anything about the coworker's personal life or sexual orientation), that individual is assuming that heterosexuality is the norm, that being in a heterosexual marriage is a norm, and that all people have the legal right to be married.

Modern heterosexism (Cowan et al., 2005; Walls, 2008) and *modern homonegativity* (M. A. Morrison & Morrison, 2002) are two other terms used to describe the less overt forms of discrimination toward LGBT people. Walls (2008) claimed that modern heterosexism involves all aspects in society in which same-sex-oriented people are marginalized while heterosexual people are celebrated. Similarly, modern homonegativity involves any prejudicial affective or behavioral response directed toward an individual because he or she is (or is perceived to be) homosexual (Cerny & Polyson, 1984; T. G. Morrison, Parriag, & Morrison, 1999).

Finally, the term *sexual stigma* refers to "negative regard, inferior status, and relative powerlessness that society collectively accords to any nonheterosexual behavior, identity, relationship, or community" (Herek, 2007, p. 906). Three types of sexual stigma are said to negatively affect LGBT people, groups, and communities: (a) enacted stigma, (b) felt stigma, and (c) internalized stigma. *Enacted stigma* describes the overt behavioral expression of sexual stigma (i.e., the traditionally overt, old-fashioned heterosexism). *Felt stigma* involves instances in which LGBT individuals may modify their behavior in order to avoid difficult and dangerous situations or enacted stigma. For instance, an LGBT person may not come out of the closet to someone in her family or personal life. Even though this family member may not have said anything overtly heterosexist or biased against LGBT people, the individual may perceive or sense a stigma or discomfort toward LGBT people and thus may not feel comfortable sharing aspects of her **sexual identity.** Finally, *internalized stigma* involves the integration of one's sexual stigma into one's value system. For example, if a person has internalized negative feelings and perceptions of LGBT people, it may be difficult for her or him to acknowledge any homosexual or bisexual feelings that she or he has. Furthermore, if a heterosexual person has internalized a sexual stigma about LGBT people, she or he may behave in discriminatory ways both consciously (e.g., using homophobic slurs) or unconsciously (e.g., not having any LGBT friends, avoiding movies or television shows with LGBT characters).

TRANSPHOBIA AND GENDERISM

Very few empirical studies in psychology have examined the discrimination that may occur toward transgender persons (Hill & Willoughby, 2005; Nadal, Skolnik, & Wong, 2012). As noted previously, hate crimes toward transgender persons are not labeled as such; instead, they are labeled as hate crimes on the basis of sexual orientation. Moreover, whereas LGBT hate crimes are underreported in general, hate crimes toward transgender persons are even more invisible and less likely to be publicized to the general society. For example, although transgender community organizations, media, and websites may keep track of the transgender people who are murdered as a result of a hate crime, these numbers rarely match those listed in police reports or presented via the mainstream media.

Two major terms are used to describe the discrimination and prejudice that transgender persons may experience: (a) *transphobia* and (b) *genderism.* Transphobia can be defined as "an emotional disgust toward individuals who do not conform to society's gender expectations" (Hill & Willoughby, 2005, p 533), whereas genderism is "an ideology that reinforces the negative evaluation of gender non-conformity or an incongruence between sex and gender" (Hill & Willoughby, 2005, p. 534). Transphobia may be a term parallel to *homophobia,* in which individuals are fearful of gay, bisexual, and lesbian people, and genderism may be parallel to *heterosexism,* which describes the subtle ways in which individuals may be prejudiced toward gay, bisexual, and transgender persons. Although it is likely that our changing society may encourage individuals to be less racist, less sexist, and even less heterosexist, it is possible that individuals (heterosexuals and even lesbians, gays, or bisexuals) may maintain transphobic or genderist views. This may be due to the rigidity of **gender roles** in U.S. society, in particular, with **gender role expectations** that dictate the way in which men and women are expected to dress, look, act, and speak in **gender conforming** ways. Furthermore, because gender conforming people tend to fixate on **gender presentation,** many may show overt fear or disgust toward any transgender person.

The few empirical studies and reports regarding transphobic discrimination that do exist have identified many of the obstacles that transgender people experience. One study found that 60% of the participants had been victimized (e.g., experiencing harassment by strangers on the street, verbal abuse, assault with a weapon, sexual assault) because of their gender identity, and 37% reported economic discrimination, such as being fired, demoted, or unfairly disciplined (Lombardi, Wilchins, Priesing, & Malouf, 2001). Another study reported how transgender individuals encountered a range of discriminatory experiences in their families; participants described everything from physical violence to open hostility and indifferent or neglectful responses from parents (Koken, Bimbi & Parsons, 2009). Many participants reported that they were forced out of their homes during adolescence (or chose to leave because of the hostile environment in which they were living), and a majority reported on the hostility with which they were met when they revealed their gender identities. Although the study concentrated primarily on transgender male-to-female women, one could hypothesize that transgender people along the gender spectrum may encounter a similar level of psychological distress when their families reject them.

Perhaps one of the most comprehensive summaries regarding the experiences of discrimination faced by transgender people was a report by the National Center for Transgender Equality & the National Gay and Lesbian Task Force (2009). This study, which included 6,450 transgender people across the United States and Puerto Rico, reported the following findings:

1. Survey respondents experience unemployment at twice the rate of the population as a whole.
2. Ninety-seven percent of those surveyed reported experiencing harassment or mistreatment on the job.
3. Forty-seven percent had experienced an adverse job outcome, such as being fired, not hired, or denied a promotion.
4. Fifteen percent of transgender people in the sample—double the rate of the general population—lived on $10,000 per year or less.

5. Nineteen percent of the sample had been or were homeless, 11% had faced eviction, and 26% had been forced to seek temporary quarters.

These alarming statistics make clear that transgender people are still experiencing extreme discrimination on both interpersonal (e.g., being discriminated against by their coworkers) and systemic levels (e.g., having higher rates of unemployment, poverty, and homelessness).

Although there is a dearth of research on transphobia and genderism, it is important to recognize the ways in which such discrimination is similar to **microaggressions**. First, some discriminatory behaviors toward transgender people may have qualities similar to **microassaults** in that the behaviors are intentional and usually conscious (e.g., calling a transgender person a *she-male* may be representative of an individual's conscious biases against transgender people). If one's biases toward transgender people turn into behaviors that are violent, they are no longer micro but are simply assaultive. On the contrary, transphobia and genderism may be similar to **microinsults** or **microinvalidations** in that they represent the unconscious or subconscious internal feelings individuals may have, which may eventually transform into discriminatory behaviors toward transgender persons. For example, if an individual believes that cross-dressing or sex change operations are wrong, then it is possible that this belief may be noticeable in her or his interpersonal interactions with a cross-dresser or transgender person (e.g., noticeably uncomfortable body language and facial expressions). In addition, because these genderist or transphobic beliefs may be unconscious, individuals may be completely unaware of their prejudices and biases and therefore may even be completely oblivious to their discriminatory actions as well.

PSYCHOLOGICAL CONSEQUENCES OF DISCRIMINATION

An abundance of previous literature has described the psychological distress and mental health problems that LGBT individuals develop as a result of overt sexual discrimination (see I. H. Meyer & Northridge, 2007, for a review). For example, researchers have cited statistics indicating that the bullying and harassment of gay men and lesbians during adolescence can be linked to suicide and suicidal ideation among LGBT youth at rates that are significantly higher than those for their heterosexual counterparts (D'Augelli, 1992; Waldo, Hesson-McInnis, & D'Augelli, 1998), and another study found a positive correlation between amount of gay-related stress exposure and depressive symptoms (R. J. Lewis, Derlega, Berndt, Morris, & Rose, 2001). Other authors have examined the *minority stress* experienced by LGBT people (i.e., the chronic, consistent stress that is related to their stigmatization and marginalization due to sexual orientation or gender identity; I. H. Meyer, 1995, 2003). Such stress can often create hostile and distressing home, work, and social environments, which may potentially result in mental health problems such as depression, anxiety, posttraumatic stress, and internalized homophobia (Herek & Garnets, 2007; Mays & Cochran, 2001; I. H. Meyer, 1995, 2003). Discrimination and stigmatization have also been related to lower self-esteem, fears of rejection, and consistent hiding or concealing of identities (Burn et al., 2005; Rostosky, Riggle, Gray, & Hatton, 2007; Rostosky, Riggle, Horne, & Miller, 2009). One study revealed that when LGBT people fail to recognize, cope with, or acknowledge discrimination, there is an increase in negative health consequences, such as higher blood pressure, more sick days taken from work, or more physician visits (Huebner & Davis, 2007). Another study reported that institutional discrimination, as operationalized by states that ban same-sex marriage, may lead to an increase in mood disorders, generalized anxiety disorder, alcohol use, and psychiatric comorbidity (Hatzenbuehler, McLaughlin, Keyes, & Hasin, 2010). So, not only do LGBT persons experience mental health disparities due to microaggressions and other forms of discrimination, but they also experience problems with their physical health.

More recently, some literature involving sexual orientation microaggressions, gender identity microaggressions, and their impact on mental health has been published. Qualitative studies have supported that when LGBT people experience microaggressions they are susceptible to myriad mental health problems, including depression, anxiety, and posttraumatic stress (Nadal, Issa, et al., 2011; Nadal, Skolnik, & Wong, 2012; Nadal, Wong, Issa, et al., 2011). Another qualitative study found that when LGBT people experience microaggressions in psychotherapy they often feel "uncomfortable, confused, powerless, invisible, rejected and forced or manipulated to comply with treatment" (Shelton & Delgado-Romero, 2011, p. 217). One quantitative study that examined the **intersectional microaggressions** experienced by LGBT people of color (LGBTPOC) found that LGBTPOC microaggressions are linked to depression and that heterosexism in racial/ethnic minority communities may be particularly harmful to the mental health of LGBTPOC (Balsam, Molina, Beadnell, Simoni, & Walters, 2011). Such studies align with the previous literature on overt discrimination toward LGBT people, which has described the various mental health disparities that LGBT people experience due to this minority stress. Although the research on LGBT microaggressions is still in its nascent stages, it is clear that experiencing any type of discrimination has an impact on mental health. Thus, it is important for people to be aware of microaggressions when they occur, in order to protect the mental health of LGBT people and that of all other members of marginalized groups.

Discussion Questions

FOR GENERAL READERS:

1. Have you experienced overt discrimination or hate crimes in your life? How have you reacted to these occurrences? How have they made you feel?
2. Have you experienced microaggressions in your life? How have you reacted to these occurrences? How have they made you feel?
3. Did your educational systems teach you about the history of LGBT people in the United States or in the world? If so, what do you remember? How do you feel about this?
4. How do you think LGBT people are portrayed in the media? How does this make you feel?
5. Do you think that LGBT people are being treated better than they were 10 years ago? 30 years ago? What can be done to improve the lives of LGBT people today?

FOR PSYCHOLOGISTS, EDUCATORS, AND OTHER EXPERTS

1. In what ways do institutional and systemic discrimination negatively affect your clients, students, or constituents?
2. What can you do in your field or organization to combat microaggressions on systemic or institutional levels?

Glossary of Key Terms

Bisexual: Describes an individual whose sexual orientation is based on her or his sexual attractions toward both genders and the identity that is developed on the basis of these attractions.

Bullying: Unwanted, aggressive behavior that involves a real or perceived power imbalance. Such behavior is often repeated (or has the potential to be repeated) over time.

Drag: Term used to describe when an individual dresses in the opposite of her or his gender identity.

Gay: Refers to an individual whose sexual orientation is based on one's sexual attractions toward one's own gender and the identity that is developed based on these attractions. The term is usually reserved for gay men; however, many women may also identify as gay.

Gender: A socially constructed identity that is usually determined by one's biological sex (or whether one has male or female reproductive organs).

Gender Conforming: The trait or identity of adhering to gender role expectations.

Gender Identity: An individual's personal sense of identification as male or female or another gender.

Genderism: The ideology that reinforces the negative evaluation of gender nonconformity or the incongruence between sex and gender.

Gender Nonconforming: The trait or identity of not adhering to gender role expectations.

Gender Presentation: The perceived gender that is assigned to a person on the basis of how she or he is dressed, looks, and/or acts.

Gender Role Expectations: The expectancy for individuals to act, speak, dress, or believe in ways that conform to what is the cultural norm of their birth sex.

Gender Roles: Expectations defined within specific societies and cultures about culturally appropriate behaviors, norms, and values for men and women, based on gender.

Gender Variance: A behavior, style of dress, or identity that does not conform to standard ideas of what it means to be a woman or man.

Hate Crime: Criminal act in which the victim was targeted because of his or her actual or perceived race, color, religion, national origin, ethnicity, disability, or sexual orientation.

Heterosexism: The negative attitudes, biases, and beliefs held by heterosexuals about nonheterosexual people, as well as the discrimination that occurs as a result.

Homophobia: An emotional disgust toward individuals whose sexual orientation is homosexual; a fear of nonheterosexual people.

Institutional Discrimination: The unfair and biased indirect treatment of an individual embedded through the operating procedures, polices, laws, or objectives of systems or large organizations.

Interpersonal Discrimination: The unfair and biased treatment between two or more individuals, based on prejudice or stereotypes.

Intersectional Identities: The unique combination of individuals' multiple social groups (e.g., race, ethnicity, gender, sexual identity, gender identity, age, religion) and the identification, experiences, and worldviews that result from this combination.

Intersectional Microaggressions: Subtle forms of discrimination that are based on individuals' multiple social identities.

Lesbian: A woman whose sexual orientation is based on her sexual attraction toward her own gender and the identity that develops because of these attractions.

LGBT: An acronym used to describe the lesbian, gay, bisexual, and transgender community. Sometimes the acronym *LGBTQ* is used to include queer and questioning people.

Microaggressions: Brief and commonplace daily verbal, behavioral, or environmental indignities, whether intentional or unintentional, that communicate hostile, derogatory, or negative slights and insults toward members of oppressed groups.

Microassaults: The use of explicit derogations, either verbally or nonverbally, as demonstrated through name calling, avoidant behavior, or discriminatory actions toward the intended victim.

Microinsults: Verbal or nonverbal communications that convey rudeness and insensitivity and demean a person's heritage or identity.

Microinvalidations: Communications that are often unconscious and exclude, negate, or nullify the realities of individuals of oppressed groups.

Modern Heterosexism: A system in which all aspects in society in which same-sex-oriented people are marginalized while heterosexual people are celebrated.

Queer: An umbrella term used to describe individuals who are not heterosexual. Although initially *queer* was an antigay epithet, many individuals have reclaimed the word as an empowering identity to identify those who identify as lesbian, gay, bisexual, transgender, or gender nonconforming.

Queer Studies: The study of issues relating to sexual orientation and gender identity, in particular, on the history and experiences of lesbian, gay, bisexual, transgender, and queer people.

Sexual Identity: The process of developing a personal sense of self as a sexual being; encompasses one's sexual orientation and gender identity.

Sexual Orientation: An individual's sense of personal and social identity based on one's sexual attractions, behaviors expressing those sexual attractions, and membership in a community of others who share them.

Sodomy: A sexual act usually involving anal or other copulation and historically involving two men, or a man and an animal.

Transgender: An umbrella term that can be used to refer to anyone for whom the sex she or he was assigned at birth is an incomplete or incorrect description of her- or himself.

Transphobia: An emotional disgust toward individuals who do not conform to society's gender expectations; a fear of transgender or gender nonconforming people.

Vicarious Traumatization: The notion that people of a certain social group will experience moderate to severe psychological distress when a member of the same social group is victimized by a hurtful, disturbing, or malicious act.

Worldview: The collection of beliefs and perspectives from which one sees and interprets the world, based on one's cultural identities and life experiences.

A Review of the Microaggression Literature

2

A s reviewed in Chapter 1, there has been a growth in literature that has supported the hypothesis that discrimination has become more subtle and covert, rather than blatant and overt. So, although it is known that assaults based on race, gender, sexual orientation, ethnicity, and other identities still occur and have detrimental impacts on oppressed groups, it has become less acceptable or "politically correct" for such interactions to transpire in everyday life. For instance, although race-based hate crimes may still be pervasive in American society, some research has found that racism in everyday interpersonal interactions has become more indirect. Such forms of racism have been labeled *modern racism* (McConahay, 1986), *symbolic racism* (Sears, 1988), and *aversive racism* (Dovidio, Gaertner, Kawakami, & Hodson, 2002). Each of these types of racism possesses two similar qualities. First, the discriminatory incidents may be more masked and may not take more obvious forms (e.g., cross burnings, lynchings) that were commonplace and, on some levels, accepted prior to the civil rights movement. Second,

DOI: 10.1037/14093-003
That's So Gay! Microaggressions and the Lesbian, Gay, Bisexual, and Transgender Community, by K. L. Nadal

although race could be easily identifiable in direct and overt racism, in subtly racist interactions both the enactor and recipient may not recognize the salience of race. For example, when James Byrd Jr., an African American, was brutally murdered by three White men in 1998, many observers could label the event as being racially motivated for many reasons, including the following three: (a) the men were identified as White supremacists, (b) they had no personal motivation for murdering Byrd, and (c) they used extreme tactics to ensure that he had a slow and painful death (Wicke & Cohen, 2009).

Contrast an extreme action such as Byrd's murder with an everyday or innocuous interaction between two parties in which one person may perceive something to be racially motivated while the other person may provide many other explanations. For example, imagine a scenario in which a White woman is riding an elevator by herself. After she moves up a few floors, the elevator stops, and an African American man enters. Right at that moment, the woman moves to the right while grabbing onto her purse tightly. People with different perspectives, experiences, and worldviews may have different reactions to and justifications of the woman's behaviors. First, some may believe that perhaps race was not involved in the interaction at all; the woman may have moved to the side of the elevator to allow the man to "have more room," and thus her behavior may even be viewed as being good-natured. In terms of the purse grasping, it is possible that the woman only coincidentally tightened her hold on her purse at the exact moment that the man entered through the door. On the other hand, others might believe that perhaps the woman was aware that she did clutch onto her purse; however, perhaps she is convinced that she would do so if anyone, of any race or gender, entered the same elevator with her. Finally, some may believe it possible that race was indeed the primary motivating factor in the woman's behavior. Perhaps she has biases or prejudices about the man because of what she has been taught about African American men by her family, her friends, or society in general. Because African American men are stereotyped in American society as being criminals (and, often, "dangerous"), perhaps her natural inclination was to assume that he might steal from her, hurt her, or both.

Regardless of the woman's intention, the man who notices her behavior may have an array of reactions. First, he may not think anything of it and may believe that she clutched her purse coincidentally, without any racial motivations. Or perhaps he does notice the behavior and attributes it to race. There is also the potential that he is accustomed to such experiences because they happen to him on a regular basis; therefore, he might claim to not be bothered by the experience. On the other hand, he may perceive the woman's behavior as being race related and may react with an array of emotions, such as anger, frustration, hurt, and sadness, *because* these types of situations occur on a regular basis.

This scenario is much different from the hate crime just mentioned, because the murder of James Byrd Jr. is more clear-cut than the elevator incident. In fact, a jury reached consensus in their decision that the murder was indeed a hate crime motivated by racism. However, in the second scenario, for which there are so many potential explanations, it may be more difficult to label the incident, confront the situation, or both. If the African American man believes that the incident was racially motivated, it may be challenging for him to "prove" his hypothesis to the woman. If he does confront her, she could deny his accusations and provide an alternative rationalization (which in turn could cause him more distress or conflict). However, if the African American man chooses to simply ignore the incident, the woman may not even be aware that her behavior has had an impact on him, and he may regret not addressing the situation. Thus, this man may find himself in a Catch-22–type dilemma in that he recognizes that there may be both positive and negative repercussions for whether he chooses to say something or remain silent. Some people may always confront microaggressions when they occur, leading to consistent arguments (and eventually psychological stress). Other people may rarely or never challenge microaggressions when they occur, which may then lead to internalized emotions such as guilt, resentment, or anger. Still others may learn to pick their battles and confront only the microaggressions that they believe might actually be worth fighting about or about which they believe the perpetrator may actually be willing to listen.

In Chapters 3 through 5, I offer more vignettes similar to the elevator example, to illustrate the complexities of microaggressions. I discuss the processes of dealing with and confronting microaggressions in more detail in Chapter 6. In the present chapter, I review the history of the microaggression literature, beginning with the work that has focused on racial microaggressions and gender microaggressions. I then highlight a taxonomy that outlines the types of microaggressions that lesbian, gay, bisexual, and transgender people (LGBT) experience in their everyday lives.

Review of the Literature on Racial and Gender Microaggressions

Psychiatrist Chester Pierce first introduced the term *racial microaggressions* in the 1970s when he described the subtle discrimination toward African Americans in the media (see Pierce et al., 1978). For the next 30 years or so, the term was described sparsely in various areas of psychology and education. For example, in 2000, researchers described the different types of microaggressions that students of color encounter on various college and university campuses (Solorzano, Ceja, & Yosso, 2000); meanwhile, one author examined the experiences of microaggressions toward Latinos in the criminal justice system, highlighting in particular the influences of color, ethnicity, and race (DeJesus-Torres, 2000). Despite these few efforts, most research involving racial discrimination during this time focused mainly on overt, blatant forms of racism, and the concept of microaggressions was generally invisible in academia.

In 2007, I was a doctoral student at Teachers College of Columbia University in New York, where I was mentored by counseling psychologist Derald Wing Sue. Under Dr. Sue's supervision, I was honored to be part of the team that reintroduced the term *racial microaggressions* in an article in the journal *American Psychologist* (see Sue, Capodilupo, et al., 2007). In this article, we described the ways that the United States has become more politically correct and how racism has become much more masked and covert. We presented a theoretical taxonomy that highlighted the different types of racial microaggressions that people of color may experience in their everyday lives. These included the following:

1. *Alien in one's own land:* Experiences in which people of color may be treated like perpetual foreigners (e.g., telling a Latina/o or Asian American, "You speak good English" or persistently asking a Latina/o or Asian American, "Where are you from?" even though they persistently respond that they are "American").

2. *Criminality/assumption of criminality:* Experiences in which people of color are stereotyped to be deviant or criminals (e.g., a police officer who pulls over an African American male driver for no reason, or a store owner who follows an African American woman around in a store while she is shopping).

3. *Second-class citizen:* Experiences in which people of color receive service that is substandard to that offered Whites (e.g., a taxicab driver who passes a person of color to pick up a White customer, a group of Latina/os or African Americans are seated at the back of the restaurant or near the kitchen when there are plenty of seats in front).

4. *Ascription of intelligence:* Experiences in which African Americans or Latina/os are assumed to be less intellectual or uneducated or when Asian Americans are assumed to be the "model minority" (e.g., when someone condescendingly tells an African American that she or he is "so articulate," when an Asian person is automatically presumed to be good at math or sciences).

5. *Assumption of inferiority:* Experiences in which people of color are assumed to be poor or in substandard careers (e.g., when

people assume that people of color reside in poorer neighborhoods or have a smaller income than Whites).

6. *Colorblindness:* Experiences in which people of color are told by Whites that they "don't see" race (e.g., after a person of color confronts a White person on a racist incident, the White person replies, "That's absurd. I don't see color; I just see you!").

7. *Denial of racial reality:* Statements in which someone invalidates the experiences with racism that people of color encounter regularly (e.g., a White person telling a woman of color that she is paranoid or "oversensitive" to racial issues).

8. *Pathologizing cultural values/communication styles:* Experiences in which people of color are viewed as abnormal or deviant for their cultural behaviors, traditions, or ways of communicating (e.g., someone tells an Asian person to "be more aggressive; you're in America now" or insults a Latina student for the cultural food she brings to lunch).

9. *Denial of individual racism:* Statements in which someone defensively denies that she or he is racist or engaged in racist behaviors (e.g., after being confronted about a microaggression, someone says, "I'm not racist. One of my best friends is Black!").

10. *Environmental racial microaggressions:* Subtly racially discriminatory messages that are communicated through institutions, media, government, and other systems (e.g., when the media portray people of color in stereotypical or negative ways, when corporations do not have any people of color in any leadership positions).

Since this taxonomy was originally presented, a number of studies focusing on racial microaggressions have emerged in the fields of psychology, counseling, and education. These include studies involving Asian Americans (Sue, Bucceri, Lin, Nadal, & Torino, 2008), African Americans (Sue, Capodilupo, & Holder, 2008; Sue, Nadal, Capodilupo, Lin, Rivera, & Torino, 2008; Watkins, LaBarrie, & Appio, 2010), Latina/os (Rivera, Forquer, & Rangel, 2010; Yosso, Smith, Ceja, & Solorzano, 2009), indigenous peoples (Hill, Kim, & Williams, 2010), multiracial people (Nadal, Wong, Griffin, et al., 2011), Filipino Americans (Nadal, Escobar, et al., 2012), and students of color in general (Sue, Lin, Torino, Capodilupo, & Rivera, 2009). Literature on racial microaggressions has even begun to emerge in other fields, including nursing (Hall & Fields, 2012), human services (Gosine & Pon, 2012), and social work (Takahashi, 2007). A racial microaggression measure, the Racial and Ethnic Microaggression Scale, which encompasses six subscales to quantitatively identify racial microaggressions that people of color may encounter in their everyday lives, has been published (see Nadal, 2011b).

While these publications and subsequent studies that have focused on racial microaggressions were emerging, dialogues regarding microaggressions that affected other marginalized groups were initiated. Sue and Capodilupo (2008) extended their microaggression framework to include microaggressions toward people of color, women, and LGBT people. In 2010, I presented a comprehensive taxonomy on gender microaggressions that was specific to women (see Nadal, 2010a). This taxonomy was based primarily on the previous literature involving everyday sexism (Swim, Hyers, Cohen, & Ferguson, 2001); overt, covert, and subtle sexism (Swim & Cohen, 1997; Swim, Mallett, & Stangor, 2004); gender harassment (Fitzgerald, Gelfand, & Drasgow, 1995); interpersonal objectification (Kozee et al., 2007); and benevolent and hostile sexism (Glick & Fiske, 2001). Six of the themes in this model were derived from Sue and Capodilupo (2008), one theme was reconceptualized, and two themes were completely new. They include the following:

1. *Sexual objectification:* Experiences in which women are viewed as sexual objects (e.g., when women are catcalled as they walk down the street, when men touch women's backs as they walk past them in a crowded bar or restaurant).

2. *Assumptions of inferiority:* Experiences in which women are viewed as intellectually or physically inferior (e.g., when women are viewed as not being capable of carrying a heavy box, when women are told that they wouldn't be good leaders).

3. *Assumptions of traditional gender roles:* Experiences in which women are presumed to maintain stereotypical gender role norms (e.g., when women are asked to cook or clean or plan the office holiday party).

4. *Use of sexist language:* Statements that subtly or overtly demean women (e.g., when people freely use the word *bitch* or *skank* to describe women).

5. *Denial of individual sexism:* Statements in which a man defensively denies that he is sexist or engaged in sexist behaviors (e.g., a man who says, "How dare you accuse of me being sexist. I have two daughters!").

6. *Invisibility:* When women receive substandard treatment to men (e.g., when a woman is overlooked for service by a male bartender at a crowded bar).

7. *Denial of the reality of sexism:* Statements in which someone invalidates the experiences with sexism that women encounter regularly (e.g., a man telling a woman that she is "angry" or "hypersensitive" to issues regarding sexism).

8. *Environmental gender microaggressions:* Subtly discriminatory messages that are communicated through institutions, media, gov-

ernment, and other systems (e.g., when the media portray women as sexual objects, when corporations do not have any women in leadership positions; Nadal, 2010a).

Eventually, studies on gender microaggressions toward women materialized, citing the various types of microaggressions that women experienced (Capodilupo et al., 2010) as well as the various ways that women reacted to these microaggressions (Nadal, Hamit, et al., 2012).

Besides race and gender, microaggression taxonomies regarding other populations began to develop. Some of these theoretical models focused on experiences of multiracial people (Johnston & Nadal, 2010), religious minorities (Nadal, Issa, et al., 2010), and persons with disabilities (Keller & Galgay, 2010). Although I was personally involved in a lot of this microaggression literature and research, as both an advanced doctoral student at Teachers College of Columbia University and, later, as an early career professor at John Jay College of Criminal Justice of the City University of New York, I wanted to ensure that the microaggressions that were experienced by LGBT people were also discussed in the literature. Thus, it became one of my professional goals to conceptualize a sexual orientation and gender identity microaggression taxonomy and to begin researching how these discriminatory experiences negatively impacted the lives of LGBT people.

Taxonomy of Microaggressions Against Lesbian, Gay, Bisexual, and Transgender People

The first step in creating a taxonomy focusing on microaggressions experienced by LGBT people was to consult with others who would be as passionate about studying the topic as I was. So I called upon David Rivera, another doctoral student of Derald Sue, with whom I had worked closely on our research team. David is a self-identified gay Latino who had previously conducted research on racial microaggressions encountered by Latina/os; he also had a solid background in LGBT issues, in particular, regarding training and education. I also called on Melissa Corpus, a self-identified gay Filipina who has conducted extensive research on lesbian and bisexual women, in particular, lesbian and bisexual women of color. Like David, Melissa had a substantial amount of professional experience in working with LGBT populations. Our task was simple: to review the previous literature on LGBT discrimination as well as to use our own professional knowledge and personal life experiences to create a list of the various types of microaggressions that

LGBT people encounter in their everyday lives. We were consciously aware that we did not have any transgender people on this task force and that all three of us identified as **cisgender**. We also recognized that we did not represent a completely diverse group of racial and ethnic backgrounds because each of us was either Latino or Filipina/o. Thus, we consulted with our personal and professional networks—which included transgender people (both **male-to-female**, or **MTF**, transgender people and **female-to-male**, or **FTM**, transgender people), other LGBT people of color, LGBT White Americans, bisexuals, and others—to create a comprehensive list of microaggressions experienced by LGBT people.

Our proposed theoretical taxonomy on sexual orientation and gender identity microaggressions cited eight distinct categories of microaggressions that may target LGBT people (Nadal, Rivera, & Corpus, 2010):

1. *Use of heterosexist or transphobic terminology:* Experiences when someone uses derogatory heterosexist or transphobic language toward LGBT persons (e.g., using terms like *faggot* or *dyke* or *shemale*, or saying things like "That's so gay!")

2. *Endorsement of heteronormative or gender normative culture and behaviors:* Experiences in which an LGBT person is expected to act or be heterosexual (e.g., a heterosexual person telling a gay individual not to "act gay in public," or a cisgender parent forcing her or his child to dress according to the child's birth sex).

3. *Assumption of universal LGBT experience:* Experiences in which heterosexual people assume that all LGBT persons are the same (e.g., stereotyping all gay men to be interested in fashion or interior design, or assuming all lesbian women to act or look "butch").

4. *Exoticization:* Experiences in which LGBT people are dehumanized or treated as objects (e.g., heterosexual people stereotyping all LGBT people as being the "comedic relief"; a cisgender man who enjoys having sex with MTF transgender women but is not open to a committed, romantic relationship with them).

5. *Discomfort with/disapproval of LGBT experience:* Experiences in which LGBT people are treated with disrespect and criticism (e.g., when a stranger stares at an affectionate lesbian couple with disgust, when a heterosexual person tells an LGBT individual that she or he is going to hell).

6. *Denial of the reality of heterosexism or transphobia:* Experiences in which people deny that heterosexism and transphobia exist (e.g., a coworker telling a gay friend that he's being paranoid thinking someone is discriminating against him, someone telling a transgender person that she should stop complaining).

7. *Assumption of sexual pathology/abnormality:* Experiences in which heterosexual people oversexualize LGBT persons and consider

them as sexual deviants (e.g., when people assume that all gay men have HIV/AIDS and are child molesters or all transgender women are sex workers).

8. *Denial of individual heterosexism:* Statements in which heterosexual people deny their own heterosexist and transgender biases and prejudice (e.g., someone saying, "I am not homophobic, I have a gay friend!").

In the upcoming chapters, I discuss examples for each of these eight categories in more depth, and I provide first-hand experiences that were shared by LGBT people in my research and in other forums. More specifically, I share some of the findings on microaggressions based on sexual orientation (i.e., microaggressions toward lesbians, gays, and bisexuals) and on gender identity (i.e., microaggressions toward transgender and gender nonconforming people). I also highlight some of the microaggressions that are based on intersectional identities (i.e., microaggressions that may be based not only on sexual identity but also on race, gender, ethnicity, religion, age, social class, or other identities).

Before I delve into these microaggressions, it is necessary to reiterate the difficulty of reacting to microaggressions, in particular, when they are not clearly heterosexist, homophobic, or transphobic. In such cases, an individual may question whether the incident occurred at all or whether it was motivated by sexual orientation or gender identity (real or perceived). Similar to the example given earlier, of the African American man in the elevator, LGBT people who experience a microaggression may choose to confront the microaggressor, to ignore it altogether, or to pick their battles and address the microaggression only if they believe doing so may actually be worth the effort. Throughout the book, especially in Chapter 6, I discuss the difficult process through which people go after they are victims of microaggressions.

Sometimes it is not readily clear whether something should be considered a microaggression or could simply be labeled as an overt form of heterosexism, homophobia, genderism, or transphobia. There are many things that can be considered. Let's first revisit the concept of a microassault, from Chapter 1, which was initially described as "old fashioned" discrimination and often manifested through name calling, avoidant behavior, or discriminatory actions toward the intended victim. One of the main differences between microassaults and traditional, overt forms of discrimination is the intention and the consciousness of the perpetrator. If an individual blatantly, intentionally, and consciously calls someone a "faggot" or a "dyke" (i.e., they are actively aware that they made the statement and they intended to ridicule or hurt someone for their sexual orientation), then this might be considered a traditional, overt form of discrimination. However, perhaps someone may use a homophobic slur in an unconscious or unintentional way, which might allow one to label it more as a microaggression. For example, when two male teens are joking with each other and they call each other "faggot," they sometimes are not even conscious that they have used the word. If confronted by a passerby or authority figure, they may realize in retrospect that they should not have used such language, but in the moment they may not have even been aware of what they were saying. Similarly, if these same two male teens were calling each other "faggot" and an LGBT person overheard the conversation, this could be considered a microaggression because the intention of the two boys was not to offend anyone around them; instead, the boys may report that they were using language that they viewed as being playful and that they were not even thinking about anyone's sexual orientation when using the word. Thus, they may not view anything wrong with their behavior and may continue with such behavior because they really do not think that any parties are hurt. Because of their lack of consciousness, intention, or both, their behavior may be viewed as microaggressive.

Throughout this book, I provide a spectrum of examples of microaggressions that may be easy to label as such. However, I also illustrate some vignettes of incidents that may straddle the fine line between microaggressions and overt forms of discrimination. In such cases, I discuss ways one can identify examples as microaggressions or not, and I provide insight into how to approach or react to each situation. Nonetheless, I hope that at this point it is becoming more evident how often these types of microaggressions occur and how they have a negative impact on people's daily lives.

Discussion Questions

FOR GENERAL READERS

1. How do you feel about sexual orientation microaggressions (or microaggressions toward lesbian, gay, and bisexual people)? Have you experienced these types of microaggressions in your life? Have you committed any of these microaggressions before?

2. How do you feel about gender identity microaggressions (or microaggressions toward transgender and gender nonconforming people)? Have you experienced these types of microaggressions in your life? Have you committed any of these microaggressions before?

3. How do you feel about racial microaggressions (or microaggressions toward people of color)? Have you experienced these types of microaggressions in your life? Have you committed any of these microaggressions before?

4. How do you feel about gender microaggressions (or micro-aggressions toward women)? Have you experienced these types of microaggressions in your life? Have you committed any of these microaggressions before?
5. Are certain microaggressions easier to deal with? If so, how, and why?

FOR PSYCHOLOGISTS, EDUCATORS, AND OTHER EXPERTS

1. What types of microaggressions do you notice most in your work with your clients, students, or constituents?
2. How do you handle microaggressions when they occur with your clients, students, or constituents?
3. How do you handle microaggressions when they occur with your coworkers or supervisors?
4. What types of microaggressions might you commit the most? How do you feel about that?

Glossary of Key Terms

Cisgender: Term that describes people who are gender conforming and/or do not identify as transgender.

Female-to-Male, or FTM: Describes transgender people whose birth sex was female but who now identify as male or along the male spectrum.

Male-to-Female, or MTF: Describes transgender people whose birth sex was male but who now identify as female or along the female spectrum.

Sexual Orientation Microaggressions: Experiences of Lesbian, Gay, and Bisexual People

3

T here are a few key studies that highlight the ways in which microaggressions may manifest for lesbian, gay, and bisexual (LGB) people. Shelton and Delgado-Romero (2011) conducted a study with 16 self-identified lesbian, gay, bisexual, or queer (LGBQ) people who were also currently clients in psychotherapy. After the participants took part in focus groups, their responses were analyzed and classified into seven major themes: (a) assumption that sexual orientation is the cause of all presenting issues, (b) avoidance and minimization of sexual orientation, (c) attempts to overidentify with LGBQ clients, (d) making stereotypical assumptions about LGBQ clients, (e) expressions of heteronormative bias, (f) assumption that LGBQ individuals need psychotherapeutic treatment, and (g) warnings about the dangers of identifying as LGBQ.

The first theme, *assumption that sexual orientation is the cause of all presenting issues,* involves instances when therapists presume that any presenting problem that their LGBQ clients have is directly related to their sexual orientation. Therapists

DOI: 10.1037/14093-004
That's So Gay! Microaggressions and the Lesbian, Gay, Bisexual, and Transgender Community, by K. L. Nadal

may hold biases that a nonheterosexual identity in itself is a problem, believing that the sexual orientations of LGBQ clients are always related to mental anguish. This can be problematic, particularly for clients who have no or limited distress related to their sexual identities. For example, if a lesbian client reveals that she is depressed because of her dissatisfaction with her career, and the therapist continually insinuates that the client's sexual orientation is a source of the tension (regardless of the client's assertion otherwise), considerable time may be spent discussing a topic that may be irrelevant. On the other hand, the second theme, *avoidance and minimization of sexual orientation,* describes instances when the therapist shows discomfort in discussing anything related to the client's sexual orientation. For example, if a gay male client begins to talk about his sexual or romantic feelings toward a male coworker and the therapist dismisses the topic or tries to change the subject, a message is sent that the client's sexual orientation is a source of uneasiness and should not be discussed.

The third theme, *attempts to overidentify with LGBQ clients,* includes instances when therapists overemphasize to their clients that they are LGBQ friendly. For example, when therapists talk excessively about their LGBQ friends or family members to their clients, one may wonder whether the motivation is to appear to be overly comfortable and whether this motivation is based on the notion that, in reality, they are uncomfortable. This may be similar to microinvalidations, mentioned in previous chapters (e.g., when people say things like "I have a Black friend" to demonstrate that they are not racist but perhaps to cover up their actual discomfort with race). The fourth theme, *making stereotypical assumptions about LGBQ clients,* involves instances when therapists presume that all LGBQ clients must act a certain way or like certain things (e.g., a therapist makes a judgment that all gay men must love the theater or that all lesbian women would be masculine, or "butch"). The fifth theme, *expressions of heteronormative bias,* consists of the ways that therapists may promote heterosexuality without recognizing they are doing so. For example, if a client notices that there is not one LGBQ-related book in the therapist's full bookcase, he or she might infer that the therapist is neither knowledgeable nor caring about LGBT issues.

The sixth theme, *assumption that LGBQ individuals need psychotherapeutic treatment,* describes therapist behaviors that suggest an unconscious bias that all LGBQ people are psychologically inept. This bias may be similar to the one that emerges from the first theme, *assumption that sexual orientation is the cause of all presenting issues.* Because the therapist believes that being LGBQ would automatically result in mental health problems, she or he assumes that LGBQ people need psychotherapy.

Similarly, the seventh theme, *warnings about the dangers of identifying as LGBQ,* involves statements that suggest biases about LGBQ people. For example, if a bisexual client comes out to her or his therapist, and the therapist replies, "Are you sure you want to enter this lifestyle?" a message is conveyed that being LGBQ is a choice and would automatically lead to a harmful or unhealthy way of living (Shelton & Delgado-Romero, 2011).

Nadal, Wong, Issa, et al. (2011) examined the ways in which LGB people react to, and cope with, sexual orientation microaggressions. They conducted focus groups with lesbians, gay men, and bisexuals. The participants reported the perceived microaggressions in their everyday lives and how they tended to react. After analyzing the data, the authors divided the reactions into three main categories: (a) behavioral, (b) cognitive, and (c) emotional. *Behavioral reactions* included different ways that LGB individuals reacted to microaggressions through their actual behaviors; for example, participants shared ways in which they were passive and did not say anything, whereas others discussed how they were confrontational and expressed their dismay to their microaggressors. *Cognitive reactions* consisted of the diverse cognitive processes that LGB individuals reported while and after experiencing microaggressions. For instance, some participants claimed that they had learned to accept microaggressions as a part of their everyday lives and that they were just conforming to societal standards. On the other hand, some participants described how they had become more empowered or resilient as a result of dealing with microaggressions. Finally, *emotional reactions* consisted of the various sorts of emotions LGB people experienced while or after encountering microaggressions; participants' emotions ranged from sad to frustrated to resentful to disappointed.

Participants also reported the various types of mental health problems they experienced as a result of microaggressions. Some participants related that experiencing microaggressions based on their sexual orientation may have been a source of their depression or anxiety; one participant described how she had developed posttraumatic stress disorder partly because of the bullying she had endured in her school. Finally, participants divulged the spectrum of systems or groups that had enacted microaggressions in their lives. They discussed how they had noticed **systemic microaggressions** in the media, in the government, in their cultural groups, in their school systems, and in their religions (Nadal, Wong, Issa, et al., 2011).

In a qualitative study that used focus groups, Nadal, Issa, et al. (2011) aimed to validate the taxonomy presented by Nadal, Rivera, and Corpus (2010). Although the original model included microaggressions based on both sexual orientation and gender identity, this study focused only on sexual orientation microaggressions and recruited lesbian, gay male, and bisexual participants (*N* = 24). After asking participants to think about the subtle types of discrimination they had encountered in their lives, the researchers used a directed content analysis to examine whether participants' responses matched those presented in Nadal, Rivera, and Corpus's (2010) model. Almost all of the original categories were supported; these included use of heterosexist or transphobic terminology; endorsement of heteronormative or gender normative culture and behaviors; assumption of universal LGBT experience; exoticization; discomfort with/disapproval of LGBT experience; and assumption of sexual pathology, deviance, or abnormality (see Chapter 2, this volume, for a brief description of most of these categories). Two of the original categories—denial of societal heterosexism/transphobia and denial of individual heterosexism—were grouped together into a new category: denial of the reality of heterosexism, and a new theme, physical threat or harassment, emerged. Participants' responses indicated that the taxonomy was indeed an appropriate representation of microaggressions experienced by LGB people.

Voices of Lesbians, Gay Men, and Bisexuals

In this section, I revisit the microaggression taxonomy presented by Nadal, Rivera, and Corpus (2010) while including the additional categories presented in Nadal, Issa, et al. (2011). With each of these categories, I provide quotes from various sources, including previous microaggression literature, examples from contemporary media and literature, and real-life perspectives that have been submitted to The Microaggressions Project (http://microaggressions.com/), an Internet blog.

USE OF HETEROSEXIST OR TRANSPHOBIC TERMINOLOGY

This theme is characterized by experiences in which LGB people are called derogatory names or teased with cruel words. It also includes heterosexist remarks that are made directly to, or around, the LGB individual. Sometimes such language is used intentionally to berate or offend an LGB person; at other times people may not even realize they are using homophobic language because it is part of their everyday speech. For example, saying "That's so gay" when referring to something that is odd, unpleasant, or unappealing is common for many people, especially youth. In 2011, actor Vince Vaughn received backlash when he used the phrase "That's so gay" in such a manner in his movie, *The Dilemma*, and refused to apologize to the lesbian, gay, bisexual, and transgender (LGBT) community because he said his intention was not to be insulting to gay people (Read, 2010). This may be similar to instances in which an individual calls another person a "fag" or a "dyke." It may not intentionally be meant to accuse someone of being a gay man or lesbian woman; instead, it may reflect the person's unconscious biases against LGB people as being bad, weak, or inferior.

On the hit television show *Glee* a well-known scene depicts a microaggression entailing heterosexist language (Murphy, Falchuk, & Brennan, 2010). Finn Hudson (played by Corey Monteith), a heterosexual high school teenager, learns he will be sharing a room with his soon-to-be stepbrother Kurt Hummel (played by Chris Colfer). When Kurt, who is self-identified as gay, decorates the room with colorful and extravagant furniture and decor, Finn becomes upset and begins to yell. Kurt screams back, "It's just a room, Finn! We can redecorate it if you want to!" Finn replies, "Okay, good! Well, then, the first thing that needs to go is that faggy lamp, and then, we need to get rid of this faggy couch blanket . . . " At this point, Kurt's father walks into the room unexpectedly and rebukes Finn for his use of the word *faggy*. Finn explains that he didn't intend to call Kurt a "fag" and that he was referring to the blanket. The incident reflects a microaggression because it demonstrates that individuals may not be conscious about their language and that their intentions may not be deliberately heterosexist.

Microaggressions involving heterosexist language have also been documented in the research. In a study my colleagues and I conducted, a gay male shared the following experience:

> I recently opened up to my friend about [being gay] and he's a guy . . . and just the other day I was at his house and we were talking about other people and he would describe them as like "faggot," and it would get to me. (Nadal, Issa, et al., 2011, pp. 243–244)

Another gay male participant in another study described how the term *faggot* is sometimes used very casually:

> For me when somebody says in the street, "Hey faggot" I look around but [then I realize] they're not talking to me. I was so worried, it's just so challenging. It's embarrassing. Even if it's not toward me, it's still embarrassing. (Nadal, Wong, Issa, et al., 2011, p. 31)

In this case, the participant was able to deduce that the term wasn't directed at him; instead, it is one that is used casually, in particular, by adolescent boys who want to tease or point out presumed weakness or femininity in other boys. Regardless of the intended target, he felt embarrassed and worried (and possibly an array of other feelings).

At other times people may use heterosexist terms and language much more directly and purposefully, with the intention of bullying or teasing. This is exemplified in a narrative by Chad Allen, an actor who is best known for 1980s television shows like *Our House* and 1990s shows like *Dr. Quinn, Medicine Woman*. In his coming-out story, he wrote about some of his experiences during adolescence:

> When I started high school, I was a full-fledged television star and girls had pictures of me pinned up on their bedroom walls. I was a teen heartthrob for God's sake, untouchable. But, it didn't matter. Somehow they knew my secret. Years before I'd ever experienced the first amazing brush of another man's lips across my own, somehow they knew. I'd hear hateful words shouted across the hall, or scribbled across my binder, "ACTOR FAG." They were like razor blades across my soul. (Allen, 2011)

Clearly, hearing and seeing such hateful words had a negative impact on the actor, which even delayed his ability to come out of the closet and be comfortable with his identity.

There have been many instances that reveal how lesbian and bisexual women (and girls) have been bullied with heterosexist language too. In one personal narrative, one bisexual woman recalls an incident during her childhood, when she was holding hands with her best friend:

> They turned, saw us holding hands, and the taunting began. One said "Chocolate and Chip, holding hands!" and the other responded "Oh gross, what lez-bos!" Today, I know that they were derogatively referring to us as lesbians. Back then, we had to demand to know, "What are you talking about?" Finally, they gave us a hint, saying that we were two of the same thing, like a chocolate chip cookie, and that it was disgusting. We should not hold hands because we were both girls and doing so made us "lez-bos." (Phillips, 2005, p.116)

It is clear that individuals often turn to heterosexist language to insult others. However, it is also apparent that such language is often ignored or condoned by passersby, sending a message that heterosexist language is harmless or acceptable. Yet the LGBT people who hear them may feel scared, unsafe, sad, and even alone.

Sometimes people may use heterosexist terms inadvertently, without recognizing the impact that they are having on people. In a news article that described the bullying phenomena with LGBT youth, Preston Witt, a gay male adult from Alabama, recalled an experience from his childhood in which such a term was used freely by students and even a teacher:

> In my elementary school during PE, there was a favorite dodgeball game of all the students called "smear the queer" . . . I still, at

that time, did not realize, "Oh, I'm gay," but the whole premise
of the game bothered me. I remember saying to the coach, "Can
we play a different game—I don't like that game. [My teacher
then made me] "the queer" [for the day] . . . The whole premise
of the game is that all the students run around and throw balls
at the student designated as the queer . . . very similar to the old
idea of stoning. (Cox, 2009)

This type of heterosexist language aligns with previous literature that has
found that some students regularly overhear homophobic or heterosexist remarks by their own teachers and other staff members (Kosciw
& Diaz, 2006). Often this language may be purposefully hurtful and
offensive, but sometimes individuals may not even be aware of the
impact of the words that they use. Regardless of intention, an underlying heterosexist bias is communicated that may especially be harmful
to LGB children who are developing their sexual identities.

ENDORSEMENT OF HETERONORMATIVE
OR GENDER NORMATIVE CULTURE
AND BEHAVIORS

This type of microaggression occurs when one conveys a message
that heterosexuality is normal while homosexuality or bisexuality is
abnormal, wrong, or unnatural. This can be expressed in overt ways
(e.g., someone saying that heterosexuality is "natural" and that homosexuality or bisexuality is "unnatural"); however, it can also come out
in subtle ways. For instance, in an entry to The Microaggressions Project
blog, an individual described a PowerPoint slide shown during a suicide
prevention workshop at a college campus that read, "LGBT people are
six times more likely to attempt suicide than normal people." Although
the presenter or the creator of the slide presentation was likely well
intended (i.e., she or he included LGBT people in their presentation,
which means that that person wanted to educate others about the population), she or he inadvertently referred to non-LGBT people as "normal," thus implying that LGBT people are "abnormal."

When it comes to these types of heteronormative messages, it appears
that women are often taught or criticized about their ways of dress
while men are often taught or criticized about their ways of behaving.
The movie *But I'm a Cheerleader* depicts a camp where adolescent girls
and boys are sent when their families suspect that they may be lesbian
or gay. In this camp, the teenagers are taught the "proper" ways to
act, talk, and dress as heterosexuals, as well as "appropriate" ways to
interact with the opposite sex and their own sex (Peterson & Babbit,
1999). Although the movie is clearly meant to be comedic and satirical,
it depicts the types of messages that are often taught in families and

by society in general. For example, a lesbian participant in one study discussed how her parents have directly and indirectly communicated these heteronormative messages:

> [My mother] knows that I'm a lesbian, but she is in denial. She doesn't want to see it, so I have to act a certain way. You know, act heterosexual, not mention anything about me having a girlfriend or anything like that to make her feel uncomfortable or make her say anything offensive toward me. So, I have to act completely different at home. (Nadal, Issa, et al., 2011, p. 244)

These types of messages are expressed not just by families but also by other members of society. One lesbian participant described an experience with a stranger:

> My girlfriend . . . she dresses a little boyish. [And this man] looks at her and . . . he kept telling her, "Why do you dress like that? You're a girl, what are you doing? You're supposed to wear, you know, girly clothes. . . . Why do you dress like a guy? Why do you look like a guy?" (Nadal, Issa, et al., 2011, p. 245)

Men also hear heteronormative messages, usually revolving around the ways in which they speak or behave. On The Microaggressions Project blog, one gay male shared that his boss once told him, "Pink nail polish, eh? Why don't you just get a rainbow flag tattooed on your forehead?" Similarly, in a collection of personal narratives, one gay man talked about the messages he had received from his family and his culture:

> When I was growing up in the Philippines, I was always teased because I was not masculine enough. I preferred to play with dolls instead of trucks or cars. I liked playing house instead of war games. I liked dressing up as girl. My first attempt at drag was to imitate my religion teacher, Sister Dolores. She asked me one day what I wanted to be when I grew up. I said I wanted to be a nun. When she looked at me confusedly, I realized I'd have to choose a different career. In that machismo culture, I was always chided to act like a man—to butch it up. I was told men don't act like girls. I was shamed for being different. (Bordador, 2010, p. 195)

Although this last example may also have many other implications due to the individual's Filipino culture and Catholic religion, it is clear that he had been ingrained with heteronormative messages from an early age.

Direct and indirect heteronormative messages can also be taught in school systems, often being conveyed by educators themselves. A recent report regarding bullying in the United Kingdom revealed that many teachers informed their students that they should "act less gay" if they did not want to be bullied (Hackell, 2011). Although the teachers who allegedly said this may have had the best of intentions, the indirect message conveyed is that acting differently from the heterosexual norm is blameworthy and even punishable. In a news report on bullying, Lisa Rivero, the mother of Josh Rivero, a gay man in Florida, recalled an experience in which a teacher had shared concerns about her son's behavior in elementary school:

> I had one teacher tell me during a parent teacher conference, "Well, I have some concerns about him that during recess he prefers to be with the girls and not with the boys . . . " I said, "Was he struggling academically because of it? If no[t], well[,] then[,] that's his decision." (Cox, 2009)

In this case, the teacher may not have realized her or his biases regarding how boys or girls should behave or whom they should befriend.

Finally, when people presume that others are heterosexual when their sexual orientation has never been announced or discussed, they are assuming that heterosexuality is the norm. For instance, when a new male employee is hired at a workplace and his coworkers make blanket comments like "Do you have a wife and kids?" his coworkers are presuming that people are heterosexual, unless told otherwise. One lesbian author described a similar experience she had at her first job:

> Questions regarding previous boyfriends, current boyfriends, and my desire to have children were on the rise from my colleagues. In addition, I was invited to express opinions regarding "controversial" topics such as gay rights, same-sex marriage, and same-sex parenting. Did I know any of those "dykes, queers, and candy-ass faggots?" (Wiebold, 2005, p. 131)

Again, although this woman's coworkers may have had good intentions in wanting to know about her personal life and political stances, they also made her feel uncomfortable when they presumed she was heterosexual. This may often cause stress for LGB people who feel the pressure to announce their sexual orientation or "come out" publicly in the workplace, even though it is never a requirement for their heterosexual counterparts to do so.

When LGB people hear (or learn) these types of heteronormative statements, they may feel uneasy, unsafe, and invalidated. Such language may not necessarily be intentionally harmful, but it can be especially damaging to LGB people who are struggling with their sexual orientation or gender identity. Individuals who are "in the closet" may assume that anyone who makes heteronormative comments (whether intentional or unintentional) views homosexuality or bisexuality as wrong, immoral, or unacceptable. This may prevent LGB people from coming out to their loved ones and, because their loved ones may be oblivious to their own heteronormative biases and behaviors, they may not understand why.

ASSUMPTION OF UNIVERSAL LGB EXPERIENCE

Microaggressions under this theme occur when one assumes that all LGB individuals are the same. One way that this may manifest is through the presumption that all lesbians have identical experiences, all gay men have identical experiences, or all bisexuals have identical experiences. The opinions may be stereotypical (e.g., all lesbians are butch or like sports, or all gay men are feminine and like fashion or theater); for example, one gay man described how a friend stereotyped him on the basis of his sexual orientation:

> One day I had asked my friend, 'cause he was on the football team, and he was the most popular, and I said, you know, "I want to try out for football." He just stood there and kind of laughed at me. I felt, you know, "What are you laughing at?" He was like, "Come on, you're gay! You can't play football!" (Nadal, Issa, et al., 2011, p. 245)

Similarly, an entry in The Microaggressions Project blog reads:

> [A coworker said] "Believe me, my son is NOT gay. He has never once touched a Barbie, he's built like a linebacker, and he's a real man's man." [That] made me feel trapped, like I couldn't explain that gender does not equal sexuality without sounding like "the mean queer."

In both scenarios there is a clear assumption that gay men are supposed to abide by certain gender role behaviors. Again, while the individual may have made the comment in jest, others felt offended, hurt, and an array of other emotions.

Bisexuals also experience stereotypes in their interactions with heterosexuals, as well as with gays and lesbians. The author of *Bi Lives: Bisexual Women Tell Their Stories* wrote:

> Bisexuality is the sexual orientation of a person who is attracted to people of both sexes. This does not mean that every bisexual person feels the need to be involved with both a man and a woman, or that they will have sex with anyone who is available to them. It does not mean, as some lesbians believe, that bisexual women are not serious about any relationship they have with a woman, because (they believe) bisexual women would place more importance on any relationship with a man. Yet these are some of the misconceptions that gay and straight people have about bisexuals. While there are bisexuals who fit these stereotypes, I have not found many of them. (Orndorff, 1999, p. 1)

Others may assume that a typical LGB experience can be applied to all. For example, it is common for people to believe that coming out of the closet is a normative and necessary experience (Brady & Busse, 1994); however, in some cultures it may be viewed as being superfluous, excessive, and gratuitous. For example, in a qualitative study with gay immigrant men from the Philippines, one interviewee stated, "The Americans are different, darling. Coming out is their drama" (Manalansan, 2003, p. 27). Because sexuality is unspoken in the Filipino community (for both heterosexuals and LGB people), this individual did not view coming out as a necessary aspect of his experience. Thus, when someone makes a judgment about an LGB person of color who does not officially come out of the closet, the individual makes the mistake of assuming that this is a common and essential experience for all. This may make an LGB person feel invalidated or abnormal because she or he has had an atypical experience.

Sometimes individuals of a certain marginalized community (e.g., ethnic minority groups, LGBT people) are expected to be familiar with everyone else in the community, even though that would be nearly impossible because that community numbers in the millions. When this occurs, there are three main possible reasons: The perpetrator (a) assumes that *all* people of the group know each other or are friends, (b) hopes to create a bond with the person, or (c) wants to appear nondiscriminatory and open minded. For example, one entry from a 22-year-old through The Microaggressions Project reads: "When friends/acquaintances feel the need to go down the list of every queer person they know upon my disclosure of my queer identity . . . I feel annoyed, pigeonholed, stereotyped, belittled." Although the intention of individuals who practice this behavior is likely to be pleasant and genuine, this experience is microaggressive because it unintentionally offends an individual, making her or him feel like a token representative member of what is in reality a large, diverse group of individuals.

Finally, microaggressions under this theme occur when LGB people are asked to serve as spokespersons for their entire community. For example, a lesbian educator described the process of conducting workshops and how people often assumed that her experience was representative of all LGBQ people: "Despite our representations of a variety of identities, we do not represent all queers and their communities: It is important that we make this distinction clear" (Glasgow & Murphy, 1999, p. 220). Just as asking people of color to be a representative for an entire group is distressful (Sue, 2010), so too is asking LGB people to do the same.

EXOTICIZATION

These types of microaggressions are evident when LGB individuals are viewed as a form of entertainment or objectified because of their sexual orientation or identity. For example, gay men may be viewed as one's source of comedic entertainment, and bisexual women may be viewed as sexual objects, communicating the message that these roles are the only purpose LGB individuals serve (Nadal, Rivera, & Corpus, 2010). Several of the participants in studies my colleagues and I have conducted shared stories of feeling exoticized. One gay male shared how people in life assumed he was living a "fantastic and fabulous" lifestyle because he is gay: "What bothers me are—where I get a little annoyed or where I feel weird about it is when I feel like they're using me as a fantasy projection for what they wish their life was" (Nadal, Issa, et al., 2011, p. 246).

Another gay male participant described an interaction in which he felt like he was expected to be an entertainer: "I feel like straight people kinda think it's funny how I behave . . . you know what I mean . . . like it's amusing to them" (Nadal, Issa, et al., 2011, p. 246).

Feeling exoticized or objectified is a very common experience for bisexual women; specifically, bisexual women may feel especially sexually objectified by heterosexual men. For example, in *Bi Lives* (Orndorff, 1999), many interviewees discussed their feelings about being with heterosexual men. One participant stated, "I'm more wary of being objectified by men than by women. When I first started sleeping with Josh, I felt it. I think he objectified me sexually in a way that I've never experienced with a woman" (p. 65). This type of sentiment was shared by a bisexual female participant in Nadal, Issa, et al.'s (2011) study, who revealed the types of interactions she tends to have with heterosexual men: "A lot of guys would think, you know, because I'm into both guys and girls that I'll be like down with the threesome kinda thing, and it's like 'Ugh, get over yourself'" (p. 247). Because women in general are so objectified in American society (and across the world), bisexual women may be stereotyped as especially oversexualized, which in turn may lead to an array of microaggressions. Also, because the perpetrators of these microaggressions may not even be aware of the impact of their words, they may continue their behavior and negatively affect other people.

A final example of an exoticization microaggression toward LGB people is when people proudly claim that they "have a gay friend." Such a statement may be considered a microaggression according to the context, the intention of the speaker, and/or how the people around them interpret it. On The Microaggressions Project blog, a gay man shared an experience about a straight female coworker who, on learning that he had a boyfriend, said, "Oh my god! Will you be my new gay best friend? We can go shopping for clothes!" He continued:

> I said "No" and walked away, confused. I don't have any interest in shopping or clothing, much less being a "gay best friend." It makes me angry that just by coming out, I can instantly be transformed into a romantic comedy stock character even when someone had seen me as a real person prior to knowing that I'm gay.

Similarly, one lesbian educator described the types of people she encounters when she conducts LGBT-related workshops: "The participants I fear the most are heterosexuals who say 'Well, I have a gay friend . . . ' Often such a comment reflects a stagnation in what should be their evolving understanding of homophobia" (Glasgow & Murphy, 1999, p. 220). In this type of situation, people may claim to have a gay friend as a way of denouncing their homophobia to others. As the educator I just quoted suggested, they may use this fact as a way of assuming that they have learned everything they need to know about LGB experiences, or believe that the experiences of their "gay friend" can be universally applied to all LGB people.

DISCOMFORT WITH OR DISAPPROVAL OF LGB EXPERIENCE

A microaggression in this category consists of instances in which a heterosexual person, whether aware or unaware, shows her or his displeasure of or apprehension toward nonheterosexual people. Historically, this may have been considered more overt, in that people were very vocal about their disdain for and condemnation of LGB people. For example, in the 1970s, Anita Bryant (an entertainer and Miss America runner-up) created a Christian group called "Save Our Children" that was committed to advocating against any gay rights laws. She publically campaigned against any state legislation that protected the rights of gay and lesbian people, stating that LGB people were immoral and would corrupt or abuse children (Bronsky, 2011). Although anti-LGB sentiment was more common during this era, it still exists, just in different forms. For example, one psychologist described how she has been told, "because homosexual acts did not result in procreation, such acts were not normal and therefore homosexuality was disordered" (Adams, 2005, p. 24). Thus, it is clear that some sentiments from over 30 years ago still exist today.

It is common for microaggressions that convey disapproval to come from acquaintances or strangers in public places; however, these may also come from family members, coworkers, and/or friends. One lesbian participant described the types of microaggressions that she had experienced in public, particularly when she was with her girlfriend:

> I was with my girlfriend on the train, and she was holding me and kissing me, and there were people sitting there, and they just made a face. They didn't—I didn't see them say anything to us. It's just the face—you can kind of tell, the manner, their facial expression is kind of like "Whoa." (Nadal, Issa, et al., 2011, p. 247)

A gay male participant shared a similar story: "One time I was kissing my boyfriend on my front porch, and this guy walked by us and started chuckling" (Nadal, Issa, et al., 2011, p. 247).

In these two interactions, the microaggressors may not be forth-right in their dissatisfaction, shock, or other negative reactions to the same-sex couples showing affection toward each other; however, their stares, glares, laughter, and facial expressions (which may or may not be conscious) may convey their discomfort with LGB people while also having a detrimental impact on the couple who experience it.

These types of disapproval microaggressions may also manifest when individuals come out to family members and friends. Sometimes this dis-approval is overt in that someone hurtfully disowns the family member or tells the person that he or she is "going to hell" or "will be condemned." Other times the experience can be bittersweet in that a family member or friend can be accepting but still say indirectly hurtful things. Actress Portia de Rossi discussed how she came out to her grandmother:

> I wasn't planning on it, but I knew I wouldn't avoid it. So she made the mistake of asking me about my love life, and I said, "It's great. I'm very, very happy, and we've been together for eight months, and everything is wonderful." And she said, "What's his name?" And I took a deep breath and said, "Ellen DeGeneres." . . . First thing she said was, "Well, this is a very bad day." It was the most honest reaction I've ever had. Then she said, "Darlin', you're not one of those." It took her two minutes of being angry and upset and frustrated and disgusted—and then she just held her arms out to me and said, "I love you just the same." (Kort, 2005, p. 46)

Although it appears that the outcome was more positive at the end of this interaction, hearing that a family member is "angry" and "disgusted" about your sexuality, or listening to a loved one deny your sexual ori-entation, retains some microaggressive qualities and may cause hurt or frustration in the LGB individual.

John O'Brien, a gay psychotherapist, shared a similar experience, reflecting upon his sexual orientation and its impact on the relationship with his family:

> My upbringing told me that being gay was wrong [or] "morally depraved." As an only son, I was expected to get married and have a son to perpetuate the family name . . . For several years, I struggled to maintain a heterosexual identity. I dated women but could never gain intimacy with them. Deep down, I knew "the unspeakable truth," that I was a gay man. Yet I had a deep-seated fear of how the process of coming out would impact relationships with my family. After coming out, my worst fears initially came true. I lost the support of my parents and initially did not have contact with them. . . . Ultimately, the relationship settled into an uncomfortable silence about my life as a gay man. "Don't ask, don't tell" was the only way to maintain a connection with them. (O'Brien, 2005, pp. 97–98)

On the basis of this narrative, it is clear that O'Brien received different types of direct and indirect messages that being gay was bad or immoral. After he did come out to his parents, they seem to not have reacted well and even halted communication with him, which could be one indication of their disapproval of his sexual identity. However, although it seems that they had eventually reinstated communication with their son, their relationship was tainted with an "uncomfortable silence" about his life as a gay man; this would likely include anything related to his romantic relationships, LGB friends, and any of his activities in the LGB community. This type of silence fits all of the criteria of a microaggression. Although O'Brien's parents are no longer divulging their discomfort with or their disapproval of his sexual orientation, silence may indirectly communicate that they are not completely accepting or celebrating of this part of their son's life.

For bisexual people, microaggressions that convey discomfort or disapproval often come in the form of others questioning their sexual identity. One bisexual woman described an experience when she felt insulted:

> I actually went to a taping of [a talk show] recently, and it was an episode about gay marriage and gay issues and [the host] had everyone in the audience wear t-shirts that they gave us that said either "straight" or "gay" or whatever on them. It was really cheesy, but they didn't have a shirt that said "bi." They had a straight shirt, a gay shirt, and then a shirt with a question mark on it. I was like, "What the fuck is this?" I'm like, my sexual orientation is *not* a question mark. I didn't like how it could be implied that I'm confused. (Nadal, Issa, et al., 2011, p. 248)

This type of situation reflects a common microaggression in which others assume that bisexual people are "confused." One bisexual woman stated, "When I was first coming out as bisexual I noticed that heterosexual and homosexual people were saying the same things to me. 'You have to make a choice. You're on a fence. You're confused'" (Orndorff, 1999, p. 111). Another bisexual woman disclosed to The Microaggressions Project:

> One thing my brother says is "I'll believe it when you don't just hook up with girls, but actually bring one home as your girlfriend." [He has a] theory that I'm not actually bisexual. I'm only 17, and figuring out my sexuality isn't easy. Made me feel like I'm making my sexuality up for attention, like I'm trying to be something that doesn't exist, or that exists, but I'm not qualified for.

When a **monosexual** individual (i.e., someone who practices exclusive heterosexuality or exclusive homosexuality) makes statements like these, it is clear that he or she has prejudicial biases against bisexual people, and although they may not realize it, their words may be especially insulting to a bisexual person's experience and identity. Similar types of microinvalidations may be common for **pansexual** people, or individuals whose sexual orientations are "gender blind" in that they can be sexually, romantically, or emotionally attracted to people of all gender identities and sexual orientations. When pansexual people are told that their sexual orientation is unfounded or illogical, they are denied their right to uphold their identities, which may often lead to feelings of invalidation and hurt.

Finally, it is crucial to note that bisexual people may experience microaggressions from others within the LGBT community. A bisexual woman described the reaction she would have from gay and lesbian friends when she entered a new relationship:

> [That] is what being bisexual is; sometimes I'll fall in love with woman and sometimes a man. This gave me my first long-term experience of what it was like to negotiate my bisexual identity with a man, the fears it raised in both him and me. I wondered if I could ever be satisfied dating just one sex. Although gay and lesbian friends were primarily happy that I found someone I loved, they couldn't completely hide their disappointment that that person was a man. Conversely, straight friends seemed a little too happy that that person was a man. (Carrubba, 2005, pp. 44–43)

This narrative exemplifies two types of microaggressions bisexual people may feel. They may feel invalidated by lesbian and gay individuals when they *are not* supported when they enter heterosexual relationships; however, they may feel invalidated by heterosexual people because they are "too" supported when they enter heterosexual relationships.

ASSUMPTION OF SEXUAL PATHOLOGY, DEVIANCE, OR ABNORMALITY

This theme includes microaggressions in which heterosexuals believe that LGB individuals are sexually promiscuous or sexually deviant. Sometimes these can take the form of comments and statements that are meant to be hurtful and demeaning. For example, when Christian fundamentalist protestors hold up signs at LGB events on which phrases like "AIDS Kills Fags" are written, it is clear that they are intending to offend the LGB people who see them or hear them. These might be considered microassaults in that they are conscious and intentional; however, depending on the context, such statements may also feel assaultive. There are some microaggressions, however, in which the perpetrator consciously decides to vocalize something without realizing the impact it will have on others. For example, one gay male participant stated, "One of the kids that I knew in high school, he just came out of nowhere and just said that all gay people have AIDS" (Nadal, Wong, Issa, et al., 2011, p. 28). Perhaps the perpetrator in this case did not realize that there were other gay people in the room; perhaps he thought he was making a factual statement. Nonetheless, his comment had an impact on the participant, and thus would be classified as a microaggression.

Many types of microinsults fall into this category. Such statements or behaviors may not intentionally or consciously be verbalized to upset or hurt the recipient; instead, the perpetrator's biases and stereotypes about LGB people are simply conveyed indirectly through their remarks or actions. For example, a gay male college student described his phone calls with his mother:

> [I] get one message. It's from my mother. I'll call her and see what she wants. "Yes, Mom, I'm practicing safe sex . . . And yes, I'm getting another AIDS test in April when I get my physical . . . Yes, Mom, I'll see you at Easter . . . bye-bye." My mother says she will be supportive of my "lifestyle" but all she does is send me "cute" articles on gay issues that she cuts out of the newspaper. I think she's very concerned that I'm going to contract AIDS and "leave her." (Meiner, 2000, p. 300)

This experience is parallel to an entry submitted to The Microaggressions Project blog in which a gay male wrote, "[For the past 5 years since I came out,] every time [when I'm home for break] my mother leaves a newspaper article about AIDS by my seat at the kitchen table. I'm 21."

Although the mothers in both of these scenarios may believe they are supportive of their sons' sexual orientation, they still maintain biases (either consciously or unconsciously) that all gay men have, or will contract, AIDS. Although there is indeed a disproportionate number of gay men who contract HIV/AIDS, assuming that this is true of all gay men is not only a stereotype but also may be considered microaggressive. Statements implying this convey that all gay men are irresponsible or are incapable of making wise decisions about safe sex. Although some of these statements (like the ones mentioned by the mothers in the last two quotes) may be well intended, they may also result in the individual feeling uneasy or frustrated, in particular, when the same types of questions are not asked of heterosexuals.

Assumptions of sexual deviance may also apply to lesbian or bisexual women. Darla Bjork, a lesbian psychiatrist, described a situation that occurred in a psychotherapy session with a heterosexual patient:

> A neighbor who knew that I was a lesbian mentioned this to [my patient] Ruth. In the next session, she confronted me and without exploring the issue adequately, I told her it was true. She became angry and frightened, stating that she wanted to be referred to another therapist because she was afraid that I would attack her sexually. I almost burst out laughing at that old stereotype of lesbians, but calmly told her that was not going to happen. (Bjork, 2004, pp. 102–103)

This experience is similar to that of a bisexual female study participant, who shared, "Well, in my case, I've actually had some friends stop being my friends, because they were like, 'Oh, since you're bisexual and you might try come on to me,' so they stopped being my friend" (Nadal, Issa, et al., 2011, p. 247). This stereotype—that a lesbian or bisexual woman would automatically hit on or sexually assault a heterosexual person—implies a bias that LGB women do not have any control of their sexual urges or desires, but it also is insulting because it suggests that these women would be attracted to any other woman, regardless of physical attractiveness level, personality, or other characteristics.

These stereotypes about women are similar to the stereotype that all gay men would be child molesters. Although a vast amount of research has found that child molesters tend to be heterosexual men with pedophilic desires for young girls, many people still stereotype gay men as pedophiles with desires for young boys. One gay male study participant, a former schoolteacher, shared, "I remember being very careful about interacting with the kids. Because I was gay, I knew that people made assumptions and kept watch over me . . . like we were all sexual predators or something" (Nadal, Issa, et al., 2011, p. 50). Although others may not have explicitly accused this man of being a child molester, their microaggressive behaviors led him to believe that they upheld stereotypes about him and felt they could not trust him around their children.

DENIAL OF THE REALITY OF HETEROSEXISM OR TRANSPHOBIA

This type of microaggression is evident when individuals deny the occurrence of heterosexism; sometimes this can occur when someone denies that she or he is homophobic, whereas at other times people can deny that heterosexism exists at all. For example, when LGB people confront perpetrators on their microaggressive behavior, the perpetrator can sometimes react defensively and assert that his or her intention was not to be offensive. Some LGB people may appreciate an explanation, but others may believe that the individual is merely creating excuses instead of admitting fault. One example includes a scenario described by a gay male study participant. At first, the interaction may be considered an exoticization microaggression; however, the second part of the interaction may be best classified under denial of heterosexism or transphobia:

> This woman came up to me one night and she said . . . I think
> I made some joke or something and she said, "Do you know who
> you remind me of?" and I knew what was coming, I just knew
> what was coming. She's like, "You're just like that Jack on 'Will
> and Grace.' You're so funny." And I looked at her, and I said,

"Ma'am, no offense, but that's actually not a compliment." And
she was like, "What do you mean? What do you mean? No, no,
I was saying you're funny, and you're cute, and you dress nice."
(Nadal, Issa, et al., 2011, p. 246)

Perhaps the gay male in this scenario would have reacted more positively
if the woman had apologized for offending him or for stereotyping him.
However, because she did not, he left feeling dissatisfied and upset.
Moreover, because this woman was unable to recognize that her statement may be based on her biases toward gay men, she may continue
to offend in the future.

Sometimes people may commit microaggressions whereby their
statements invalidate LGB people's realities, in particular, in overcoming the heterosexist discrimination they encounter on interpersonal
and systemic levels. One lesbian study participant related an anecdote
in which her professor invalidated the realities related to her same-sex
relationship:

My professor, who is overseeing my dissertation in [chemistry],
really wants me to become a professor of [chemistry]. And I tried
to explain to him that it wasn't very easy for me, that there
are very few jobs, and they are all like in Ohio or Oklahoma or
in places I personally wouldn't want to live. And also I have a
partner, who because of her visa situation is tied to [New York],
and I tried to explain to him. I can't just get married to my partner
and take her with me where I go because of federal laws, the
Defense of Marriage Act. And so I didn't appreciate his guilt trip
when I decided to leave [academia] and his sort of lack of understanding around, "Do I give up my personal life and who I am
and maybe go to a place where I have to be closeted just because
he think I should?" And I would say his lack of understand might
be a subtle form of discrimination. (Nadal, Issa, et al., p. 249)

Finally, sometimes LGB people (and people of other marginalized groups)
do not report discrimination because of their fear of how others will
react. For example, many children will not tell their teachers or principals about bullying because they fear they may somehow be blamed
for their actions. Lisa Rivero, the above-mentioned mother of a gay
son, discussed how she had tried to talk to school officials about her son
being bullied. In a news article, she said, "I spoke with principals over
the years and got the typical responses: 'Oh well, he needs to toughen
up' or 'Oh, it's usually his fault'" (Cox, 2009).

PHYSICAL THREAT OR HARASSMENT

Microaggressions that fall into this category can be classified as microassaults in that they are overt discrimination or assaults in nature
but the aggressor does not physically harm the individual and may

not even have intended to in the first place. For example, in a focus group conducted by Nadal, Issa, et al. (2011), a participant reported that she had been teased and harassed and had received death threats because of her sexual orientation. Although such death threats may be viewed as overt microassaults and perhaps even as hate crimes, the harassment and bullying that ensued may be viewed as more microaggressive.

In another study, a gay male participant described a situation that left him feeling uneasy:

> I was at a hotel party . . . and the night before we had a good time. The next morning, there were some really rough dudes . . . This guy asked me if I was gay and I was like, "Yeah." And he backed up out of his chair and he said, "Oh, we're all walking around in our boxers here, 'What were you thinking?'" I didn't know what was going to happen but I felt a little uncomfortable . . . a little bit unsafe. (Nadal, Wong, Issa, et al., 2011, p. 30)

Although the participant did not identify any outright physical threats, he felt uncomfortable based on the tone and behaviors of the man.

Similarly, a gay male college student wrote about how his fraternity brothers found out about his sexuality and wanted to kick him out of the fraternity:

> Members and alumni begin to fear that the Iowa Delta chapter of Sigma Phi Epsilon will be labeled as the "gay house." They fear they will lose potential new membership to other houses. To them the only "logical" choice, instead of acceptance and support, is to make the faggot's life miserable, and they find a loophole in the bylaws to deactivate me. They hurl slurs and verbally harass me, my friends, and my parents. Threats of physical violence become frequent. Due to my circumstances, I am deactivated, but of course a repeal process is never explained to me. (Meiner, 2000, p. 301)

Again, although the narrator does not reveal any physical abuse or assaults that took place, feeling unsafe and being threatened can have a profound impact on people's mental health and psychological well-being.

ENVIRONMENTAL MICROAGGRESSIONS

Finally, environmental microaggressions comprise elements in the systems or institutions that send denigrating messages to LGBT individuals. For example, when watching television shows that do not portray any LGBT individuals or portray them only in a negative or stereotypical light, some individuals may feel invalidated or insulted. This category is endorsed by research on sexual stigmas (Herek, 2007) that claims that sometimes LGBT persons just "feel" unable to disclose their sexual orientation or identity because of an unsafe environment, but not because of any specific heterosexist event that was targeted at them. This may parallel the experiences of people of color and women who feel invalidated when they are in environments where Whites or men are celebrated and viewed as the norm or the elite, while people of color and women are invisible.

Previous research has found that environmental microaggressions occur in various systems, such as schools, the government, and the media. For example, a female study participant described one heterosexist school policy she encountered:

> I remember I had a guy friend—he kissed another guy, he just kissed a guy and they gave him detention, they would give detention at any moment like doing anything with the person of the same sex and then they would say, "You know, you should keep that to yourself because parents will complain, students will complain" and I'm like "Why would they complain[,] it's not like I'm doing anything to them" and they're like, "No, it's wrong, you shouldn't do it because it makes other people uncomfortable." It actually bothered me because why can't I be myself, you know, it shouldn't be a problem. If other people can have boyfriends you know . . . really promiscuous people making out in the hallway, you're trying to get to class and . . . they just keep doing whatever they're doing on the lockers and everything but if I was to hold hands with my girlfriend it would be like "What are you doing?" (Nadal, Wong, Issa, et al., 2011, p. 36)

Another participant described how he perceived heterosexist micro-aggressions in government:

> I was in the Army and they have the . . . "Don't Ask, Don't Tell" rule. Well, you're there and you feel like freakin' terrified if any-body found out that you were that way. So that really pissed me the hell off. So, I just kind of kept to myself, you know. I mean, if at some point I develop a close knit relationship with one of my battle buddies, then I'm pretty much need to shut up and keep your mouth like this [gesture of zipping lip] and just don't let it get out there. (Nadal, Wong, Issa, et al., 2011, p. 36)

Messages from the environment that being LGB is bad or deviant can cause significant distress and have a negative impact on the self-esteem of LBG individuals. Moreover, these microaggressions create an unsafe environment for LGB people while also promoting the notions that heterosexuality is the norm and heterosexist biases are acceptable.

Case Studies

I now present three case studies that illustrate the potential effects of microaggressions on LGB individuals.

THE MICROAGGRESSION OF SILENCE WITHIN FAMILIES: THE CASE OF NICOLE

Nicole is a 28-year-old White, Irish American lesbian woman who grew up in a suburban neighborhood outside of Philadelphia, with her parents, her older brother, and her younger sister. Nicole has always known that she was a lesbian, and she came out to her parents when she was a junior in college. Initially, her parents were shocked and asked her a lot of follow-up questions, like "Are you sure?" and "How do you know you're gay if you've never had a boyfriend?" She replied, "Of course I'm sure!" and asked her father, "How do you know you're straight if you've never had sex with a man?" and her mother, "How do you know if you're not gay if you've never had sex with a woman?" Although their interactions with her were awkward at first, Nicole's parents both told her that they loved her and would try to learn to accept her "decision."

Since coming out 8 years ago, Nicole has noticed that her parents have never made any direct mention of her sexuality, usually changing the topic when she talks about LGBT-related political issues or tries to tell them about the various LGBT community events she attends. Her parents have never said anything overtly homophobic to Nicole, yet she feels sad and invalidated because they do not make the same efforts that they do with her heterosexual siblings. She observes her parents consistently asking her brother and sister when they plan on getting married, whether they're dating anyone special, and when they plan on "giving them grandchildren." Meanwhile, neither of her parents has asked Nicole about her dating life, whether she has plans of having a family, or whether she will be able to "give them grandchildren."

Nicole recently began a serious romantic relationship with a woman named Andrea and is considering bringing her home to meet the family for Thanksgiving. Because she has never brought a girlfriend home before, Nicole is extremely distressed by the situation. Although she is able to talk to Andrea and some friends about how she is feeling, she decides to seek a psychotherapist to guide her on whether she should bring her girlfriend home and whether she should confront her parents about her perceptions of their discomfort with her sexuality. In therapy sessions, Nicole is able to connect to her feelings of anger, sadness, and disappointment with her parents. She is able to explore her jealousy of her siblings because of how they are favored because of their heterosexuality. She also begins to realize that having a lack of explicit support from her parents is almost as hurtful as not having support from them at all.

MICROAGGRESSIVE ENVIRONMENTS
AND BULLYING: THE CASE OF DANIEL

Daniel is a 14-year-old Mexican American high school freshman who lives at home with his mother, his father, and 12-year-old sister. The family lives in a typical middle-class, predominantly Mexican American neighborhood in a small southwestern town. The high school Daniel attends is also predominantly Latina/o, with about three fourths of the students being Mexican American. Because the community in which he lives is small, Daniel has known most of his classmates since he was a child. However, at present Daniel has very few friends, in particular, few male friends, as other boys consistently tease him or bully him because they assume he is gay.

The bullying began several years ago, when Daniel started to become more involved in the arts (particularly in theater and dance) and to develop close friendships with girls. During his physical education classes, Daniel was often the last to be picked for teams; the boys often called him a "sissy" or a "fairy" and told him that he "played sports like a girl." Sometimes his teachers heard these comments, but they usually ignored them and told the kids to concentrate on the game. Daniel usually tried to brush off these hurtful statements in public; however, when he got home, he often cried alone in his room, without being able to tell anyone in his family about what happened that day.

In high school, the bullying continued, and Daniel tried to find excuses to skip class, in particular, gym class, so that he wouldn't be teased. He also had to learn to avoid certain areas of the school because he knew that bullies gathered there, often laughing at him or mumbling insults as he walked by. In his other classes he often heard homophobic comments (by both teachers and classmates) that made him feel insulted and sad. For example, in his sex education class, his teacher was discussing the issue of families and marriage. When another student raised her hand and asked about same-sex marriage, the teacher responded, "No; we'll only be learning about normal families in this class." A month or so later, in his social studies class, his teacher asked students to bring in clippings about relevant news to discuss in class. When one of Daniel's classmates brought in an article about the repeal of the Don't Ask, Don't Tell law, the teacher said, "I know I wouldn't want to sleep in close quarters with a homosexual." While the rest of the class laughed, Daniel pretended to laugh too, so that others wouldn't suspect he was gay.

Numerous other incidents like this continued at his school, and Daniel continued to feel disheartened and alone. He didn't want to tell his friends what he was feeling because that would mean that he would have to admit to being gay—something he wasn't even 100% certain about anyway. He became so depressed that he found himself crying himself to sleep and sleeping for 10 hours every night. His family noticed this behavior but didn't know what to do. When he told his mother that he wanted to kill himself, she panicked and took him to the emergency room.

MICROAGGRESSIONS WITHIN THE LGBT COMMUNITY: THE CASE OF SEAN

Sean is a 32-year-old Vietnamese American man who works as a licensed clinical social worker at the local LGBT community center in an urban city in the Midwest. When Sean first took the job, he was very excited to work there, especially because he had a passion for working with LGBT people and advocating for their mental health needs. When Sean was hired, he outed himself immediately as a bisexual man to his supervisor, Jennifer. He asked her if there were other openly bisexual people who worked at the center. Jennifer, an African American lesbian, informed him that there were bisexual female employees but that she was not aware of any openly bisexual men. However, she assured him that the work environment was very "bisexual friendly" and very diverse in every other way.

When Sean started meeting his coworkers, everyone was very friendly with him. People oriented him to the office protocols and gave him a brief history of everything he needed to know. Although he liked everyone in the office, Sean realized that most of his coworkers assumed he was gay, because of the subtle comments he heard them make. For example, in one of his staff meetings, there was a discussion about how to make the center more accessible and welcoming to underrepresented groups within the LGBT community, in particular, to transgender people and people of color. When someone raised her hand and asked, "What about the bisexuals?" a male coworker named Ben said, "Well, we have lots of bi women here, and we all know that bisexual men don't exist!" While most of the people laughed, Jennifer awkwardly looked at Sean, wondering if she should say something. After sharing brief eye contact with each other, they both remained silent.

Situations like these continued in the workplace for the next few months. Sean decided not to say anything because he figured that they were simply being ignorant and because he was accustomed to hearing **monosexist** language in every other aspect of his life. A few months later, Sean began dating a woman named Sophia. When he brought her to an office social gathering, he introduced her to his coworkers as his girlfriend. Some of them were polite but had puzzled looks on their faces. Some coworkers asked incessant (yet indirect) questions to both Sean and Sophia about their relationship. One asked Sophia whether she was bothered that Sean had been sexually involved with men; another asked Sean whether he liked having sex with men or women more. Both Sean and Sophia were uncomfortable with the questions but answered them politely. However, Ben, one of Sean's coworkers, was vocal about his disapproval, stating, "So when did you *become* bisexual?" Sean angrily replied, "I've *always* been bisexual, and you'll always be a jerk." He then walked away even more furious than before.

Case Study Discussion

As the three cases demonstrate, microaggressions toward LGB people can take many forms. In the first case study, we were introduced to Nicole—a lesbian woman who does not feel that her parents support her sexual identity. Although she does not have any tangible evidence to support this (i.e., they have never said anything overtly homophobic to her since she came out to them), she recognizes that their behavior toward her is different from that toward her heterosexual siblings. This type of situation is difficult to address, for many reasons. First, because there is a lack of LGBT-supportive behaviors (instead of the presence of overtly homophobic statements or actions), Nicole may question whether she is being oversensitive to the issue or whether she really does perceive a reality. As a result, she may have difficulty in confronting her parents because she may be afraid that they may dismiss her accusations or tell her she is being paranoid. Second, because this conflict occurs within families, there are many other factors to take into consideration, including dynamics with other family members, the family history, communication styles, and an array of differing worldviews. Although racial microaggressions are less likely to occur within families (i.e., because a majority of families are monoracial and comprise people of the same race), microaggressions toward LGBT people are quite common within families because there is usually only one LGBT family member (Nadal, Wong, Issa, et al., 2011). Finally, it may be challenging to confront microaggressions within families because individuals may want to avoid family conflict and tension. So, although Nicole is currently bothered by her situation with her parents, she may choose to hold back her feelings in order to maintain harmony within the family.

In the second case study, we further our understanding of the relationship between bullying and microaggressions through the case of Daniel, a 14-year-old high school freshman who has been bullied for several years, primarily because of his involvement in the arts and his friendships with girls. Most of the bullying is extremely overt (e.g., his classmates call him names like "sissy" or "fairy"); however, some of the bullying may be more difficult to label if he did want to tell an authority figure (e.g., when his classmates laugh when Daniel walks by in the hallway—how can he prove that it is directed toward him, or that it is malicious?). Moreover, there are many ways in which the bullying is perhaps condoned (e.g., his teachers not punishing students for using homophobic terms toward Daniel), as well as ways that microaggressions may lead to an unsafe environment for Daniel and other potential LGBT students (e.g., teachers making heterosexist comments, perpetuating harmful stereotypes about LGBT people, or both). Perhaps one of the reasons why the situation has become so intense is that Daniel has not been able to discuss his experiences with anyone. Although his family and small group of friends seem generally supportive of him, he may not want to talk about his experiences with them because it may force him to acknowledge that he is gay. Thus, like many young people who struggle with their sexual identity, he may repress all of his feelings, which eventually would take a toll on his mental health.

The third case study describes a microaggression that may often occur within the LGBT community: microaggressions against bisexual people. As mentioned earlier, bisexual individuals are often labeled (by both heterosexual and homosexual people) as "confused," incapable of maintaining monogamous romantic relationships, or overly sexual. Bisexual men in particular are often viewed as "pretending" to be bisexual instead of fully accepting a gay identity. A scene from the popular television show *Sex and the City* has the four main characters talking about the bisexual man that Carrie Bradshaw (played by Sarah Jessica Parker) is currently dating. Carrie, perplexed by bisexuality, states, "I'm not even sure *bisexuality* exists. I think it's just a layover on the way to Gaytown" (Bicks & Thomas, 2000). Although this was likely meant as a joke (because the show is a comedy), biases such as these may be considered microaggressive because they invalidate the existence of bisexual men while also enabling microaggressions against bisexuals (as exemplified by the microaggressions encountered by Sean).

Sean has devoted his career to working with LGBT people and advocating for their mental health. However, at his workplace, several jokes and other types of comments are made that promote people's views of **monosexuality.** Sean tries to ignore these types of biased views but begins to feel upset as they persist on a semiregular basis. Because these types of microaggressions occur between members of two marginalized groups, addressing them may be complicated. For example, bisexual women have reported feeling microaggressed by lesbians, and lesbians have reported feeling microaggressed by bisexual women (Nadal, Wong, Issa, et al., 2011). However, because both groups are oppressed by heterosexual society, two outcomes may occur. First, it may be difficult for individuals to recognize when they are the perpetrator of microaggressions because they are also the victims of such incidents and, second, some people may argue that these types of microaggressions might feel less threatening than those coming from the group with **power** and **privilege** (e.g., heterosexuals). Thus, it is possible that Ben (Sean's gay male coworker) may have difficulty admitting his bias against bisexuals because he is of a minority status himself (i.e., he is a gay man who is discriminated against by heterosexuals). Perhaps Sean may have ignored or excused these comments because they were coming from gay or lesbian people instead of from heterosexuals (whose comments he may view as being more oppressive). Perhaps a microaggression committed by someone from a **target group** (e.g., LGBT people, people of color, women, persons with disabilities) may feel differently than a microaggression committed by someone of a **dominant group** (e.g., heterosexuals and cisgender people, Whites, men, or able-bodied people) because of the power and privilege involved. Either way, it is important to recognize that microaggressions can occur even within marginalized communities and can still be hurtful to their recipients.

A few themes are apparent in all three of these case studies. First, in each case study some incidents are much more blatant and obvious, whereas others might be well intentioned and not malicious in any way. For instance, when Nicole's parents ask her if she is "sure" she is a lesbian, their intention may not be to insult her; instead, they may just be concerned about their daughter's well-being and want to ensure that she is happy. Similarly, when Sean's coworkers ask him and his girlfriend Sophia relentless questions about their relationship, their intention may not be to judge Sean or Sophia; instead, they may be well intentioned and simply curious.

In each of the case studies several people serve as support systems for the individual: Nicole has her girlfriend, Andrea, and her psychotherapist; Daniel has his family and an intimate group of friends; and Sean has his girlfriend, Sophia, and his supervisor, Jennifer. Sometimes these individuals appear to be helpful (e.g., Nicole's psychotherapist seems able to guide her in working through her issues), sometimes they seem stumped on how to react (e.g., Jennifer is unclear whether she should address the microaggression at the staff meeting), and sometimes they may not even know what is going on at all (e.g., Daniel's parents are not even aware he is being bullied). Having allies during the experience any type of discrimination can be very beneficial for two reasons: (a) They can help validate one's perceptions, feelings, and realities; and (b) they can advocate for the victim of microaggressions so that the individual does not feel that he or she always has to fight alone. Perhaps if all individuals had more social support, they would be better able to better cope with the microaggressions, which may then lead to optimal mental health.

Finally, in each of the case studies, the reactions of all three individuals reflect the wide range of processes and responses that people have when dealing with microaggressions. Daniel, the gay teenager who is persistently bullied, has tried to avoid the perpetrators of microaggressions while repressing his true emotions when the microaggressions do occur. Nicole, the lesbian whose parents are not openly supportive of her sexual identity, has chosen to seek mental health treatment and is debating whether to confront her parents about her feelings. Sean has chosen to ignore the microaggressive comments he hears in the workplace; however, it seems that he is no longer able to contain his emotions and finally unleashes how he is really feeling about his coworker's biased remarks. Regardless of how each situation is ultimately handled, each individual still experiences distress.

Discussion Questions

FOR GENERAL READERS

1. What types of sexual orientation microaggressions do you believe are most common? Which types of sexual orientation micro-aggressions are most harmful or hurtful?
2. Do you believe that sexual orientation microaggressions that come from other LGB people are less harmful or hurtful than microaggressions that come from heterosexual people?
3. What types of microaggressions do you believe occur more often with lesbian women? with gay men? with bisexual women? with bisexual men?
4. What types of sexual orientation microaggressions do you notice in various institutions (e.g., your workplace or school) or systems (e.g., government, media, religious)?
5. How could systems and institutions (e.g., government, school systems, media, policies) assist Nicole, Daniel, and Sean in their experiences with microaggressions? How could these systems have been helpful in the past to prevent these microaggressions altogether?
6. Have you ever committed a sexual orientation microaggression as a perpetrator? Were you aware of your behavior? How do you feel about this today? When you were reading each scenario, what were some of the feelings that arose for you?
7. What would you do if you were in Nicole's situation? Daniel's situation? Sean's situation?

FOR PSYCHOLOGISTS, EDUCATORS, AND OTHER EXPERTS

1. In what ways might you improve your cultural competence in working with LGB people?
2. What techniques or methods would you use in working with Nicole, Daniel, or Sean?
3. What types of countertransference issues would you have in working with Nicole, Daniel, or Sean?

Glossary of Key Terms

Dominant Group: A group of people in a society with greater power and privilege due to their majority status or historical authority.

Monosexist: Discriminatory on the basis of exclusive heterosexuality and/or exclusive homosexuality as the only legitimate or right sexual orientation. A related term is **monosexism:** the act of believing or promoting exclusive heterosexuality and/or exclusive homosexuality as the only legitimate sexual orientation.

Monosexual: One who identifies as exclusively heterosexual or homosexual.

Monosexuality: The belief in exclusive heterosexuality or exclusive homosexuality.

Pansexual: An individual whose sexual orientation is gender blind in that she or he has the potential to be sexually, romantically, or emotionally attracted to people of all gender identities and sexual orientations.

Power: The ability to define reality and to convince other people that it is their definition as well.

Privilege: A right, favor, advantage, or immunity specially granted to one individual or group and withheld from another.

Systemic Microaggressions: Subtle forms of discrimination that are perpetuated through various systems (e.g., government, educational systems, media, religion).

Target Group: A group of people in a society with less power and privilege due to their minority status or historical marginalization.

Gender Identity Microaggressions: Experiences of Transgender and Gender Nonconforming People

4

As there is for sexual orientation microaggressions, there is a dearth of research on gender identity microaggressions, not only because there is a lack of literature on microaggressions overall but also because there is a limited amount of literature focusing on transgender people in general. In the PsycINFO database (which archives all psychology-related literature from 1877 to the present), a keyword search of *transgender* in December 2011 yielded only 1,712 entries; the same search revealed only 21 entries that include the keywords *transgender* and *discrimination*. Many of these articles may not even be reflective of transgender experiences but instead were included in the search results because the term *lesbian, gay, bisexual, and transgender* (LGBT) was used. Although authors tend to use this umbrella term, it has been a trend for most types of LGBT-related articles in the social sciences to focus in particular on gay men, with some literature focusing on lesbians (Meezan & Martin, 2003). Thus, many articles are assumed to be applicable to transgender people when in fact they do not include any **trans** participants in their research.

DOI: 10.1037/14093-005
That's So Gay! Microaggressions and the Lesbian, Gay, Bisexual, and Transgender Community, by K. L. Nadal

As a result, readers may presume that the experiences of transgender individuals are exactly the same as the experiences of lesbian, gay, and bisexual (LGB) people, and therefore they do not learn anything about transgender people. Because of this, it is important to review some basic terminology associated with transgender people, in order to better comprehend members of this community while recognizing how microaggressions may affect them on systemic, institutional, and interpersonal levels.

In Chapter 1, I defined some basic terms, including *transgender* (an umbrella term that can be used to refer to anyone for whom the sex she or he was assigned at birth is an incomplete or incorrect description of her- or himself), *gender identity* (i.e., an individual's personal sense of identification as male or female or another gender), and *gender nonconforming* (i.e., the trait or identity of not adhering to gender role expectations). All three of these definitions are important because they help us to understand who is included in the transgender community. Although *cisgender* people (i.e., individuals who are gender conforming) tend to think of transgender people as all being **transsexuals** and others who physically transition, the transgender community can also include individuals who do not conform to any gender at all or who identify with a third gender. For example, **genderqueer** is an umbrella term that applies to people who self-identify neither as a man or woman or who self-identify as both a man and a woman.

Furthermore, people who **gender bend** (also known as **gender benders**) may also be classified under the transgender umbrella. Gender benders may include **drag queens**, **drag kings**, and **cross-dressers** who may dress in gender nonconforming ways often, occasionally, or once in a while. For example, a drag queen or king may gender bend only during stage performances, and a cross-dresser may reserve gender bending for special occasions or nights out on the town. Sometimes individuals who gender bend do not identify as transgender or LGBT. In fact, many may view themselves as heterosexuals who have a more fluid gender identity, thus further supporting the fact that gender identity and sexual orientation are independent concepts and self-identities.

Learning these definitions is also necessary because it helps one grasp why microaggressions (and overt discrimination) toward transgender individuals are so common. Because most Western societies accept, promote, and teach others a **gender binary,** many cisgender people may have difficulties in recognizing that there are alternative ways to experience or express gender, other than exclusively female or exclusively male. This gender binary may promote heteronormativity, in which all people are expected to act in accordance with their birth sex and gender roles. As demonstrated by the many examples in Chapter 3, LGB people have described how others judged, mocked, or punished them when they behaved in gender nonconforming ways (e.g., boys who acted effeminately or girls who participated in traditionally masculine activities). For trans people, however, this gender binary may result in even more microaggressions because others may be extremely uncomfortable that these individuals' identities, physical appearances, or both do not match what is traditionally considered "male" or "female."

The gender binary may affect various subgroups under the transgender umbrella differentially. First, gender presentation is a huge factor in understanding one's experiences with discrimination. As mentioned in the Introduction, **pre-op** transgender people (i.e., those who do not medically transition or have gender reassignment surgery) may have difficulty in "**passing**" as their self-identified gender (i.e., their physical appearance does not match the gender with which they identify or with which they feel most comfortable). As a result, **cis** people may hold prejudicial attitudes toward these individuals, which may lead to microaggressions and more overt forms of discrimination. On the other hand, **post-op** transgender people (i.e., those who do medically transition or complete gender reassignment surgery) and those who opt for hormonal treatment may have an easier time in "passing," which may reduce the discrimination they experience. However, this may result in microaggressions in which they are assumed to be cisgender (e.g., a coworker who does not know a post-op transgender person's history may make a transphobic remark).

It is crucial to be aware that there are many reasons why transgender people do not undergo reassignment surgery or hormone treatment: they may not have access to hormones, they may not have the financial resources, or they simply do not feel the need to physically transition. Because transgender people are often kicked out of their homes as youth (Koken, Bimbi, & Parsons, 2009) and have difficulty gaining employment because of discrimination (National Center for Transgender Equality and the National Gay and Lesbian Task Force, 2009), they may have difficulty earning enough money to sustain their lives, let alone pay for hormone treatment. Furthermore, when they do not have access to full-time jobs, or their employers do not provide transgender-friendly health services, they may not have the resources to get the treatment that they need. Third, some transgender people simply view a medical or hormonal transition as unnecessary. Some of these individuals are comfortable with the fact that their physical bodies do not match their transgender identities or feelings. Others recognize that because they do not have the resources to attain the medical treatment to transition, they learn to be comfortable with maintaining their biological sex. Finally, those who identify as gender nonconforming may be comfortable with their physical bodies but not want to be identified as either male or female; thus, transitioning into the opposite of their birth gender may be neither salient nor required.

Moreover, because of the gender binary, transgender people who do transition may experience discrimination based on their perceived gender or gender presentation. For example, male-to-female (MTF) transgender women who pass may begin to encounter microaggressions similar to those committed against cisgender women (e.g., they may be sexually objectified, viewed as intellectually or physically inferior). Meanwhile, female-to-male (FTM) transgender men, who are now presumed to be cisgender men, may be expected to adhere to the same rigid gender roles as cisgender men (e.g., they may be expected to be emotionally strong, masculine, or chivalrous). So, although transgender people all along the spectrum can encounter gender identity microaggressions, it is clear that perceived gender itself can heavily influence one's experiences with discrimination.

Only one known study focused specifically on the impact of gender identity microaggressions on transgender and gender nonconforming people. Nadal, Skolnik, and Wong (2012) used a qualitative, focus group method with transgender female and male participants ($N = 9$) to classify the spectrum of gender identity microaggressions. Similar to previous studies on LGB individuals, Nadal, Skolnik, and Wong used several categories that validated the taxonomy presented by Nadal, Rivera, and Corpus (2010), including the following nine: (a) use of transphobic and/or incorrectly gendered terminology, (b) endorsement of gender normative and binary culture or behaviors, (c) assumption of universal transgender experience, (d) exoticization, (e) discomfort with/disapproval of transgender experience, (f) assumption of sexual pathology/abnormality, (g) denial of the existence of transphobia, (h) physical threat or harassment, and (i) denial of individual transphobia. (See Chapter 2 of this volume for a brief description of each of Nadal, Rivera, and Corpus's original categories.) In Nadal, Skolnik, and Wong's study, however, one category emerged that was significantly different from the LGB studies: denial of bodily privacy. This type of microaggression describes the various ways that transgender people's bodies are often objectified or exoticized, in particular, through others' insidious and entitled questions. Overall, participants' responses demonstrated that the taxonomy was an appropriate representation of microaggressions experienced by transgender and gender nonconforming people.

Voices of Transgender and Gender Nonconforming People

Similar to the previous chapter, this next section begins by revisiting the categories based on the microaggression taxonomy presented by Nadal, Rivera, and Corpus (2010); however, here I focus on the microaggressions from the perspectives from transgender people. I also provide examples from my own research (e.g., Nadal, Skolnik, & Wong, 2012), contemporary media and literature, and other real-life perspectives that have been submitted to the Internet blog The Microaggressions Project (http://microaggressions.com/).

USE OF TRANSPHOBIC TERMINOLOGY

This category of microaggressions includes instances when others use denigrating language about or toward transgender people. Sometimes transphobic or genderist language was used intentionally to insult or berate a transgender person. In one study, a transgender man talked about an incident he had experienced before fully transitioning:

> I remember one time before I transitioned when I first moved to New York; I was on the train with my roommate, who was a non-transgender woman of color. A young African-American guy was like, "Yo, yo . . . is that a dude or is that a woman?" (Nadal, Skolnik, & Wong, 2012, p. 65)

A transgender woman mentioned a similar microaggression involving transphobic language:

> I was walking one time to the post office and I had just recently had my lips done and a little five-year-old kid said, "Daddy, daddy. Hey daddy, that's a shemale." So he never referred to me as a man. He referred to me as . . . a shemale. (Nadal, Skolnik et al., 2012, p. 65)

In both cases, it is clear that the enactor of the microaggression was conscious about his action. Although they may not have intended to directly offend the transgender individual, their transphobic words were hurtful and insulting. Even more disheartening is that the second example includes a transphobic remark made by a young child, which signifies that children can learn hurtful language at an early age.

Sometimes people may use transphobic or genderist language that is unconscious and unintentional. For example, it is common for cisgender people (heterosexual and even LGB people) to use the word *tranny* when describing transgender people. One individual from The Microaggressions Project described being called a tranny by a friend. The cisgender friend told another, "She's too sensitive. Why should she get upset at me for calling her what she is?" The individual said, "[It] made me feel awful. Like calling me slurs is okay because I'm trans and that I'm overreacting for being hurt by it." This example demonstrates that even good-hearted people who believe that they are accepting of transgender people may use language that is offensive and hurtful.

The use of incorrect gender pronouns can also be considered trans-phobic language. In a narrative about growing up with a transgender parent, one author described how she purposefully used to use the incorrect pronouns to express her disdain for her father's transition into a woman:

> In public, we became adept at blowing pronouns. Today I still slip up sometimes and call Dana [my biological father who has transitioned into a transgender woman] "he" or "him," but back then we did it on purpose, to show Dana that we still thought of her as a man, a husband and father, not this strange new woman who wore frilly, fancy sweatsuits and pink lipstick and who spoke in an artificial-sounding falsetto. Every time my mother or I said "he" or "his" in public, Dana would respond with a dirty look, an elbow in the ribs, or a kick under the table. (Cicotello, 2000, p. 135)

The intentional action of using the wrong pronoun may be considered a microassault in that the author was conscious of her behavior and desired to offend her father. However, the author mentions how she still "slips up" and uses the wrong pronoun, even after becoming more accepting of her transgender parent. Perhaps this type of behavior may be viewed as a microinsult because it is unintentional and not meant to be malicious.

Microaggressions in which people use incorrect pronouns can also manifest in the media. When Chaz Bono, the transgender male son of Sonny Bono and Cher, became a contestant on ABC's *Dancing With the Stars*, several figures in the media shared opinions that were either blatantly or subtly transphobic. One of the more vocal critics was Dr. Keith Ablow, a news reporter for Fox News. In one article, he wrote the following:

> Chaz Bono should not be applauded for asserting she is a man (and goes about trying to look like one) any more than a woman who believes she will be happier without arms, has them re-moved and then continues to assert that she was right all along. (Ablow, 2011)

As he continued on a diatribe that belittled Bono and all transgender people, Ablow consistently used the word *she* to refer to Bono, regard-less of Bono's identification as a man. Whether Ablow was intentional in his use of the pronoun, the act of dismissing someone's **preferred gender pronoun** would be considered microaggressive.

Similarly, on E! Television's *Chelsea Lately*, host Chelsea Handler and several panelists also discussed Bono's participation in *Dancing With the Stars*. For several minutes, three of the four comedians commented on Bono being a "he/she" while also making jokes about Bono's genitalia.

The Gay and Lesbian Alliance Against Defamation released the following statement:

> The "humor" utilized by others hinged solely on using both male and female pronouns to describe Bono and reducing his identity down to his anatomy in order to ridicule him. In doing so, they are effectively making a mockery of anyone who identifies as transgender and contributing to the already dangerous and hostile climate many transgender people face. (Kane, 2011)

In this instance, it is clear that the comedians were intentional in using their transphobic language when referring to Bono. If confronted, they may respond that they were simply "being funny" or that "it was just a joke." However, hearing such language can be damaging both to transgender people (who may feel dehumanized and ridiculed) as well as to cisgender people (who may learn that it is acceptable to make jokes at transgender people's expense).

ENDORSEMENT OF GENDER NORMATIVE CULTURE AND BEHAVIORS

This theme describes instances in which transgender people are expected to subscribe to the gender binary, by subscribing to a gender normative culture and participating in gender normative behaviors. Often such comments are not meant to be malicious; people may believe that they are simply stating their opinions and that their thoughts match what most other people think. Furthermore, these types of statements are usually based on a person's biased assumption that there are two rigid genders that need to be upheld. For example, on an episode of ABC's *The View* in 2007, the cohosts were discussing how they felt about children who wear clothes that are stereotypically intended for the opposite sex (e.g., boys who wear dresses), especially at school. While many of the cohosts did not see a problem with such behavior, Sherri Shepherd proclaimed, "Not in *my house*! Not in *my house*! Not in *my house*! My son isn't putting on dresses! Girls wear dresses! When he's 18, he can do what he wants, but not in my house!"

It is clear that Shepherd has biased opinions about what is considered normative for boys and for girls. Although gender normative comments such as these may affect all people (including LGB people, as mentioned in Chapter 3), transgender people may experience these types of microaggressions in unique ways. There are times when transgender people are encouraged to "stay" with their birth gender. At other times they are stereotyped as not being capable of doing something that a cisgender person would be able to. They are also presumed to not be "real" men or women regardless of their physical, medical, or psychological transitions.

In one study, a transgender man (who was still transitioning) described how his coworkers questioned his ability to do physical work: "[My coworker] said, 'This is a man's job type thing, you know'" (Nadal, Skolnik, et al., 2012, p. 67). Perhaps this comment was made because his coworkers didn't assume he was masculine enough; perhaps they still stereotyped him as being a woman who would not be capable of completing a physically arduous task. Similarly, in the movie *Transamerica* there is a scene in which the main character, Bree Osbourne (played by Felicity Huffman), is at dinner in a restaurant with her family. Although Bree identifies and presents as a woman (and despite the fact that there are other people at the table), her mother expects Bree to be chivalrous and pull out her chair for her as she sits down. The underlying message communicated in this scene is that Bree is "still a man" and is thus expected to engage in the same chivalrous behaviors that are expected of cisgender men.

Through The Microaggressions Project, a transgender woman reported a similar type of experience:

> My mother contends that my sister, who is cis, needs to learn how to cook, something she's never said to me, a trans woman. I'm angry that my mother thinks women are obligated to be domestic and that she's only trying to get my name and pronouns right instead of trying to see me as a woman. [As I write this] I am 27, six years after I came out.

Although it appears that the mother of the transgender woman in this example may make conscious efforts to be careful about using her correct name and pronouns, it still appears that the mother does not view her as a "real woman" because she does not expect her to uphold the same gender roles as her cisgender sister. Whereas a cisgender woman might find her mother's gender role expectations to be microaggressive or sexist, this transgender woman simply wants to be treated as any other cisgender woman would.

Additionally, through The Microaggressions Project a few transgender FTM men have described comments that have been said to them. One transgender man shared that a cisgender woman at his liberal church said, "But you're so cute! Why do you want to be a boy?" He stated that the comment made him feel "completely worthless, completely erased." Similarly, a gay transgender FTM man shared how cisgender gay men have told him, "What's the point of being a gay trans man? Why didn't you just stay a straight girl?" He revealed that the statements made him feel "vulnerable, invisible, and defeated." In both of these examples, the individuals' intentions may have been genuine and innocent in that they believed they were asking a viable question. However, in doing so, they invalidated the transgender individual's gender identity and revealed their hidden biases that transgender identities are invalid and that identifying with one's birth gender is preferred.

Finally, sometimes transgender people experience microaggressions in which others treat them like their birth gender instead of as their self-identified gender. For example, one female (MTF) transgender participant described one romantic relationship she had with a man:

> I went out with a guy, also, at first when he thought I was a woman, when he thought I was a woman, he would open the car door for me. He would do this, he would do that, he would bring me flowers, and when I told him that I was transgender, he stayed with me, I'm not going to say he didn't. But when we would fight he would say, "But you're a man, why should I treat you this way?" (Nadal, Vargas, Meterko, Hamit, & McLean, 2012, p. 134)

Again, although the cisgender man in this scenario may have seemed to be somewhat accepting of the transgender participant, he still did not view her as a "real" woman. He chose to be chivalrous and generous with her when he was happy with her; however, he chose to be mean and degrading when he was upset with her.

ASSUMPTION OF UNIVERSAL TRANSGENDER EXPERIENCE

These types of microaggressions occur when individuals presume that all transgender people are the same. Many of these assumptions can be based on negative stereotypes that are learned through religion, the media, and other sources; others may be based on generalizations from past personal experiences. For instance, in the movie *Transamerica,* when one of the characters, Toby, learns of the protagonist's transgender identity, he makes a comment alluding to the notion that transgender people could not be Christian. In response, Bree (the protagonist) replies, "My body may be a work-in-progress, but there is nothing wrong with my soul." Often it is assumed that LGBT people could not possibly be religious or spiritual because they are "choosing" something that others believe to be "against God's will." However, as Bree affirms in the quote above, transgender people are just as moral and good as anyone else.

Sometimes transgender people are stereotyped on the basis of what is viewed in the media. One author wrote about how there is a disproportionate amount of transgender women who are portrayed as sex workers on television and in movies:

> The popular assumption that trans women deliberately transform ourselves into sexual objects also explains why we are so frequently depicted in the media as sex workers.

> The fact that trans female sex workers have reached the status of "stock characters" is of particular interest, as such depictions are at complete odds with other cissexual presumptions about transsexuality. Media representations of trans people that do not involve sex work typically go out of their way to stress the fact that transsexuality is an extraordinarily rare phenomenon, and to promote the idea that transsexuals are sexually undesirable. So it is unclear why, being as rare and undesirable as we supposedly are, we seem to make up such a significant percentage of sex workers on TV and in the movies. (Serano, 2007, p. 261)

This stereotype—that transgender women are sex workers—parallels a narrative from a transgender woman in a study my colleagues and I conducted. She described going to the police station when she and another transgender friend were victims of a crime. She stated, "The detectives in the victim's unit asked if we were prostitutes. So I said, 'I'm not a prostitute, why are you saying that? He said, 'Because all you transsexuals are all prostitutes'" (Nadal, Skolnik, & Wong, 2012, p. 65).

Another transgender participant described how people assume that after transitioning, all transgender people would have the same experiences, identities, lifestyles, and interests:

> In my experiences, [people] play certain male gender roles that are like super normative and I'm just like, "No, I don't play that. That's not me." There's so much of that that exists that it's hard to figure out how do you balance between being who you are and wanting [to] be respected and also not want [to] complicate it as well. (Nadal, Skolnik & Wong, 2012, p. 65)

Thus, it is clear that cisgender people have some stereotypes about transgender people that they assume are true of all people within the transgender umbrella. Again, although perpetrators of these microaggressions may be well intentioned, they in fact are communicating their true feelings of judgment or disapproval of transgender people.

EXOTICIZATION

Many microaggressions occur when transgender people are dehumanized or treated like objects. Often these microaggressions happen when transgender people are viewed as sexual objects instead of human beings with any feelings. A Latina transgender woman in one study discussed how men often treat her:

> [Men often tell me], "You're not girlfriend material.
> All I want from you is that sexual asset and that whole
> thrill of being with a transsexual and go on with my life

and act like you never exist." Now, not only am I being objectified and sensationalized, I'm being less than human. (Nadal, Skolnik, & Wong, 2012, p. 66)

When transgender people are not being sexually objectified, they are viewed as "tokens" : token girlfriends, token boyfriends, or even token friends. One participant shared, "Even if they don't even like you, just because you're a tranny, they want you in their collection" (Nadal, Skolnik, & Wong, 2012, p. 66).

Finally, there are many ways in which transgender people can be viewed as unique or bizarre instead of being viewed as people. For example, in the movie *The Crying Game,* one transsexual character's transgender identity was revealed to the audience when her penis was shown during a love scene with a cisgender male character. The movie caused quite a stir at the time because it was one of the first times that a transgender female character was portrayed in a mainstream movie as being "beautiful"—a word that was even used by the film's director. Although the movie's plot included several other dramatic and suspenseful storylines, I found it interesting that reviewers used words like "comedic," "sexual extremism," and "perverse" to describe the film (Kotsopoulos & Mills, 1994). Because of this one transgender character and her "big secret," the movie was viewed as comedic, perhaps signifying that cisgender people view transgender people as perverse individuals who exist for their entertainment. Furthermore, Jaye Davidson, who played the transgender character Dill, was nominated for an Academy Award for Best Actor, which led to several forms of transphobia in the media. For example, film critic Gene Siskel argued that Jaye Davidson deserved an Oscar because he had "two roles to play: first, a woman, and then, the character Dill" (Kotsopoulos & Mills, 1994). Such commentary can be construed as transphobic because it supports that male and female actors are expected to play only roles that match their birth gender and that anything else along the spectrum would require exceptional talent. It also exoticizes transgender people as being a unique species because they do not conform to a gender.

DISCOMFORT WITH OR DISAPPROVAL OF TRANSGENDER EXPERIENCE

Often microaggressions based on discomfort with or disapproval of the transgender experience may be conscious in that the individual is aware of her or his uneasiness. At other times these microaggressions may be unconscious in that the perpetrators are not even aware they are reacting or acting in such a way. Sometimes these types of microaggressions may be unintentional in that the individuals may know that they are uncomfortable but do not understand the negative impact such microaggressions have on the person.

For example, a transgender participant in a study my colleagues and I conducted shared a story in which both a classmate and a romantic interest showed disapproval of her transgender identity:

> I was in school and was getting to know this gentleman. I didn't feel comfortable in telling him that I was transgender because I wasn't too sure how I [felt] with him yet. There was this girl in my class who I had thought she knew I was transgender because we go to the gym together. She tried to question my gender and she [also] found out I was talking to that gentleman. One day, I happened to walk down the same block as he was and he moved to the left and I kept moving forward. He waved "hi" but it was like he was ashamed, like I was a disease. I was definitely hurt. In the end, I found out she told him that I was a man. (Nadal, Skolnik, & Wong, 2012, p. 66)

So, although neither the classmate nor the romantic interest directed hurtful or discriminatory language to the participant, their avoidant behaviors demonstrated their discomfort with and/or lack of acceptance of her.

A transgender male participant described a feeling he gets when interacting with certain cisgender people:

> I pay real close attention to how I get treated in different spaces. I noticed that when I'm in an environment with mostly straight but sometimes also queer men, who know of my transgender history, the ways in which they treat me versus the way in which they treat non-transgender men are like absolutely very clear. (Nadal, Skolnik, & Wong, 2012, p. 66–67)

This type of scenario demonstrates a subtle type of microaggression—the type that may be hard to define or articulate. Because it may be more difficult to point out (i.e., it is often a feeling that a person gets), it may be more challenging to confront an individual regarding any microaggressive behaviors.

This type of subtle, unspoken microaggression may be common for transgender people when they try to find employment. For example, one transgender woman described why it is so difficult for her to get hired:

> I remember a lot of them looking at me . . . and taking the paper. I gave them my resume, and "If we have an opening we'll call you." Even though in the window it says "Now Hiring," they go, "If we have an opening we'll call you." So they would say that but they didn't just come out and go "how dare you, hell no we ain't gonna hire you." But they did say it, it was just they watch what they say cause there were witnesses. (Nadal, Vargas, et al., 2012, p. 132)

Again, although the person perceived that the employer was assuming something prejudicial toward transgender people, the lack of evidence may leave the individual feeling confused or paranoid.

A respondent on The Microaggressions Project blog shared a comment that was made by a family member:

> Well, you can't reasonably expect health care providers to know anything about your situation. I mean, you're transsexual, and that's pretty weird. I don't know why you're so upset about this. You should really be more tolerant of people who don't get it.

The individual in this interaction clearly was conscious of what she or he was saying, yet the intention may not have been to hurt or offend the transgender person; instead, the intention may have been to provide explanations to the transgender person regarding the type of discrimination she or he experiences. Despite this, calling transsexuals "weird" clearly demonstrates the individual's discomfort with and disapproval of transgender people.

Also on The Microaggressions Project blog, one participant described an instance in which she overheard a mother say, "We're not going near the drag queens!" at an LGBT pride parade and festival, in a "generally [LGBT]-friendly town." The participant reported feeling "awkward and sad that somebody would teach their child to hate and fear . . . [and] confused that somebody with those feelings would attend a Pride festival in the first place." Although the sexual orientation of the woman who made this comment is not known, this incident exemplifies the types of microaggressions that can occur within the LGBT community. Because LGB people are the victims of heterosexist discrimination (and microaggressions), they may not recognize the privilege they have as cisgender people or understand how their biases against transgender people may lead to microaggressions.

ASSUMPTION OF SEXUAL PATHOLOGY, DEVIANCE, OR ABNORMALITY

This category includes microaggressions in which transgender people are assumed to be sexually pathological, deviant, or abnormal. Similar to the examples shared in Chapter 3, regarding LGB people, transgender people may be assumed to be sexually promiscuous or be diagnosed with HIV/AIDS. A transgender woman in one study revealed the following experiences:

> A lot of men objectify or sensationalize me for being transgender and the first thing is "Will you suck my dick?" And I'm like you know, I don't even like oral sex so why don't you just say "Hello, my name is . . . " (Nadal, Skolnik, & Wong, 2012, p. 68)

Similar to the earlier example, in which a police officer assumed that all transgender women are sex workers, this incident suggests that people assume that transgender women are overly sexual or engage in deviant sexual behavior.

Another transgender woman shared an encounter in which an emergency medical technician (EMT) accidentally came in contact with her blood: "She said, 'I have kids, I can't believe this. Oh my God. I touched that person! I touched that person's blood. I touched that person's blood'" (Nadal, Skolnik, & Wong, 2012, p. 68). It is clear that this EMT was reacting differently to this participant than she would to a cisgender person. EMTs likely encounter blood on a regular basis; thus, to react so negatively with a transgender person's blood may exemplify her bias toward transgender people or her specific stereotype that transgender people would have HIV/AIDS.

DENIAL OF THE REALITY OF TRANSPHOBIA

This category of microaggressions involves instances (most often statements) in which cisgender people deny that transphobia and discrimination are realities in the life of transgender people. Often these types of invalidations may be well intentioned in that the person simply wants to provide a rationalization for the transgender person. For example, in an example given earlier, a relative told a transgender person, "I don't know why you're so upset about this. You should really be more tolerant of people who don't get it." This type of statement can be invalidating to the transgender person who experiences such bias and discrimination on a regular basis. A cisgender person does not know what it is like to be transgender; neither does she or he know what transphobic discrimination feels like. Thus, when invalidating a trans person's experiences, cisgender people communicate that trans people's perceptions are unworthy or irrational.

On The Microaggressions Project blog, one transgender individual shared a microaggression that led the individual to feel "depressed, guilty, ashamed, angry." When the individual described worry about being transgender, the individual's cisgender "girlfriend expressed indignation because 'nothing bad has ever happened' to [the transgender person] personally." The transgender person continued, "As if my fears about rejection and/or violence would only make sense if I had been seriously attacked." Similarly, another respondent on the blog revealed posting a rant on Facebook regarding a transphobic joke made on a popular television show; the person's friend replied, "Those things are terrible, but you really just have to ignore them. Just let it go and it will go away on its own." In both of these experiences, the microaggressor may have intended to be helpful. In the first, the individual's cisgender girlfriend may have made such a comment as a way of being optimistic that the transgender person has never been physically assaulted. However, in doing so, she may have made the transgender person feel invalidated because the threat of physical assault is a reality that transgender people encounter regularly. In the second instance, the Facebook friend's intention may have been to encourage the individual to "not be so sensitive," but the person ends up silencing the transgender person, who simply wanted to express frustration about transphobia in the media.

Finally, a transgender participant in one study described the reaction she got from a friend after being verbally assaulted on the street: "I went home, I started crying and my friend said 'Don't feel bad.' And I said, 'But didn't you just see what happened?'" (Nadal, Vargas, et al., 2012, p. 134). Again, perhaps the friend in this scenario was simply be trying to be supportive and encouraging, perhaps even hoping that the individual would not dwell on a negative and obviously hurtful event. However, such a comment may invalidate the transgender person, who simply wants a friend to comfort her and to authenticate that she has a right to feel the way that she does.

PHYSICAL THREAT OR HARASSMENT

Similar to the threatening behaviors toward LGB people that were described in Chapter 3, microaggressions that involve physical threat or harassment do occur toward transgender people. Again, if a behavior were clearly assaultive (i.e., it connotes clearly intentional, overt, physically abusive behavior or emotionally abusive behaviors), it would not be considered microaggressive. For example, in the movie *Boys Don't Cry*, which tells the story of Brandon Teena, the transgender male teen who was assaulted, raped, and killed for being transgender, the actions of the perpetrators are clearly hate crimes. However, physically threatening or harassing microaggressions directed toward transgender people may include instances in which an individual may not necessarily feel that his or her life is in danger; instead, he or she may feel extreme discomfort because the perpetrator is creating a hostile or emotionally unsafe environment.

In a scene in the movie *To Wong Foo, Thanks for Everything, Julie Newmar*, Chi Chi Rodriguez, a drag queen played by John Leguizamo, is being followed by several of the male citizens in a small rural town. Although the young men do not overtly tell Chi Chi that they disapprove of her or intend to harm her physically, it is clear that Chi Chi feels very threatened by their hostile body language. Another young male townsperson comes to "rescue" Chi Chi from the tense situation, but it was clear there was a potential for something awful to happen.

However, nothing did occur, so the men's behavior would not be classified as an assault but even though there was no overt physical or verbal harassment, the event could potentially be labeled as a microaggression.

This type of microaggression has also been documented in the research. For example, in one study, a transgender woman described an experience in which she felt extremely uncomfortable because of the threatening behavior of others:

> I can remember when just walking in the street . . . I could have been with my friend and someone could have said. . . . "Those are men . . . " And they would actually walk up to us . . . . You know . . . All make faces, laugh and tell other people in front of us. Some people would come up to us . . . call us names . . . and that can happen from time to time. When I used to live in the projects, I also had a very hard time . . . And every time I walked out, I swear even little kids, they would say "You got balls!" You know, everyday it was a horror story. . . . parents would tell their kids like 6 years old 7 years old. . . . [they're] so young. . . . A lot of the guys used to . . . you know. . . . I used to walk by . . . and they would be like. . . . "No that's a dude" . . . and then "No that can't be," those would come up to me and look at me . . . it was always really hard for me. (Nadal, Skolnik, & Wong, 2012, p. 68)

In this scenario, the behaviors of the perpetrators are intentionally and consciously hurtful. However, these may be considered microaggressions; they cannot quite be classified as harassment because they consist of comments that are often said under people's (even little children's) breath. Although physical and emotional assaults traditionally are viewed as criminal behavior, the types described by transgender study participants may not actually "qualify" and thus may be classified as microaggressions.

DENIAL OF BODILY PRIVACY

This microaggression category appears to be unique to transgender people; it is not pervasive in research on LGB individuals. Transgender people across the spectrum are often subjected to intrusive, personal questions about their body parts. Because transgender people are often in various stages of transition, many cisgender people may feel privileged in finding out about transgender people's bodies. When cisgender persons "discover" a transgender person's biological makeup, they often feel angry or betrayed that the transgender person did not tell them initially. However, Bree Osbourne, the main character of *Transamerica*, said it best when she proclaimed, "Just because a person doesn't go around blabbing her entire biological history to everyone she meets doesn't make her a liar."

I have found, in my research, that it is common for transgender people to be asked very private questions about their bodies. One transgender woman (MTF) shared the following:

> I'm very open about being transgender inside the school and [an acquaintance] went and told some students . . . "That's a man," and the students looked at me and were like, "What, that's not a man. Look at her face and she has breasts. That's not a man." So, they were standing and looking at me like if I was a circus freak, you know . . . as usual. (Nadal, Skolnik, & Wong, 2012, p. 69)

A transgender man shared a similar experience:

> This guy was like, "Yo, is that a dude or is that a woman" and I was like, "All right, okay. Let's see how far this goes." And then he came up to me and said, "Yo, yo, you have a dick or pussy? A dick or pussy?" And I was just like, "Why does it matter?" (Nadal, Skolnik, & Wong, 2012, p. 70)

Finally, in another study with transgender participants, one FTM participant shared, "I would hear coworkers snicker behind my back at work and had friends at college who would ask what was in my pants. Not cool" (Singh & McKleroy, 2011, p. 38). Being on display and susceptible to public commentary is invalidating, dehumanizing, and belittling for transgender people. Cisgender people who make such statements may not realize how much their words affect the transgender people who hear them.

SYSTEMIC MICROAGGRESSIONS

Finally, previous research has found that transgender people experience a significant number of systemic microaggressions in their everyday lives (e.g., Nadal, Skolnik, & Wong, 2012). Although other groups—namely, people of color, women, LGB people, and people with disabilities—experience numerous microaggressions through systems, institutions, and environments, there are many microaggressions that seem to affect transgender people specifically. For example, there is an array of disparities in educational attainment, employment, and socioeconomic status that affect all of the aforementioned marginalized groups. Transgender people, however, experience not only these but also additional obstacles. Some of the major systemic microaggressions that have been reported in the past have included the following areas: public restrooms, the criminal justice system, health care, and government-issued identification.

It is a common, everyday struggle for transgender people to decide which public restroom to use. If they use the restroom of the gender with which they identify, they risk being viewed as intruders and accused of being sexual predators or deviants. If they use the restroom of the gender with which they do not identify, they may also be harassed by individuals who believe they don't belong there. One transgender male participant shared this dilemma:

> When I use the bathroom, I tend to withdraw and use the
> handicap bathroom. People are always looking at me like . . .
> Their perception of me is like "Just use the male bathroom."
> And I'm thinking . . . do I wanna engage with my male co-workers
> who might freak out? Or if I want to use the women's bathroom . . .
> what that brings up for women and seeing my presence in there.
> (Nadal, Skolnik, & Wong, 2012, p. 72)

Although using a public restroom may seem innocuous to cisgender people, this very simple everyday behavior may cause distress for a transgender person.

Regarding the criminal justice system, transgender people are often placed in prisons and other facilities on the basis of their birth sex, not their gender. This may lead to inappropriate activities, like strip searches by individuals of the opposite gender or harassment by law enforcement officers. One transgender participant described an experience of being arrested and strip searched in front a group of other arrestees, and a transgender woman participant recalled the treatment she received in prison when she and her transgender friend were the victims of a crime:

> "Can you hurry up and write your statements? Because it's late
> and we all have families. So do you wanna write a statement or
> do you want to leave?" And I just said [to my friend] "Write your
> statement because something happened to you" and so she was
> gonna write it . . . and the detectives were passing by and they
> said . . . (singing) "Transformers . . . men up in disguise" . . .
> Just like that. . . . I said "What the hell?" . . . I said "These are
> the detectives . . . Wait, wait, wait . . . Don't write anything.
> They're gonna throw this in the garbage—they want us to leave."
> (Nadal, Skolnik, & Wong, 2012, p. 73)

Although many groups may experience discrimination within the criminal justice system, the type encountered by transgender people is usually much more overt and vocalized.

Transgender participants have described the types of microaggressions that they experience within the health care system. Often they are met with interpersonal microaggressions (i.e., specific health care workers enacting microaggressions), but sometimes there are systemic microaggressions in which the system displays its lack of competence in serving transgender people. One transgender female participant described the following experience:

> The ambulance lady came to pick me up. And she asked me
> when was the last time I got my period. And I looked at her and
> I said "I don't get no periods, sweetie, I'm transgender." Once I
> told her that, as soon as they put me in the chair in the hospital,
> she told ALL the doctors what I was, ALL the nurses, and every-
> body came up to me looking at me. And the pain kept on getting

stronger. I started getting agitated. I started going crazy. I got up, ripped the IV off with the blood gushing and I flipped on all of them. I said "You know what, I'm not here for ya'll to look at me and to find out what the hell I am. I am here for you to help me." (Nadal, Skolnik, & Wong, 2012, p. 74)

The transgender person in this scenario simply needed medical assistance, yet the second her transgender identity was discovered, she was treated as less than human. Although none of the doctors or nurses explicitly said anything discriminatory to her, she felt belittled and dehumanized.

Concurrently, the health care system in itself may be transphobic in that it does not address the needs of transgender people. For example, most insurance companies do not cover transgender-related medical costs (e.g., hormones, gender reassignment surgery). One participant in a study with transgender people of color disclosed the following:

There are transgender-specific issues such as access to medical care and hormone treatment. It is unaffordable to pay for hormones when it costs $25 for [a] one-month supply. Health insurance does not always cover it, and if it is, it is very minimal. The problem is also with obtaining hormones, like one day you're in and one day you're out. (Bith-Melander et al., 2010, p. 215)

This quote makes clear that social class may play a role in the transition process for transgender individuals. However, even transgender individuals from higher socioeconomic status families may be disowned by their families, which may lead to difficulties in paying medical costs. So, systemic microaggressions in the health care system may potentially affect transgender people of all social classes.

Finally, participants have described how government-issued identification is a major challenge because of the requirement to report gender. One participant shared this story:

I have to get my passport redone and I literally have to make an Excel spreadsheet. Its like, well, in order to get my passport gender marker changed, I have to first submit a letter to the Selective Service explaining why I'm not eligible for the draft. Then, I have to get a copy of my birth certificate, which I don't have because it says the wrong name and gender, so I can't use it. So, I have to first change that. And then I would have to go the Social Security . . . uhhhh. . . . as I think about it, I was like "Ohhh my God . . . I have a migraine." (Nadal, Skolnik, & Wong, 2012, pp. 74–75)

Case Studies

I next provide three case studies that help illustrate the types of microaggressions transgender individuals experience.

SYSTEMIC MICROAGGRESSIONS:
THE CASE OF DESTINY

Destiny is a 17-year-old Filipina American (MTF) transgender woman who lives in a major metropolitan city on the West Coast. She is the youngest of four children (with one older brother and two older sisters who are 5 to 8 years older than she). Destiny was born a biological boy named Dennis. Because her father was out of the picture, her single mother had always worked full-time, and her older siblings spent a lot of time taking care of their youngest sibling. When "Dennis" was 4 or 5 years old, she loved playing dress-up with her sisters. Because her mother did not buy her any dresses, she would ask her sisters if she could try on their clothes and makeup. They granted her requests and enjoyed putting on short performances for each other, while participating in their own fashion photo shoots and fashion shows.

When Destiny was a young adolescent, she thought that maybe she was a gay man, mainly because she knew she was attracted to other boys. However, as she grew older she started to realize that playing dress-up wasn't just a phase—it was something with which she felt most comfortable in every aspect of her life. She started to buy her own makeup and dresses and started to dress as a woman in private, when her family was not at home. By the time she was 16, she felt more comfortable wearing women's clothing in public, and she eventually told her sisters and two of her close friends that she felt transgender. Luckily, all were supportive of her.

Destiny is about to start her senior year in high school and decides that she wants to live her life as a woman. At the urging of her sisters, she first comes out to her older brother and her mother at the same time. While they were definitely shocked (her mother cried hysterically at first) and confused (her brother said, "Are you sure you're not just gay?"), they both told her that they would support her decision but that it would take them a while to get used to it. When Destiny mentions that she wants to finish high school as a woman, her mom begs her not to, saying, "It will be too hard for you! I don't want you to get hurt." However, Destiny assures her that she is ready and that she doesn't want to live a lie anymore.

To prepare herself for her senior year of high school, Destiny sets up a meeting with Dr. Kaner, her high school principal. When Destiny shows up to the meeting dressed as a woman, Dr. Kaner looks at her irritably but allows her into his office. Destiny then tells him that she is transgender and that she wants to live her life as a woman. She also states that she wants to make sure that the school knows and that they are able to provide a safe environment for her. Dr. Kaner responds by saying, "I can't promise you that it's going to be safe. Kids will be kids." He adds, "Plus, it's your decision to dress like that, so you can always choose to dress as a normal person if you don't want to get into any trouble." Destiny is shocked by his lack of support but asks, "Well, I was wondering if I could use the faculty bathroom from now on, because I know they have private unisex bathrooms." He replies, "No, you still have to use the men's bathroom; we can't make special requests for any student." Destiny nods in understanding, leaves his office, and cries when she gets to her car.

UNINTENTIONAL, TRANSPHOBIC MICROAGGRESSIVE LANGUAGE: THE CASE OF JAN

Jan is a 25-year-old African American transgender, gender nonconforming person who identifies as neither male nor female. Although Jan was born a female at birth (named Jennifer), Jan has always felt different from other family members, friends, and classmates. As a child, Jan refused to wear the dresses that Jan's mother often wanted Jan to wear, opting to dress in more **gender neutral** clothing, like sweatshirts and jeans. Most people just assumed that Jan was a lesbian, based mainly on Jan's gender presentation (which for most of Jan's childhood was as a "butch" teenage girl). However, Jan never identified as being gay or lesbian; instead, Jan always just felt "neither." Also, because Jan knew that others would be confused or not accepting toward Jan's identity, Jan decided to keep on checking off any "female" boxes on applications and forms, just because it was easier.

Jan went to college in a state that was several hours away from Jan's family. Moving far away was important for Jan because it would give Jan the opportunity to explore romantic and sexual relationships, as well as **gender expression,** differently, because Jan would not have to worry about running into family members or friends. During the first week of school, Jan thought it would be best to meet other LGBT students, so Jan decided to go to the university's LGBT resource center and attend a LGBT pride club meeting. When Jan first started making friends, Jan disclosed as one who self-identified as transgender and gender nonconforming. Most of the other students in the organization identified as lesbian and gay; Jan was the only one who identified as transgender. Despite being the only one, Jan tried not to let this be bothersome; in fact, Jan just assumed that there were very few transgender people altogether and was happy to just be around LGBT people. However, in order to ensure that transgender issues were being addressed in the organization, Jan decided to run for one of the elected officer positions, and won.

One of the things Jan had always been clear about with new friends or acquaintances was that Jan did not identify as either female or male and therefore would prefer not to be called a gendered pronoun (e.g., "she" or "he"). Instead, Jan asked to simply be referred to as "Jan." When Jan mentioned this at the first board meeting, everyone was respectful about the request and promised Jan that they would abide by this. Jan was thankful for their sensitivity, even though Jan had to occasionally gently correct them each time they used a gendered pronoun.

Despite everyone else's promise to abide by Jan's request, people still referred to Jan as "she" or "her" whenever they made mention of Jan. For example, Ethan, the president of the organization, said, "So, you all know we have a new board member, Jan. I was wondering if someone can help to familiarize her with some of the basic procedures?" Before others could volunteer, Jan politely smiled and corrected the mistake, playfully saying, "Remember, it's just Jan!" Ethan, embarrassed, apologized and continued to ask for a volunteer before continuing with the meeting. These subtle mistakes transpired a few more times at the meeting with others. Similarly, Jan would lightheartedly interrupt whoever was speaking, while correcting them in the same way as with Ethan. Each time, the individual would apologize and the meeting would continue. However, by the fourth or fifth time that Jan was correcting the individual, Jan began to wonder if people were starting to get annoyed by the disruptions or if others even really cared about Jan's feelings regarding preferred gender pronouns. Jan decided not to say anything for the rest of the meeting, even though others referred to Jan as "she" a few more times.

After the meeting, Jan decided to talk to Ethan, the president of the organization, who is a gay White cisgender male. Jan shared feeling like the others were not taking the request seriously and that their actions made Jan feel marginalized, invisible, and upset. Ethan apologized, stating that he didn't want Jan to feel this way. He then added, "I think people have trouble not referring to you as a 'she' because you look like a woman. Maybe if you had surgery or took hormones or something, people might be able to remember to not use pronouns." Jan could not believe that Ethan had spoken those words, and Jan was even more baffled that he didn't realize that what he was saying was hurtful and offensive. Instead of arguing with him, Jan meekly stated, "Okay, I see how it is" and walked away. Eventually, Jan quit attending the LGBT pride meetings altogether.

MICROAGGRESSIONS ENCOUNTERED BY THOSE WHO PASS: THE CASE OF SID

Sid is a 41-year-old transgender man (FTM) of Native American and Irish descent. Sid had always known that he was transgender. In fact, he came out to his parents when he was 17, and he began hormone treatment on his 18th birthday. Though initially shocked, his parents eventually became supportive. However, because they were a working-class family, they told Sid that he would have to pay for his own medical expenses. So, while going to college, Sid lived at home and worked two part-time jobs, in order to save whatever money he could. By the time he graduated, at age 26, he had saved enough money to finally have his gender reassignment surgery.

After graduating from college with a double degree in computer sciences and visual arts, Sid decided to pursue a career in graphic design. He worked for several smaller companies in more entry-level positions before becoming hired as a project coordinator for a major fashion magazine, where he has been working for the past 1.5 years. Sid enjoys his job very much and has made several friends in his company. However, he often wonders if anyone recognizes that he is transgender. When he was hired, Sid decided not to tell anyone about his history. He always thought to himself that if cisgender people do not announce that they are cisgender, then he does not need to announce his transgender identity to anyone, either. Upon meeting him, most people likely assume that Sid is a cisgender man and would not have any indication that he was born a female at birth. While people may stereotype him as being a gay man, because of his sensitive and compassionate interpersonal style, Sid "passes" very well.

Over the past year, Sid has started to become more acquainted with a couple of coworkers who are around his same age. Many of these coworkers, who are cisgender, heterosexual women, have expressed a desire to spend time with Sid outside of work. One week, one of his coworkers, Liz, invited Sid to come to a friend's birthday party that was taking place at a gay bar. She told Sid, "Oh, my gosh, you're going to love it; there are these trannies who host this drag show at midnight. It's hilarious!" Sid, who did not know how to react, was initially silent. Liz, who noticed Sid's discomfort, stated, "I hope you're not offended that I assumed you were gay. You are, right?" It was at this moment that he decided to out himself to Liz, explaining, "Hey, Liz, I really like you and would like to get to know you better, but there is something you should probably know about me." He went on to tell her that he was transgender and taught her that the word *tranny* is actually offensive. Liz apologized for being insensitive, stating that she "really didn't know better." She thanked him for sharing his history with her, and she ended by proclaiming, "I wouldn't have even known. You look like a normal man!"

Case Study Discussion

As the three cases demonstrate, there are many ways in which microaggressions toward transgender people can manifest. In the first scenario, Destiny began to discover her transgender identity when she was a young child. When she played dress-up with her older sisters, she started to realize that this was not a phase—it was something that felt normal and right for her. Although she did experience some family microaggressions (e.g., her brother asked her, "Are you sure you're not gay?"), most of the microaggressions in this scenario occurred when she met with her high school principal, Dr. Kaner. In general, Dr. Kaner is very dismissive of Destiny, implying that he cannot do anything to protect her from harassment or discrimination. He also presumes that Destiny's transgender identity is a "choice"—invalidating her reality and self-concept. Finally, although the school was not built to accommodate to transgender students (e.g., there are no gender-neutral restrooms), Dr. Kaner makes no attempts to assist Destiny, communicating that transgender people are unimportant or not worthy of being helped. Because of all of these microaggressions, Destiny feels extremely distressed, likely not knowing how she will be able to make it through her senior year of high school.

In the second case, we learn of Jan, an individual who identifies as a gender nonconforming person. Although Jan was born biologically as a female (and currently presents physically as female), Jan would prefer to not be referred to as any gender. At an LGBT student organization meeting, Jan shares the preferred gender pronoun with which Jan would like to be identified and, initially, Jan's peers agree. However, when others have difficulty obliging this request, Jan tries to discuss this with the president of the organization, who is eventually dismissive, suggesting that Jan should undergo surgery or take hormones so that people would not be confused. This type of conflict signifies that even well-intentioned LGB people are capable of engaging in gender identity microaggressions. It also signifies that people may often blame the transgender person, even though they are the ones who are guilty of committing a microaggression. Because many cisgender people may view transgender people's requests as being inconvenient, it may be difficult for them to change their behaviors. For example, many cisgender family members and friends of transgender people may slip up with transgender people's new names or pronouns. Perhaps an occasional slip-up may be more tolerable by a transgender person if the perpetrator recognizes it immediately (and independently) and apologizes for it right away. However, if people do not recognize the hurtful behavior, or make adjustments to their behavior, transgender people may feel as if their feelings or identities are not valid or accepted.

The third and final case study describes how some transgender people may pass, which may lead to specific types of microaggressions that people who cannot or do not pass may not encounter. So, although people's discomfort may be more identifiable with nonpassing transgender people, transgender people who do pass may experience microaggressions because others do not even recognize that they are transgender. In this case, Sid has been working at a company for over a year, and no one knows that he is transgender. When his coworker Liz invites him to a birthday party at a gay bar, a few microaggressions occur. First, she uses the word *tranny* very casually when describing the drag queens who host a show at the bar. Although she probably used the word in jest (because it is a term that is commonly used among gay men), it can be an offensive term to transgender people. Second, when Liz assumes that Sid is "probably" a gay man, she forces Sid to out himself, instead of allowing him to share his sexual identity (both his sexual orientation and his gender identity) at his own accord. Perhaps he would have divulged this information on his own independently and when he felt most comfortable; however, he now feels obligated to tell Liz all about his history, when he perhaps does not want to. A final micro-aggression is when Liz tells Sid that she thought he was a "normal man"— signifying that being transgender is abnormal and that being cisgender is normal. Although Liz may have intended this to be a "compliment" (i.e., to tell Sid that he passes very well), it can be construed as a reflection of biases about transgender and gender nonconforming people.

In each of the case studies the intentions of the perpetrators may or may not be malicious. Dr. Kaner, the high school principal, may not directly want to upset Destiny by failing to accommodate her needs at school; instead, he may genuinely believe that he is making the fairest decisions by not "favoring" anyone. Ethan, the LGBT college student organization president, may sincerely believe that he is justified in telling Jan that Jan's requests for not using gender pronouns is unreasonable. He may not intend to be hurtful; instead, he may feel he is standing up for himself against what he perceives as an irrational desire. Finally, Liz, the coworker, may honestly believe that she did not say anything offensive to Sid. She may believe she was trying to be kind in reaching out to her coworker, whom she wanted to get to know better. When Sid outed himself to her, she may feel apologetic about using the word *tranny* because she did not know there was anything wrong with using the word. Thus, it appears that unless Liz was confronted (or unless others pointed out her microaggressive behavior), she would not have even recognized any fault. This is likely a common experience for the majority of cisgender people, whose transphobic biases are unconscious because they have learned overt and covert transphobic messages that are embedded in every aspect of society.

Discussion Questions

FOR GENERAL READERS

1. What types of gender identity microaggressions do you believe are most common? Which types of gender identity micro-aggressions are most harmful or hurtful?

2. What types of microaggressions do you believe occur more often with transgender women (MTF)? With transgender men (FTM)? With gender nonconforming people?
3. What types of gender identity microaggressions do you notice in various institutions (e.g., your workplace or school) or systems (e.g., government, media, religion)?
4. Have you ever committed a gender identity microaggression as a perpetrator? Were you aware of your behavior? How do you feel about this today?
5. When you were reading each scenario, what were some of the feelings that arose for you?
6. What would you do if you were in Destiny's situation? Jan's situation? Sid's situation?
7. How could systems and institutions (e.g., government, school systems, media, policies) assist each character in their experiences with microaggressions? How could these systems have been helpful in the past to prevent these microaggressions altogether?
8. Do you believe that gender identity microaggressions that come from other LGB people are less harmful or hurtful than gender identity microaggressions that come from heterosexual people?

FOR PSYCHOLOGISTS, EDUCATORS, AND OTHER EXPERTS

1. In what ways might you improve your cultural competence in working with transgender or gender nonconforming people?
2. What techniques or methods would you use in working with Destiny, Jan, or Sid?
3. What types of countertransference issues would you have in working with Destiny, Jan, or Sid?

Glossary of Key Terms

Cis: Shortened version of the word *cisgender*.
Cross-Dresser: Individual who wears clothing that is typically worn by the opposite gender.
Drag King: A cisgender woman who dresses, and usually acts, like a man, usually for the purpose of entertaining.
Drag Queen: A cisgender man who dresses, and usually acts, like a woman, usually for the purpose of entertaining.
Gender Bending: Informal term to describe the behavior of actively transgressing or defying traditional gender roles.

Gender Binary: The belief that there are only two genders: male and female.

Gender Expression: The manner in which people perform their gender roles.

Gender Neutral: Description of something or someone as being unassociated with female or male.

Genderqueer: Umbrella term for gender identities other than cisgender female or cisgender male.

Passing: Ability to be regarded as a member of the sex or gender with which one identifies.

Post-Operation, or **Post-Op:** Describes transgender people who complete gender reassignment surgery.

Preferred Gender Pronouns: Pronouns that individuals desire to be used when others are referring to them. Examples include *she, he, ze,* or the use of no pronoun at all.

Pre-Operation, or **Pre-Op:** Describes transgender people who do not complete gender reassignment surgery or who are in the process of completing gender reassignment surgery.

Trans: Shortened version of the word *transgender.*

Transsexual: Individual who uses various interventions to medically transition into the gender with which he or she most identifies.

Intersectional Microaggressions: Experiences of Lesbian, Gay, Bisexual, and Transgender People With Multiple Oppressed Identities

5

One of the principal difficulties in understanding microaggressions is determining whether such instances occurred because of one singular identity (e.g., one's sexual orientation) or because of multiple identities (e.g., one's sexual orientation and one's race). Throughout this book there have been many examples of microaggressions that are primarily due to singular identities, yet perhaps some of the examples may have also been influenced by one's multiple identities. Let's revisit two of the microaggression incidents that I described in the Introduction. First, there was the case of same-sex couple Stephanie and Debbie, who attended Stephanie's 10-year high school reunion. Stephanie, who is Asian American, and Debbie, who is African American, were both "jokingly" propositioned by one of Stephanie's male former classmates, after he assumed that Stephanie was a lesbian instead of bisexual. Also recall the case of Agnes, a 20-year-old transgender Latina woman (male-to-female [MTF]) who was harassed by a campus security

DOI: 10.1037/14093-006
That's So Gay! Microaggressions and the Lesbian, Gay, Bisexual, and Transgender Community, by K. L. Nadal

guard because her identification card did not match her current gender identity.

Although both of these cases clearly involve microaggressions on the basis of sexual orientation or transgender identity, perhaps other social identities were also a factor. In the first scenario, perhaps both race and gender influenced the microaggression. Would Stephanie and Debbie have been propositioned (and subsequently objectified) if they were both men? Could there be a possibility that the male classmate exoticized both of the women because of their racial backgrounds, which led to his sexual proposition? In the second scenario, could it be possible that race and age (and maybe even social class) influenced the microaggression? If Agnes were White, or older, would she have had an easier time getting through security? Although her social class may not be as obvious as, for example, her race, could it be possible that she would have been treated better if the security guard had perceived her as being wealthy or upper class? It is entirely possible that these other identities did indeed have an influence on the ways these individuals were treated; however, because these identities were not clearly addressed or articulated, this question may be much more difficult to answer, leaving the victim feeling particularly confused and emotionally distressed.

In this chapter, I discuss *intersectional microaggressions:* those microaggressions that are encountered as a result of one's intersectional or multiple identities. First, I discuss power and privilege as a way to understand the complexities of intersectional identities, in particular, within the lesbian, gay, bisexual, and transgender (LGBT) community. Next, I provide a brief review of the previous literature on intersectional microaggressions. Finally, I highlight the experiences of LGBT people of color, LGBT people of various religious groups, LGBT people with disabilities, and LGBT people with other marginalized identities.

Understanding Power and Privilege in the LGBT Community

In Chapter 3, I introduced the concepts of power and privilege. *Power* in its most general form can be defined as the ability to define reality and to convince other people that it is their definition too. On the other hand, *privilege* refers to a right, favor, advantage, or immunity specially granted to one individual or group and withheld from another. Throughout the text, I have written about how LGBT people may have less power and privilege due to the heterosexism and genderism that occurs at systemic, institutional, and interpersonal levels. It is important, however, to recognize that power and privilege do exist within the LGBT community itself, which then creates a culture of what is considered normative and results in an array of dynamics between various LGBT subgroups.

First, it becomes necessary to acknowledge that although research on LGBT-related topics has been minimal for the past century in the United States and abroad, the majority of the existing LGBT literature has focused almost exclusively on able-bodied, cisgender, White American gay men and lesbian women (Meezan & Martin, 2003). Thus, throughout the history of LGBT people in the United States, people who belong to these groups have unconsciously set the cultural norms, behaviors, and standards of beauty for everyone else, regardless of race, gender, gender identity, ability, and other identities. For example, LGBT people who are able-bodied, cisgender, gay, male, and White American are often viewed as having the most power and privilege in the community. The higher the number of these descriptions someone identifies with, the more power and privilege she or he will have. When someone identifies with few or none of these descriptions, the less power and privilege she or he will have.

Let us now discuss how this might manifest within the LGBT community. Let us first consider the standard of beauty that has been predominantly promoted in gay male culture: the young, able-bodied, thin or athletic White American man. In this case, there are many people with financial or institutional power who enable this standard of beauty to continue: the film and television producers who only cast actors who fit this type in gay media, the owners of gay bars and restaurants who only hire staff members that fit this type, the editors of gay male magazines who only use these types of models, the owners of gay establishments who do not install wheelchair-accessible ramps, and the managers or bouncers of gay clubs who refuse to admit others who do not fit this description. At the same time, individuals who do fit this picture (in particular, those who match all of these characteristics) hold power and privilege without even recognizing it. They have the power of assuming that their experiences are the norm and that their physical looks are most desirable. They also are likely to receive certain privileges (e.g., rights, favors, advantages) without even recognizing it. For example, they may not even consciously realize that they have an easier time getting admitted into certain establishments; that they get better treatment by bartenders, restaurant servers, or others; or that certain magazines and establishments cater to them. Meanwhile, any other gay male who does not fit that description (e.g., gay men of color, gay men with disabilities, gay men who are overweight or obese, gay men who are older or elderly) may feel deficient, inferior, or second class; may be treated as such; or both.

Furthermore, it is necessary to emphasize that, as with any social identity, individuals with privilege may not recognize they have privilege (see McIntosh, 2003). For instance, able-bodied people in general may not think twice about wheelchair access to buildings. Because they have the privilege of belonging to the dominant group of other able-bodied persons, they may unconsciously uphold the expectation that most buildings will have entrances and walkways that they can utilize. Unless someone points out the privilege to them, they may live their life not realizing the ways in which their lives are easier because of the group to which they belong. Moreover, when someone is oppressed in one identity but privileged in another, it may be even more difficult for that person to recognize the power and privilege he or she has. For example, when a gay White man feels marginalized and oppressed because of the many ways in which heterosexism has negatively affected his life, it may be difficult for him to recognize the ways that he has privilege because of his race or his gender. When a lesbian woman of color feels marginalized or oppressed because of the many ways in which both racism and heterosexism have negatively affected her life, she may not be able to easily recognize the power or privilege she has that a transgender person or a person with a disability would not. Because of this, it is important for people of any marginalized or target group to recognize that there are likely to be other social identity groups in which they do have power and privilege. Otherwise, people may remain defensive and be unable to hear or validate the realities of others.

Discussing the types of power and privilege in the LGBT community may help elucidate the types of dynamics and tensions that may occur. Sometimes LGBT people with other marginalized identities (e.g., LGBT people of color, LGBT people with disabilities, elderly LGBT people) may feel excluded, disconnected, or isolated by other LGBT people with privileged identities (LGBT White Americans, able-bodied LGBT people, LGBT young adults), leading to even further isolation in the LGBT community. Other times people with these privileged identities may be genuinely oblivious to the ways that they are privileged, which may then lead to microaggressions that are often unconscious or unintentional. Thus, it is important for all individuals to recognize the areas in which they have power and privilege as well as the domains in which they have less power and privilege. In doing so, dialogues can continue within the LGBT community, which ideally will result in more unity and less marginalization.

Previous Literature on Intersectional Microaggressions

Now that we have learned more about power and privilege within the LGBT community, let's discuss the two best-known studies that focused on intersectional microaggressions toward LGBT people of color. The first is a quantitative study conducted by Balsam, Molina, Beadnell, Simoni, and Walters (2011), who created the LGBT People of Color Microaggressions Scale in order to understand the types of micro-aggressive experiences that LGBT people of color may encounter in their everyday lives. On this 18-item self-report scale LGBT people of color answer questions regarding racism in LGBT communities, heterosexism in racial/ethnic minority communities, and racism in dating and close relationships. Balsam et al.'s preliminary findings included the following three: (a) gay and bisexual men of color scored higher (i.e., they reported higher numbers of racism and heterosexism in all three categories) than gay and bisexual women, (b) lesbians and gay men scored higher than bisexual women and men, and (c) Asian Americans scored higher than African Americans and Latina/os. Thus, this research supports the notions that LGBT men of color may perceive or experience more inter-sectional microaggressions than LGBT women of color, that people of color may perceive or experience more intersectional microaggressions than bisexual people of color, and that Asian American people of color may perceive or experience more intersectional microaggressions than African Americans or Latina/o people of color.

The second major study that focused on intersectional micro-aggressions toward LGBT people of color was conducted by me and my research team at John Jay College of Criminal Justice of the City University of New York. Nadal, Davidoff, et al. (2012) conducted a qualitative research project that examined intersectional microaggressions. Using the focus group data garnered from previous microaggression studies involving women (Capodilupo et al., 2010; Nadal, Hamit, et al., 2012); lesbian, gay, and bisexual (LGB) people (Nadal, Issa, et al., 2011; Nadal, Wong, Issa, et al., 2011); transgender people (Nadal, Skolnik, & Wong, 2012); multiracial individuals (Nadal, Wong, Griffin, et al., 2011); Mus-lims (Nadal, Griffin, et al., 2012); and Filipino Americans (e.g., Nadal, Escobar, et al., 2012), we aimed to identify participants' experiences with microaggressions that were based on more than one identity. With 80 participants in 19 focus groups, participants were initially asked only about microaggressions based on one identity (e.g., the Muslim partici-pants were asked specifically about microaggressions based on being Muslim). However, in the ensuing discussion, many participants also described how other identities influenced their experiences with microaggressions (e.g., the Muslim male and female participants described different ways in which they had experienced microaggressions because of their religion and gender). The analysis led to eight main themes: (a) *exoticization of women of color;* (b) *assumption of gender-based stereotypes for lesbians and gay men;* (c) *disapproval of LGBT identity by racial, ethnic, and religious groups;* (d) *assumption of inferior status of women of color;* (e) *invisibility and desexualization of Asian men;* (f) *assumption of inferiority or criminality of men of color;* (g) *assumption of gender-based stereotypes for Muslim men and women;* and (h) *women of color as spokespersons.*

Of these themes, two directly involve sexual orientation and gender identity and share experiences from LGBT people: (a) *assumption of gender-based stereotypes for lesbians and gay men* and (b) *disapproval of LGBT identity by racial, ethnic, and religious groups.* The former involves microaggressions in which all lesbians are assumed to act "butch" and not feminine. For example, one female participant shared the following:

> I often have people be like "Oh well you're very feminine, so how are you a lesbian?" But yeah I get that a lot where people say that I'm too feminine to be gay and I'm like, "That has nothing to do with it . . . like, not all lesbians are like really butch" . . . or they didn't seem happy because I'm not a butch lesbian. [They think] I'm a porn star lesbian where I only do it for the attention of guys. And I'm like, "If I wanted guys to notice me, I'd actually, like, pursue the guys." (Nadal, Davidoff, et al., 2012)

Similarly, gay men identified microaggressions in which they were presumed to be feminine or uninterested in traditionally masculine activities. One male participant shared the following:

> I'm one of the only guys in the area and I feel like the women always compete for me to give them compliments on what [they're] wearing. [Laughter]. Like . . . if I actually, I said to someone, "Wow, I really love that dress." She was like, "Oh my God, if you love this dress, then it must be really great."

He went on to describe a common stereotype of gay men but one that many gay men do not fit:

> I know so many gay men who dress terribly . . . like my ex. He dresses terribly. He couldn't tell you what was on the runway last season . . . He didn't know from Adam what was trendy or cool, you know what I mean. He didn't care. So like, I happen to be a gay man who kinda does, but there are lots really dull [gay guys] who dress as sloppy as straight boys. And there are straight guys who are like beautifully dressed all the time. (Nadal, Davidoff, et al., 2012)

Another theme, *disapproval of LGBT identity by racial, ethnic, and religious groups,* involved microaggressions that LGBT people of color and

LGBT Muslims experienced by their families and ethnic/religious communities. As one male participant in an LGB group simply stated, "If you're a minority gay, it's way worse" (Nadal, Davidoff, et al., 2012). Many participants described how their families and friends did not accept them because of the rigid culture or religion to which they belonged. Others described how culture prevented them from coming out to their families, but how they were unable to do so, feel accepted, or both, because of their cultural identities. For example, one young woman explained, "My family doesn't really know I'm bisexual. But it's because they're Latin. I tried once to tell my mom, and she stopped me right there when I tried to tell her" (Nadal, Wong, Issa, et al., 2011, p. 34).

Although the remaining themes did not include perspectives from LGB participants, they may have implications for LGBT people. First, the theme of exoticization of Asian American women may apply to the lives of lesbian, bisexual, and transgender women who are (a) exoticized because of their race, gender, and sexual identities and (b) exoticized by heterosexual men and by LGBT women and men. For example, when a Latina transgender woman in one study was told by a cisgender male that she was not "girlfriend" material (Nadal, Skolnik, & Wong, 2012; see also Chapter 4, this volume), perhaps this happened not just because of her gender identity but also because of her race or ethnicity. Previous studies have found that Latinas (Rivera, Forquer, & Rangel, 2010), Asian American women (Nadal, Escobar, et al., 2012; Sue, Bucceri, et al., 2010), and African American women (Sue, Nadal, et al., 2008; Watkins, LaBarrie, & Appio, 2012) are exoticized by heterosexual men for different reasons (e.g., Latinas are often viewed as being "sassy" or "spicy," whereas Asian American women are viewed as being "Madame Butterfly"–type characters or as sexually submissive). Perhaps this dynamic is common not only between lesbian, bisexual, and transgender women of color and heterosexual men but also between them and White lesbian and bisexual women, other lesbian and bisexual women of color, and **transamorous** men.

Second, in regard to the theme *invisibility and desexualization of Asian American men*, which was initially reported in a previous study on microaggressions with Asian Americans (see Sue, Bucceri, et al., 2010), one gay Asian American male revealed how Asian American men are viewed as the least desirable in the gay male community:

> If you mention that you're an Asian, it's like listening to crickets on the Internet. I mean, gay men are just that shallow. Particularly Caucasian . . . So, it's a little hard. It's like thinking, damn! I can't even get laid on the Internet! (Nadal, Davidoff, et al., 2012).

Similarly, a gay male participant in a study of microaggressions experienced by Filipino Americans shared his perceptions of how Asian Americans are portrayed in the media: "Can't we just see one really butch Asian male? We are not all feminine" (Nadal, Escobar, et al., 2012, p. 164). Both of these examples demonstrate that Asian American males experience racial microaggressions not just in general American society but also within the LGBT community.

Three final themes may be applicable to the lives of LGBT people of color, but they may need to be further explored in future research involving intersectional microaggressions. First, with the theme *assumption of inferior status of women of color*, it is possible that LGBT women of color may feel even more distress when they are viewed to be intellectually, physically, or socially inferior because of their race, ethnicity, gender, and sexuality. For example, if an African American lesbian woman receives substandard treatment in her workplace by her supervisor or coworkers, one may wonder whether this is due to her race, ethnicity, gender, sexual orientation, or some combination of these. Similarly, aligning with the theme *assumption of inferiority and criminality of men of color*, it is possible that gay, bisexual, and transgender men of color (who experience microaggressions in which they are stereotyped as being inferior or criminally deviant) may experience intensified distress because of their **dual minority status**. Perhaps they experience both racism and heterosexism on an everyday basis, which may in turn negatively influence their mental health. Finally, in applying the theme *women of color as spokespersons* (or LGBT women of color specifically), future researchers may examine whether these individuals experience multiple or **dual minority stress** when they are asked to be the spokesperson for their multiple groups. So although their counterparts who do not hold these multiple oppressed identities (e.g., heterosexual people of color, White LGBT individuals) may be asked to be spokespeople for one group, such a request may be even more distressful for an individual with multiple oppressed identities, who may feel obligated to represent several groups of marginalized people.

It is important to acknowledge that the themes that emerged from Nadal, Davidoff, et al.'s (2012) study by no means represent the various types of intersectional microaggressions that exist for all groups of people. Because the sample was limited, skewed in certain directions, and did not specifically concentrate on LGBT people, many other themes could have emerged. For instance, because the study did not include focus groups specifically targeting African Americans, Latina/os, or people with disabilities, those groups' perspectives may have not have been voiced or recognized.

Given that so little research has examined intersectional microaggressions experienced by various groups, I will draw from other sources (mainly previous research and contemporary narratives) to demonstrate the types of encounters these individuals might have; specifically, you will hear voices from LGBT people of color, LGBT people of religious groups, LGBT people with disabilities, and LGBT people of other marginalized identities.

Voices of Lesbian, Gay, Bisexual, and Transgender People of Color

The literature that has focused on the experiences of LGBT people of color—namely, Black/African Americans, Latina/os, Asian Americans, Pacific Islanders, and Native Americans (Akerlund & Chung, 2000; Balsam et al., 2011; Chan, 1989, 1992; Chung & Szymanski, 2006; Conerly, 1996; Greene, 1994; Harper, Jernewall, & Zea, 2004)—has been growing. However, some authors have noted that the majority of these articles pertaining to LGBT people of color have focused on the *deficit model;* that is, they concentrate mainly on the negative aspects of their experience, including substance abuse, HIV/AIDS, and health disparities (Akerlund & Chung, 2000). For example, many studies have described how Latino gay men and other Latino men who have sex with men experience a higher prevalence of health problems than White gay men and White men who have sex with men (see Ibañez, Van Oss Marin, Flores, Millett, & Diaz, 2009, for a review).

Despite this, some notable studies have examined the types of discrimination that LGBT people of color experience within American society in general, within the LGBT community, and within their own racial and ethnic communities. For instance, some studies have found that LGBT people of color feel excluded or treated as second-class citizens in predominantly White LGBT spaces (Diaz, Bein, & Ayala, 2006; Greene, 1994; Han, 2007, 2009; Ibanez et al., 2009; Sohng & Icard, 1996) and that LGBT people of color may experience racism in their dating lives and sexual or romantic relationships (Han, 2009; Ibañez et al., 2009; Mays, Cochran, & Rhue, 1993; Phua & Kaufman, 2003; Wilson et al., 2009). On the other hand, LGBT people of color may also feel excluded or treated as second-class citizens within their racial and ethnic communities, in particular, by heterosexual group members who want to deny or silence their sexuality or those who overtly discriminate against them (Chan, 1989, 1992; Chung & Szymanski, 2006; Conerly, 1996, Nadal & Corpus, 2012). Although they may not have been labeled as such, many of the examples provided fall into the category of microaggressions.

Through my own review of academic literature, contemporary narratives, and media, I have found that there are a few major themes that tend to have an impact on people of color. Because this is not an empirically based analysis, it may not be a complete depiction of the experiences of all LGBT people of color. Furthermore, because of the limited literature on experiences of transgender and bisexual people of color, as well as other "invisible" racial and ethnic minority groups, these themes may not be exhaustive. I hope, however, that these examples will serve as an introduction to the intersectional microaggressions experienced by LGBT people of color and may potentially inspire future qualitative and quantitative research.

EXCLUSION WITHIN LESBIAN, GAY, BISEXUAL, AND TRANSGENDER COMMUNITIES

Previous research has found that LGBT people of color encounter exclusion in the LGBT community primarily because it tends to be a predominantly White LGBT community. Previous research (e.g., de la Luz Montes, 2003, Diaz et al., 2006; Han, 2007, 2009; Mays et al., 1993; Nadal & Corpus, 2012; Phua & Kaufman, 2003) has highlighted the racial politics within the LGBT community in regard to social scene, romantic relationships, and online dating. For example, in one study, a gay Asian American male participant described the types of microaggressions he experiences in the LGBT community:

> It's not so blatant, I mean, people don't come up to you and call you "chink" or anything like that. But it's definitely there, you can feel it . . . Like little things, like if a lot of Asians go to a bar, then they start calling it a "rice bar" or something. And like the personal ads that say, "No Asians," or whatever, so it makes it hard to approach guys at bars because you never know if they're going to reject you because you're Asian. (Han, 2009, p. 276)

In one narrative, a lesbian Filipina American shared a similar sentiment about feeling excluded:

> When it came to the lesbian community, I also felt slightly out of my element, but in a different way. I was (and am) always that one Filipina. Living in New York City, the lesbian social scene consists of bars that are primarily full of White girls. (Corpus, 2010, p. 190)

Similarly, in a study with gay and bisexual Latino men, one male participant shared the following:

> Well, my experience in growing up in a gay world . . . it's kind of almost like if you are not Caucasian, you do not even deserve to be gay, in the sense of . . . you know, like what are you doing here in these kinds of clubs? These are gay Caucasian kinds of clubs, and unless you go to a specific Hispanic club, I personally feel that you're not treated equally, not only as an individual, but because you are [a] different, you know, race. You can also

be homosexual, which I would think would be enough of a
unity, [but] just because you are gay like someone else does not
unify you to any kind of organization or group. It's not enough.
I feel . . . it's almost like a hindrance being Puerto Rican . . . to be
accepted in the gay community. (Diaz et al., 2006, p. 213)

Finally, a gay African American male in one research study shared his
experience:

I would go into a bar . . . behind young Whites who looked a hell
of a lot younger than me, and they would have no problem getting
in. Whereas, I would be stopped and they would ask for at least
two forms of ID. Also, just the attitudes of the bartenders. They
would wait on others before they would wait on me . . . and it
really saddened me because I thought we were all gay, we were
all fighting for equality. You know, we would pull together. But I
found more overt racism among White gays than I did among just
Whites period . . . which really upset me. (Loiacano, 1989, p. 69)

In all four of these examples it is clear that the narrators perceive subtle
racism in the LGBT community. Perhaps these types of microaggressions are so prevalent in the LGBT community because the general
LGBT culture (e.g., organizations, social scenes, community groups)
tends to be normed after White culture, communication styles, and
standards of beauty, regardless of the actual racially diverse makeup
(Ward, 2008). Because of this norming it is possible that LGBT White
Americans may not even be aware of the subtle racism that occurs,
in particular, the ways in which LGBT people of color are expected to
conform to White norms.

What you see on television and other visual media may best exemplify the environmental microaggression normalization of Whiteness
in the LGBT community. With the exception of one television show
(*Noah's Arc*), most of the well-known "mainstream" lesbian or gay
American television shows (e.g., *Will and Grace, The L Word, Queer as Folk*)
focus on the lives of lesbian and gay characters who are White Americans.
One author wrote about this lack of diversity in depictions of lesbians in
the media: "Lesbian bar representations in the twentieth century depict
bars as primarily white spaces. Save for a few nonwhite women, the
women who populate the lesbian bars . . . are white" (Hankin, 2002,
p. 112). Similarly, when the television show *Queer Eye for the Straight
Guy* premiered in 2003, there was some controversy not only because
of the lack of diversity on the show (Jai Rodriguez, a multiracial Latino,
was the only non-White person on the show) but also because the lone
African American (James Hannaham) was fired after just a few episodes.
The consistent lack of LGBT people of color in the media may promote the underrepresentation of LGBT people of color in the general
LGBT community while also discouraging LGBT people of color (young

and old) from feeling comfortable in coming out to their families and communities.

EXCLUSION WITHIN COMMUNITIES OF COLOR

Previous empirical research has found that LGBT people of color often feel excluded from their racial and ethnic communities, which may not be accepting of their sexual identities (Chan, 1989, 1992; Greene, 1994; Nadal & Corpus, 2012). For example, Gloria Anzaldúa (1999), a Latina lesbian writer, discussed how she feels excommunicated from her racial and ethnic community because of her sexual identity:

> As a *mestiza*, I have no country, my homeland cast me out; yet all countries are mine because I am every woman's sister or potential lover. As a lesbian I have no race, my own people disclaim me; but I am all races because there is the queer of me in all races. (pp. 102–103)

Similarly, Dr. Michael Mobley, a gay male African American counseling psychologist, described a time when he felt excluded and hurt by a friend and colleague (a heterosexual African American woman). When the two were to give a presentation, he noticed that she had removed all of the PowerPoint slides that were related to sexual orientation. When Mobley confronted her, she said, "Michael, I cannot be gay affirming." He wrote:

> Hearing this, I was immediately shocked, angered, and I felt a deep sense of disbelief followed by an internal rage. My gay cultural identity was being deleted, denied, and dejected in my very presence . . . I feared that [she] represented one of those African Americans who gave lip service to being friends with an African American lesbian, gay, or bisexual (LGB) person but in reality was obviously not fully comfortable and accepting due to "the church." (Mobley & Pearson, 2005, p. 89)

Although the interaction eventually led to an intense discussion as well as a deeper friendship between Mobley and his colleague, this type of conflict represents one that is very common between LGBT people of color and heterosexual people of color (in particular, those who are religious). Because many communities of color (especially African Americans, Latina/os, and Asian Americans) are so influenced by discriminatory views of LGBT people, it may be particularly difficult for LGBT people of color to feel accepted in these communities. When their heterosexual family and ethnic community members discriminate against LGBT people of color, it may be especially hurtful because of the knowledge that these individuals know firsthand what it is like to experience exclusion and discrimination due to racism.

DENIAL OF EXISTENCE IN COMMUNITIES OF COLOR

In addition to being excluded, there are many ways in which LGBT people of color are denied their sexual identities. In 2007, when President Mahmoud Ahmadinejad of Iran claimed "In Iran, we don't have homosexuals" at a gathering at Columbia University in New York (Alizadeh & Johnson, 2011), it was not the first time that non-Western countries viewed homosexuality as a "Western problem." This denial of the existence of LGBT people of color can occur on all levels, such as community organizations, groups, and families. Carla Trujillo, a Chicana/Mexican American lesbian, wrote:

> The issue of being a lesbian, a Chicana lesbian, is still uncomfortable for many heterosexual Chicanas and Chicanos, even (and especially) those in academic circles. Our culture seeks to diminish us by placing us in a context of an Anglo construction, a supposed *vendida* [traitor] to the race. (Trujillo, 1991, p. ix)

It is evident that the narrator may feel that she is on the receiving end of microaggressions because of her sexual orientation, even by peers who are likely to be oriented to racial and other social justice issues.

Microaggressions may also occur within families in which parents and other relatives deny that their loved one is really LGBT. Many LGBT people of color describe the fear in coming out to their family members. For instance, in a study with transgender people of color, one African American transgender man stated, "It's shocking when you know your very own family might not be around to accept who you really are" (Singh & McKleroy, 2011, p. 38). Other times LGBT people of color do come out to their families but are met with dismissal or denial. For example, in a personal narrative, Melissa Corpus, a self-identified gay Filipina woman, described the following situation:

> I thought I came out to my mom when I was 24 years old, but apparently I didn't. You see, in my household (and in many other Filipino households), coming out doesn't really mean anything. It just encourages my mom to work harder at being in "denial" that I'm gay. I can't blame her. She's genuinely worried that I won't be saved by Jesus. Since I came out, I've been receiving Catholic prayer books, rosaries (that she got blessed by her priest at St. Athanasius), and panties on a frequent basis. In her indirect way of communicating to me, her subtext has always been clear. She believes prayer could solve everything, even my sexuality. (Corpus, 2010, p. 188)

Similarly, in a study that included Black and South Asian gay men in Britain, participants from both subgroups described how they perceived White gay men to be more accepted by their families and communities; for example, one Pakistani man shared,

> [The] fact that being gay is now "accepted" amongst the White British culture whereas with Asian, Black etc. it is still a taboo subject and in that way it is harder for some gay people from ethnic minorities to "come out." (McKeown, Nelson, Anderson, Low, & Elford, 2010, p. 847)

In both of these scenarios it is clear that people of various racial/ethnic groups may have difficulty coming out to their families because of their family members' unwillingness to accept their sexual identities, because of their family's religion or culture, or both.

DENIAL OF RACISM IN LGBT COMMUNITIES

Because of the "White norm" in the LGBT community, it is common for LGBT people of color to feel as though racism goes unaddressed and is sometimes even denied. For example, in a study with African Americans, one lesbian Black woman described her perceptions of the general LGBT community:

> Some of us (women of color) end up dropping out of planning groups or raising hell. We might want to work on the racism that's going on there, but racial issues are tough, and people don't really want to talk about them. (Loiacano, 1989, p. 68)

Similarly, in the previously noted narrative by a gay female Filipina American woman, she stated:

> As diverse as NYC is, it has always been clear that being Asian American and gay and a woman meant you had to find your niche within these dichotomous places. It's the feeling of constantly juggling and adapting—the feeling that one had to be a chameleon and adjust to whatever surrounding she was in. The sad thing is that it seems like my "lesbian community" does not even recognize this plight that I may experience. I've felt invalidated by White lesbian women who claim that racism is nonexistent in the lesbian community. (Corpus, 2010, p. 190)

These types of denial of racism are similar to the previous microaggression literature that describes how people of color who are often invalidated on their racial realities (e.g., Sue, Capodilupo, et al., 2007). When the experiences of LGBT people of color are invalidated, it may cause them to feel even more alienated within the LGBT community.

EXOTICIZATION

As mentioned earlier in this chapter (and in previous chapters), there are many ways in which people of color are exoticized in general society. Previous research has suggested that Asian American women are viewed as being sexually submissive (i.e., they are obedient to their sexual and romantic partners) or as being Madame Butterfly–type characters in that they are sexually conniving or odd (Nadal, Escobar, et al., 2012; Sue, Bucceri, et al., 2009). Meanwhile Latina women are viewed as being sexually provocative or "sassy" (Rivera et al., 2010), whereas African American women are sometimes perceived as being sexually seductive, "Jezebel" characters (J. A. Lewis, 2010). It is likely that LGBT people of color experience exoticization in similar yet nuanced ways to these general stereotypes, as a result of the intersections of their racial and sexual identities.

First, as previously stated, Asian American men in general are stereotyped as being demasculinized or effeminate. As a result, gay and bisexual Asian and Asian American men are often said to uphold similar stereotypes as Asian and Asian American women in that they are viewed as sexually submissive or obedient "bottoms" (i.e., those who would be the recipients of anal sex), feminine and dainty (i.e., small in stature and smooth skinned, with small penises), while sometimes also being viewed as different from "normal" White gay men. For example, gay Asian American men have described how they often feel exoticized by White men. One gay Asian American man described his perceptions of "rice queens," or gay White men who fetishize gay Asian American men.

> A rice queen is a White guy, usually a White guy, who
> likes Asian men. That's the short definition. But then
> there's the whole stereotype of what a rice queen is supposed
> to be. He's the older White guy who's not so attractive and
> he goes for younger Asian guys because that's all he can
> get. But then, the counterstereotype is that Asian guys
> go for rice queens because that's all they could get.
> (Han, 2009, p. 276)

On the other hand, Latino gay and bisexual men may not be viewed as sexually submissive; however, they are often oversexualized in that they are stereotyped as being "hot Latin lovers," or they are hypermasculinized in that they are viewed as being ultramasculine, dominant in bed, or having large penises. For example, in one research study, a gay Latino male shared the following:

> With some White gay men it's like they see you as, again, a piece
> of meat. Something they could go to bed with, you know, they
> had their Latino boy or whatever and I've been in situations
> where I start talking and they're like, "Oh, you can think, too?"
> (Diaz et al., p. 213)

One author wrote about how lesbian and bisexual women of color, in particular, Black and Latina lesbians, are often exoticized in the media:

> Exoticized Black lesbian bar patrons repeatedly appear in pulp
> fiction, journalistic exposés, and scientific studies . . . Most
> notable are the bar scenes in [the movies] "Living Out Loud"
> and "Boys on the Side." [The] White heterosexual protagonist
> in "Living Out Loud" "finds herself" after being caressed by
> scantily clad women of color in a lesbian bar. In "Boys on the
> Side," the multicultural depiction of the lesbian bar contributes
> to the film's overall fetish of the Southwest's Hispanic culture.
> (Hankin, 2002, p. 113)

Given all of these examples, it is evident that LGBT people of color may feel objectified within the general White LGBT community because of stereotypes about their race or ethnicity. These types of microaggressions may further lead to a sense of exclusion within the LGBT community while perpetuating the previously noted normalization of White standards of beauty within the LGBT community.

MICROAGGRESSIONS BASED ON BOTH RACIAL/ETHNIC AND SEXUAL IDENTITIES

Finally, some microaggressions may make LGBT people of color feel marginalized or discriminated because of the intersection of their racial/ethnic and sexual identities. Sometimes they may be treated as second-class citizens or intellectual inferiors, and sometimes they may be assumed to be criminal or pathological. When these types of experiences occur, the individuals may be unclear whether the microaggression occurred because of one of their social identities, both their racial/ethnic and sexual identities, or some other combination with other factors (e.g., age, social class). For example, one African American transgender MTF described how she feels negatively stereotyped because of her race, ethnicity, and gender identity:

> Society put me in a place where I am a minority and doesn't
> think I have the talent or potential because of who I am
> [racially/ethnically]. When I was a child, [I] didn't think my
> ethnicity was anything to be proud of—I was looked down on
> because I was Black. And then being transgender made it even
> worse. Now that I am older, I am proud of everything I am.
> I am an African American transsexual woman. No one can
> tell me I am less than anyone else. That helps me no matter
> what bad things happened to me. Some days, just getting out
> of bed is a revolutionary act to deal with the world. And I
> *make sure* I get out of bed. (Singh & McKleroy, 2011, p. 38)

Similarly, a Latina transgender MTF woman described how she reacts to people who may treat her negatively because of both her race and gender identity:

> I decided that just because I was transsexual Hispanic woman
> didn't mean that people could treat me any type of way. I didn't
> know if anyone would ever love me. I realized that I had to fight
> just to live my life as who I am—in school, at work, with my
> family, everywhere! That's also why I knew I couldn't just
> stay in an abusive relationship. I had to accept myself 100%.
> (Singh & McKleroy, 2011, p. 38)

Both of these quotes demonstrate three main themes that relate to LGBT people of color. First, it may be impossible to examine only singular identities when understanding experiences of LGBT people of color. Although in some situations a singular identity may be a primary factor when microaggressions occur, the individual is still a person of color, which may influence the situation as well. For instance, if a transgender woman of color is called a derogatory, transphobic slur, her transgender identity may be the primary factor behind the discriminatory statement. However, perhaps the intention of the perpetrator was to be even more hurtful or offensive because of the transgender woman's race (or age, social class, and/or physical appearance, etc.).

Second, one's dual minority identity may also influence one's ability to react to, and cope with, the incident, which in turn may affect one's mental health. For example, one study found that Black and Latina lesbian and bisexual women who accepted discrimination in their lives and did not discuss discrimination with others were more likely to be diagnosed with psychiatric disorders and that Black lesbian and bisexual women in particular were likely to be diagnosed with mood and anxiety disorders when they accepted discrimination and did not talk with others about their experiences (McLaughlin, Hatzenbuehler, & Keyes, 2010). Thus, it is especially necessary for LGBT people of color to turn to their support systems when they experience discrimination, in order to maximize their mental health outcomes.

Third and finally, because LGBT people of color hold these dual minority statuses, it is evident that they may be more cognizant of the different ways they navigate certain communities than their counterparts with only one marginalized identity (e.g., LGBT White people, heterosexual people of color). LGBT people of color may be more able to identify racism in the LGBT community than LGBT White people, while being able to identify heterosexism in their families and communities of color than heterosexual people of color. As a result, further research should examine whether these individuals encounter more microaggressions, perceive more microaggressions in their lives, and/or are more distressed because of the higher prevalence of encountering or perceiving these microaggressions.

Voices of Lesbian, Gay, Bisexual, and Transgender Religious Group Members

Because most major religions are not accepting of LGBT people in teaching or leadership positions—or, in many cases, even as members of the religious community—there are many intersectional micro-aggressions that can be experienced by LGBT people of various religious groups. First, it is necessary to acknowledge that discrimination toward LGBT people is still explicit and blatant in many ways. For example, it has been documented that many gay men in the Church of Jesus Christ of Latter Day Saints (aka the Mormon Church) are forced to undergo **conversion therapy,** as a way to "cure" them of their homosexuality (Beckstead & Morrow, 2004). As a result, it may be very difficult for members of the Mormon Church (and other Christian religions) to come out because they have been taught explicitly that their sexuality is "an abomination," "sinful," or "evil." Many times, these anti-LGBT sentiments that are preached in the Christian religions are based on passages from the Bible, many from the Old Testament. Often referred to as the "clobber passages," these verses are taken from biblical stories such as the creation narrative in the Book of Genesis, the story of Sodom and Gomorrah, and the holiness code in the Book of Leviticus (Bulokhov, 2009). One of the more famous clobber passages is Leviticus 18:22: "Thou shalt not lie with mankind as with womankind: It is abomination."

Teachings with anti-LGBT sentiments are explicitly conveyed in other religious works, too. For example, the Mormon Church preaches,

> Homosexual and lesbian activities are sinful and an abomination. . . . Unnatural affections including those toward persons of the same gender are counter to God's eternal plan for His children. You are responsible to make right choices. Whether directed toward those of the same or opposite gender, lustful feelings and desires may lead to more serious sins. All Latter-Day Saints must learn to control and discipline themselves. (Church of Jesus Christ of Latter-Day Saints, 1990, p. 15)

Hearing such explicitly homophobic teachings in any religion may cause psychological distress to anyone who may be questioning his or her LGBT identity. As a result, many individuals may experience immense amounts of guilt and shame if they stay with their religion and often choose to leave their religious group altogether (Beckstead & Morrow, 2004; Goodwill, 2000).

Much as there is for the literature on LGBT people of color, there is a dearth of research on the experiences of LGBT people from various religious groups. Thus, in the paragraphs that follow I highlight a few themes that are similar to the existing literature with LGBT people of color. I attempt to include a spectrum of examples from various subgroups of the LGBT community, including perspectives from LGB and transgender people, as well as experiences of those from Christian, Jewish, and Muslim faiths. Again, this is not an inclusive list because not all groups are represented; thus, it is important for more research to emerge in this area.

EXCLUSION FROM THE RELIGIOUS COMMUNITY

When LGBT people are also religious, they may often question whether they are "good people" because they may have learned from their religious teachings that same-sex sexual acts and relationships are sinful. One gay male, who was studying to become a priest in the Catholic Church, wrote the following:

> This head-on collision between the truth about myself and the church propelled me to one of the deepest crises of the spirit. Can I be a good person and still be gay? Can I serve God and still be gay? Can I be gay and still be Roman Catholic? Although I loved the Roman Catholic Church, with the emergence of this new consciousness about my sexuality, I somehow felt I was being kicked out of my spiritual home. Thus, I eventually I gave up my aspiration to become a priest, and ultimately left the church altogether. I did not leave with hate or bitterness, but I left believing it was necessary for my own spiritual survival. (Bordador, 2010, p. 196)

Although the Catholic Church does indeed disapprove of homosexuality, it appears that it was not necessarily anything that was explicitly said by another Catholic that led this individual to leave the church. Instead, the unspoken environment in which LGBT people and experiences are condemned was one in which he did not feel comfortable. Thus, he felt part of a community while at the same time feeling excluded and the recipient of microaggressions.

There may not be anything explicit in Islamic teachings that describes negative perceptions of LGBT people. For example, in one study, a Muslim participant shared:

> I can't see anything in the Qur'an that says homosexuality is wrong . . . The Qur'an says many things are a sin . . . All it needed to do was have one line that says it is a sin, and it doesn't do that. (Minwalla, Rosser, Feldman, & Varga, 2005, p. 119)

It is clear, however, that the Muslim community may not be accepting of LGBT people. In the same study, which focused on the perspectives of LGBT Muslim people, one male participant described the following experience:

> When I was probably 17 or 18, I was struggling because I was
> attracted to men. There was a sense of guilt . . . I found a mosque
> in the neighborhood that I would go to every Friday, and I found
> a group of people that were pretty religious, . . . that was for me
> an escape from feeling guilty . . . because I didn't know who to
> talk to about my feelings so I kind of concealed them, stored
> them away . . . So, at 17, 18, and 19, that's when I was kind of
> very religious. [It let me] escape from socializing from my cousins,
> even with my parents, because each time we met as an extended
> family, there was talk about girls or marriage—it was just too
> much for me. That was a good escape from those pressures.
> (Minwalla et al., 2005, p. 118)

Thus, it is clear that even though Islam does not rely on traditional
writings to condemn LGBT people, the heteronormativity it promotes
may isolate those who question their sexual identities. In this case,
the participant may not have been told explicitly that he was bad or
that homosexuality was evil, but he was pressured with subtle heteronormative communications that he should marry a woman and live a
heterosexual life. Such messages may be just as damaging or hurtful
when someone is struggling with her or his sexual identity.

USE OF RELIGION AS AN INTERVENTION

When LGBT people of color do come out to their families, family members may react in many ways. It appears that one common reaction from
family members who are religious is to have some sort of religious intervention as a way to "eliminate" the homosexuality from their loved one.
As described earlier, many gay Mormons have reported being forced to
undergo conversion therapy by their families or church leaders when
their sexual identities were discovered. In the movie *Prayers for Bobby*,
Sigourney Weaver plays Mary Griffith, a devout Christian mother in a
traditional White American middle-class family who discovers her son
Bobby's gay identity. Instead of accepting him, she turns to the church
and encourages him to do the same. In one scene in the movie, she claims,

> Homosexuality is a sin. Homosexuals are doomed to spend
> eternity in hell. If they wanted to change, they could be healed
> of their evil ways. If they would turn away from temptation, they
> could be normal again if only they would try and try harder if it
> doesn't work. (Mulcahy, 2009)

Because of this lack of acceptance by his family, Bobby eventually
commits suicide. After this tragedy, Mrs. Griffith aims to become more
educated on LGBT experiences and later becomes an activist in the
LGBT community. However, this story reflects a situation in which a
family member turns to religion as a way of coping with family members
who come out of the closet.

Some research has highlighted similar experiences LGBT people have had regarding religious interventions. For example, in a study with transgender people of color, one MTF participant shared,

> I don't consider myself a religious person. A punishment from my mom was being forced to read passages condemning homosexuals to hell. She thought I was gay, but being forced to read that hurt me. I am a very spiritual person though. Eventually, I established own personal relationship with my creator that I don't have to justify to anyone who I am. My spirituality helps me with that—practicing meditation and having faith that I am not a mistake [as a transgender person of color]. That gives me hope—the terrible things that have happened to me don't have to *become me*. (Singh & McKleroy, 2011, p. 39)

Meanwhile, in a study with LGBT Filipino Americans, one gay male participant revealed,

> I started coming out to cousins, female cousins, not male cousins . . . except for one . . . but then about last year, all my cousins wanted to have a family intervention. It became religious in scope. I think that the hardest blocks to coming out was the religious aspect. (Nadal & Corpus, 2012, p. 7)

Although these interventions might be well intentioned (i.e., family members are genuinely concerned about their LGBT loved one's soul and well-being), they are examples of microaggressions that may occur as a result of intersectional identities. If the families of these LGBT individuals were not religious, these types of microaggressions would likely not occur, at least not on the part of family members.

MICROAGGRESSIONS BASED ON BOTH RELIGIOUS AND SEXUAL IDENTITIES

Aligning with the previously described experiences of LGBT people of color, LGBT people of religious minority groups may encounter microaggressions that may be due to both their religious and sexual identities. Simply stated, when they experience certain microaggressions from others, it may be because of their religious identity, their sexual identity, or both concurrently.

For example, one Jewish lesbian woman described the treatment that she received in her academic department as an untenured professor:

> Christian literature showed up at my office door. A student asked to pray with me and prayed that I give up not only my "homosexuality" but also my Judaism, as she hoped I would "accept Jesus as my savior." The chair of my department informed me that calls were received demanding my dismissal. While the faculty all openly supported me, my file for retention, tenure, and promotion . . . was questioned. It was suggested that I remove all evidence of the

scholarly and professional work I had been doing on gay and lesbian issues from the file. I refused. (Dworkin, 2005, p. 66)

Similar to the previous discussion on the intersectional identities of LGBT people of color, this narrative exemplifies the multiple microaggressions experienced by a person who has several minority identities. First, it is evident that this professor was experiencing both overt and covert discrimination, and the microaggressor(s) may or may not have had malicious intentions. For example, when a Christian person encourages another to become a Christian, the former's intentions may not be malicious; she or he may genuinely believe that they are being kind and compassionate and "saving" the other person (Nadal, Issa, et al., 2010).

Second, this example demonstrates how difficult it is to separate one's multiple identities when understanding one's experiences with microaggressions. Did the narrator experience this microaggression because she is Jewish, a lesbian, a woman, or because of some combination of all of these traits? Would her experiences with religious microaggressions be different if she were heterosexual, and would her experiences with sexual orientation microaggressions be different if she were Christian? Because of the complexities of microaggressions toward individuals with multiple oppressed identities, it is likely that these individuals may experience psychological distress that goes above and beyond the stress that is experienced by individuals with singular minority identities.

Voices of Lesbian, Gay, Bisexual, and Transgender People With Disabilities

Another group within the LGBT community that is neglected both in general society and within the LGBT community itself is LGBT people with disabilities. In the most general terms, *disability* is "the expression of a physical or mental limitation in a social context, the gap between a person's capabilities and the demands of the environment" (Pope & Tarlov, 1991, p. 1). Disabilities can be physical (e.g., being blind, deaf, or using a wheelchair for mobility) or mental (e.g., one who has cognitive or intellectual deficiencies). In the past, there has been a focus on the "impairment" or "pathology" of people with disabilities; today, however, psychologists and other mental health practitioners tend to support person–environment approaches, which state that a number of external and environmental factors (that go above and beyond one's bodily capabilities) influence people's experiences (Pledger, 2003).

Because of this, it is important to recognize that a disability is merely a part of a person's experience and should not be the only way in which that person is defined or understood.

A growing amount of literature has been focusing on the types of institutional discrimination people with disabilities experience in the workplace (see Bruyère, von Schrader, Coduti, & Bjelland, 2010, for a review), yet there is a dearth of research on the ways in which people with disabilities are discriminated against in their everyday lives. Only one known study focused on the types of microaggressions that people with disabilities face. Keller and Galgay (2010) described a number of microaggression themes that people with disabilities encounter. Some of these include the following five: (a) denial of identity (e.g., when people overemphasize one's disability, instead of allowing her or him to identify as a human being), (b) denial of privacy (e.g., when people ask intrusive questions about people's disabilities), (c) desexualization (e.g., when a person with a disability is assumed to be **asexual**), (d) patronization (e.g., when people tell people with disabilities how "heroic" they are for accomplishing mundane tasks), and (e) second-class citizenship (e.g., when a person with a disability receives secondary treatment than an able-bodied person). It is likely that LGBT people with disabilities encounter these types of microaggressions. One might wonder, however, whether one's sexual orientation or gender identity may exacerbate one's experiences with microaggressions.

In this next section, I include a few themes that have emerged in narratives from LGBT people with various disabilities, including those who use wheelchairs for mobility, those who are blind or deaf, and those with cognitive deficiencies. Similar to other people with multiple oppressed identities, there is a lack of research on the microaggressions toward this group. In fact, there are very few representations of LGBT people with disabilities in the media and general society altogether (Guter & Killacky, 2004). The few articles that do focus on this community tend to concentrate on gay men and lesbian women who are predominantly White American and cisgender. Thus, I reemphasize that the following examples are limited and much more research should be conducted so that the voices of this community can be heard.

EXCLUSION WITHIN THE LESBIAN, GAY, BISEXUAL, AND TRANSGENDER COMMUNITY

Similar to other marginalized subgroups within the LGBT community, LGBT people with disabilities may feel excluded by their able-bodied counterparts. One lesbian woman with a disability wrote eloquently about this exclusion:

> Sometimes, however, we are not "invited" to be part of our own gay community. This happens when events are not accessible, when there are no lesbian bars that are wheelchair accessible, when only part of a bookstore can be accessed, or when our fellow lesbians and gay men assume that we don't exist and can't even conceive of having a relationship with us. (Field, 1993, p. 18)

Likewise, in an article written about LGBT people with disabilities, one blind gay man stated,

> The LGBT community is not really inclusive when it comes to the disabled . . . While that's not a problem exclusive to the gay community, it is made worse with their fixation on beauty and perfection. A disability, no matter what it is, makes you imperfect.

He continued, "I can accept it if I'm not liked for my personality, but it ticks me off when someone won't talk to me just because I'm blind" (Aterovis, 2006).

Similarly, another gay male with a disability shared how he was treated like a second-class citizen within the LGBT community:

> I decided to finally come out of my shell after two years, be active in the community and socialize. What I have found is the moment I'm asked what I do for a living and I tell them I'm disabled, the conversation stops as if I have the plague . . . This has been coming from people who are so mad that they are being treated as a second-class citizens for not being allowed to marry, yet they treat people in just the manner they are screaming about. (Broverman, 2009)

Feeling excluded in the LGBT community may also lead to negative views of romantic partners. For example, one gay deaf young man shared the following:

> I refuse to have a hearing partner, because hearing people sometimes view Deaf culture with disdain and have no respect and understanding. They don't like our culture or are not able to fully appreciate it. My future life, relationships and everything, it is a big question. (Sinecka, 2008, p. 481)

These perspectives make it clear that not feeling included by other LGBT people can be hurtful and isolating.

MICROAGGRESSIONS IN HEALTH CARE AND REHABILITATION SETTINGS

Several LGBT people with disabilities have reported perceiving microaggressions because of their sexual orientation while in a health care or rehabilitation setting. In a study that focused on lesbians with disabilities who go to rehabilitation therapy, participants described how discrimination is subtle but still felt. For example, one woman reported, "There wasn't a lot of really blatant, you know, 'We don't like dykes and get out of our hospital' kind of stuff, but there was a clear sort of critical-ness of people's expressions and lack of understanding" (Hunt, Milsom, & Matthews, 2009, p. 174). Another woman shared how she perceives health care workers who discover her sexual orientation: "Then when they figure it out, you can sort of see the looks, you can see the level of uncomfortability" (Hunt, Milsom, & Matthews, 2009, p. 174).

Sometimes health care workers create a heterosexist environment that prohibits LGBT people from feeling comfortable in expressing their sexual identities. In a different study that focused on lesbians with dis-abilities, one participant described her perceptions of the heterosexist biases of health care workers:

> There was some level of uncomfortability definitely in the psych hospital because when my partner would come and visit we were the only couple there that was gay and people would stare. . . . The staff, they just didn't really want to talk about it. They were more into straight people who've got kids and were married. (Hunt et al., 2006, p. 169)

Similarly, another lesbian with a disability described,

> And, uh, it's just that sort of atmosphere where if I had said anything when we were talking about family members and husbands and wives or their lack of understanding or whatever the effect on them, I could never, ever have brought . . . [my partner] up. (Hunt et al., 2009, p. 174)

Finally, when health care workers assume that LGBT people's partners are merely siblings or friends, they communicate that hetero-sexual marriage is the norm. For instance, one lesbian described a sce-nario that occurred with a physician: "He asked if she was my sister, and [my partner] didn't feel comfortable, so she interjected that she was a friend. . . . We didn't feel free to put it out there" (Hunt et al., 2009, p. 175). In Chapter 3, I described this type of microaggression as an "endorsement of heteronormative culture and behaviors"; for example, asking a woman, "Do you have a husband and children?" assumes that she is heterosexual and interested in raising children. Nonetheless, all of these examples point to the need for health care workers to become more culturally competent when working with LGBT people, par-ticularly LGBT people with disabilities. Although health care workers (especially those involved in rehabilitation therapy) may have learned to be compassionate and competent in working with individuals with disabilities through education and exposure, they must also be compas-sionate and competent in relation to their clients' sexual identities.

DESEXUALIZATION

LGBT people with disabilities, much like their heterosexual counterparts, may also be viewed as asexual or not sexually attractive as a result
of their disabilities. For example, one gay blind man shared, "Whenever
I hang out at a gay bar, particularly if I've never been there before and
people don't know me, a lot of times people look at me as a casual friend,
but not much else" (Aterovis, 2006). Being excluded in this way may feel
distressing because LGBT people with disabilities can be (and feel) just
as sexual as their able-bodied counterparts. Furthermore, when LGBT
people with disabilities are **desexualized**, they may feel even more
isolated and distant from the general LGBT community.

For people with cognitive or developmental disabilities, sexuality is
something that is often avoided altogether, in particular when same-sex
sexual acts are involved. For instance, in a study that examined perceptions of health care staff who work with people with developmental disabilities, one participant described how the institution responded when
two men were found having sex: "The local day center found a couple
having sex in the shed and guess what the day center did to deal with
the problem? They took down the shed. I think that says it all, doesn't
it?" (Abbott & Howarth, 2007, p. 119). Although it is possible that the
institution is uncomfortable when any of their clients have sex, there is
a possibility that they are especially uncomfortable when a person with
a developmental disability identifies as LGBT or engages in same-sex
sexual acts. Thus, such an instance could be considered an intersectional microaggression because it is based on both disability and sexual
orientation.

ENVIRONMENTAL MICROAGGRESSIONS

Although there are many interpersonal microaggressions that people
with disabilities may face regularly, it is evident that there are a number
of environmental microaggressions that may have a negative influence
on their everyday lives. Wheelchair access may be a huge obstacle for
many individuals with disabilities and make them feel excluded not
only in general society but also within the LGBT community. One lesbian
with a disability wrote about her feelings about the **ableism** that she
perceived in her workplace:

> My partner uses a wheelchair for mobility, and this added
> another level of complexity to the social aspects of the organi-
> zational environment. For example, departmental celebrations
> and events that included significant others were often hosted in
> inaccessible environments. The failure to attend to additional
> disability-related accessibility issues resulted in an air of exclusion.
> (Wiebold, 2005, p. 133)

On the other hand, one author recalled an scenario involving ableism within the LGBT community:

> I am reminded of a store owner who once remarked to me that his store didn't need a ramp because "people in wheelchairs don't come here." Right! And there is no homophobia in North Bay, because homosexuals or "people like that" apparently don't live there! Well, of course they do, but they may not be "out" because people's attitudes are as inaccessible as an unramped store. (Field, 1993, p. 19)

Another major environmental microaggression that may occur for LGBT people with disabilities involves the health care system. One lesbian with a disability described a difficult situation that she and her partner had because their relationship was not legally recognized:

> To fill out my disability forms, [my partner] could help me, but she couldn't go seek out my info. No one would give it to her, so I had to go. . . . It would have been great to say, "Here, go get me that information." (Hunt et al., 2009, p. 175)

A final environmental microaggression that LGBT people with disabilities may experience is invisibility. One of the reasons why this community goes unnoticed is because both of their identities (i.e., as LGBT people and people with disabilities) tend to be overlooked in our heterosexist and abelist society. In a collection called *Queer Crips: Disabled Gay Men and Their Stories,* the editors gathered short stories, poetry, and other writings to share the intersectional identities of those who are "queer" (i.e., gay, bisexual, transgender) and "crip" (i.e., with a disability). In their Introduction, they wrote of the need for the stories of LGBT people with disabilities to be told:

> As queer crips, we've been isolated from society at large and even from one another, by underemployment, institutionalization, poverty, and internalized cripophobia. All these factors have not merely discouraged us from telling our stories, they have [brainwashed] us into believing we have no stories to tell. . . . Fearing we are wordless, it becomes easy for us to believe we are worthless. (Guter & Killacky, 2004, p. xviii)

When LGBT people with disabilities are invisible in the media (and in society in general), many people from this community may feel invalidated and isolated, which may in turn have a negative impact on their mental health and self-esteem.

MICROAGGRESSIONS BASED ON BOTH DISABILITY AND SEXUAL IDENTITY

As with the other intersectional identities presented in this chapter, some microaggressions may be influenced by both one's disability and one's sexual identity. In these types of situations, the micro-aggressor may be behaving in such a way because of the individual's disability, that person's sexual orientation or gender identity, or some combination of both. In a performance piece, one author wrote about a scenario of something that a woman said to him, a gay man with a disability:

> You have to understand that the choice that you have made in your life is a sin. Your body is crippled, because it is crippled with sin. Don't you see? If you go to church God will help you. God can heal you. God gave you a disability, because he knew that you were going to be gay. Now don't take offense at what I'm saying. (Walloch, 2004, p. 3)

This type of statement may be considered a microaggression because the woman asks him to not "take offense" at what she was saying. She may genuinely believe that her comment would be helpful for the speaker and that she was helping him to find God and "cure" him. This example also demonstrates an intersectional microaggression in that her bias is based on both his disability and his sexual orientation.

A gay, deaf young man described how both of his identities nega-tively affected his relationship with his father:

> My parents did not try to tell me what was going on most of the time and I felt lost. My father did not care; I don't remember him trying to educate me or bring me up. He could not cope with the fact that first, I am Deaf, and second, that I am gay. Therefore our relation broke down. My dad does not accept that I am gay, just does not accept it! (Sinecka, 2008, p. 480)

In this case, it appears that the narrator's father already had such a dif-ficult time with his deafness that their relationship became even more strained when he came out as gay, too. Either way, this type of scenario exemplifies the dual minority stress that LGBT people with disabilities encounter in their everyday lives.

Finally, there are times when people with intersectional identities feel like they are not fully understood or accepted because others can-not grasp both identities. For example, in a study with lesbian women with disabilities, several participants described how some mental health counselors "get it" and how some do not. One woman reported the following:

> Gay professionals that I tried to go to cared about the disability and stuff and had never done their own work on that, so I couldn't go to them, and straight people couldn't deal with the lesbian thing. I've never found anybody who could get the lesbian and the disability pieces together. (Hunt, et al., 2006, p. 169)

Another woman stated, "Talking about disability was not something they were comfortable with and my treatment modalities . . . I mean

I sensed that immediately and then talking about being lesbian was secondly [their] least [favorite topic]" (Hunt et al., 2006, p. 169). In these cases, both participants perceived that their counselors were uncomfortable in addressing sexuality and disability. When clients in therapy have to worry about their counselors' biases about their social identities, they may feel invalidated and find it difficult to build a rapport with their therapists. They may also leave treatment altogether, which means that the reason that they went to therapy (e.g., depression, anxiety) would remain unaddressed.

Voices of Elderly and Aging Lesbian, Gay, Bisexual, and Transgender People

Another subgroup within the LGBT community that is often marginalized and victimized by microaggressions is the elderly and aging LGBT population. Because the U.S. Census does not accurately account for LGBT people in their data collection, it is difficult to know the exact number of elderly LGBT individuals in the country. One report estimated that 1.4 million to 3.8 million Americans over age 65 are LGBT, based on the typical estimate that LGBT people comprise 5% to 10% of the total U.S. population; the same report projected that by 2030 the population will expand to approximately 3.6 million to 7.2 million people (Grant, 2009). In recent years, there has been a growth of literature on elderly LGBT individuals, describing a range of sociocultural issues that these individuals may experience (see Stein, Beckerman, & Sherman, 2010). One of the biggest issues is living in isolation; research indicates that three fourths of this population live alone (Adelman, Gurevitch, de Vries, & Blando, 2006; Rosenfeld, 1999) and are less likely to have adult children or other family members to care for them during times of illness (de Vries, 2009). Another major issue for elderly LGBT people is that they encounter a great amount of institutional discrimination, in particular, regarding health insurance, medical care, social services, and housing. For example, according to the National Gay and Lesbian Task Force (2011), some of the major issues affecting this population include the following:

▪ Social Security pays survivor benefits to widows and widowers but not to the surviving same-sex life partner of someone who dies.
▪ Medicaid regulations protect the assets and homes of married spouses when the other spouse enters a nursing home or long-term care facility; no such protections are offered to same-sex partners.

▪ Tax laws and other regulations of 401(k)s and pensions discriminate against same-sex partners, costing the surviving partner in a same-sex relationship tens of thousands of dollars a year, and possibly more than $1 million during the course of a lifetime.
▪ Basic rights, such as hospital visitation or the right to die in the same nursing home, are regularly denied same-sex partners.

Given these factors, it is evident that there are many ways in which elderly LGBT individuals are not being treated as equally or fairly as their heterosexual counterparts.

Moreover, elderly LGBT individuals face many interpersonal microaggressions as well. For example, one report stated the following:

> These seniors are "twice-hidden" due to social discrimination on two levels: ageism and homophobia or heterosexism. LGBT seniors often face antigay or gender discrimination by mainstream elder care providers that renders them "invisible" and impedes their access to vitally important services. At the same time, LGBT elders frequently confront ageism within the LGBT community and the organizations created to serve the community's needs. (Funders for Lesbian and Gay Issues, 2004)

The dual minority status of being an LGBT person and an elderly person can lead to three types of discrimination: (a) ageism within the LGBT community, (b) heterosexism and transphobia within the elderly community, and (c) discrimination on the basis of dual or multiple identities that they could feel throughout general society.

Although an "out" LGBT community in the United States is still fairly new and developing, ageism has become a major divider between the younger and the older. One author wrote, "There is a great emphasis on youth, especially in the gay male community, but it exists throughout society. Youth is highly sexualized so that the uses and appeal of it may be overly emphasized" (Jones, 2001, p. 14). Youth is promoted in almost every aspect of the LGBT community through norms of social behaviors and standards of beauty. In terms of normalized social behaviors, it may be viewed as stereotypical for young LGBT people, in particular, gay and bisexual men and transgender women, to be "partygoers" who frequent bars and clubs. Gay and bisexual men are also stereotyped as also being "gym obsessed," which is likely due to individuals' desires to uphold the community's standards of beauty. As mentioned earlier, standards of beauty for gay and bisexual men focus on the intersection of race, physique, and age. One article cited how one 71-year-old gay man considers himself to be part of the generation of "invisible men" who "are gay men older than 60 (or 50, 40, even 30, depending where you frequent) who get overlooked in the quest for the 'hot young thing' on the dance floor" (Buhl, 2008).

Age influences standards of beauty for other aspects of the LGBT community as well. For instance, in one study with transgender women MTF sex workers, participants described how much aging was a factor in their ability to be perceived as attractive by clients. One participant revealed, "It's not like before, it's not like I enjoy doing [sex work] now. And each day that passes by I'm trying to walk away from it because I'm getting older and I don't know, I think I value myself a little more now" (Nadal, Vargas, et al., 2012, p. 140). Although this ageism may actually be healthier for this transgender woman in that it prevents her from turning to sex work as a means of survival, it demonstrates how much youth and beauty are emphasized in regard to transgender women in general.

Although ageism exists in the heterosexual community, such microaggressions can be particularly hurtful to an LGBT person who at one point may have felt very connected and involved in the LGBT community. Many of these now-elderly LGBT individuals were at the forefront of the Stonewall riots in New York or the forming of the Castro neighborhood in San Francisco in the 1960s. These individuals have been arrested, harassed, and beaten for standing up for their beliefs. Some watched their friends die in the name of civil rights. Thus, being isolated and excluded by younger LGBT people can be especially distressful for older LGBT people, who know that they paved the ways for the equal rights that young LGBT adults benefit from today.

On the other hand, elderly LGBT individuals also experience overt and covert discrimination in nursing homes and other health care settings. In one article, a health care worker described how some elderly LGBT people even go back "into the closet" to avoid microaggressions or unfair treatment:

> "Fearing discrimination, gay and lesbian seniors will resist services such as nursing homes, yet because they don't have others to fall back on they tend to go into nursing homes earlier," she said. "And there, they feel pressured to go back in the closet. In addition, we've heard that some home health care aides, when they learn that their client is gay, sit and read the Bible to them, in order to 'save' them." (Buhl, 2008)

In one study that focused on elderly LGBT people and their perceptions of the health care system, several participants described the discrimination that they fear. One participant shared, "I have to think very carefully about the possible repercussions when I let each doctor know, because I have been discriminated against and worse" (Stein et al., 2010, p. 429). Another participant added,

> I'm afraid to have a stranger in my home, someone who may be very anti-gay, and then what if they find out about my life and now they're in my home regularly, and could somehow take advantage or mistreat me. (Stein et al., 2010, p. 429)

Because of this fear of being discriminated against (either blatantly or covertly), many older LGBT individuals may actually prefer to be isolated or alone. For example, one said, "I feel I'd be better off home and alone than feeling humiliated by other residents or even worse, the people I'd depend on for my health care, my medicine" (Stein et al., 2010, p. 429).

In addition to the discrimination that elderly LGBT people may face in both the communities of elderly individuals and in the LGBT community, there are many ways they may be discriminated against, not only because of the intersection of their sexual identities and age but also because of the intersections of other identities as well. For example, transgender senior citizens may face discrimination because of their gender identity, their age, or both. One report described one of the obstacles faced by transgender elderly people:

> What nearly all transgendered elders have in common is a body that does not "match" their clothing, presentation, and/or identity. Transsexual genital surgeries only began in the 1940s and 1950s, are extremely expensive and seldom covered by insurance, and—especially in the case of female-to-male transsexuals—have often produced less-than-satisfactory results. Therefore, even transsexual elders are likely to have genitals and (perhaps) other physical features that are not congruent with their sense of who they are. That means transgendered elders will tend to be extremely reluctant to use services—even emergency medical care—that require disrobing. (Cook-Daniels, 2003)

Thus, transgender elderly people may have more obstacles to worry about than do LGB elderly people. Not only might they face discrimination based on heterosexism in health care settings and ageism in the LGBT community, but they must also be concerned about how they can keep up their hormone treatment or how they can deal with discrimination when care workers do not know about their gender identity.

Elderly LGBT people of color may also experience additional stress due to their racial/ethnic minority status. One article revealed some of the difficulties faced by elderly LGBT people of color:

> Minority gay aging is more challenging to understand and deal with than gender issues, because it is complicated by additional societal discrimination, lower income levels, more chronic impairment, greater concerns about financial and functional independence, and even less research targeted to minority gay aging. (Haber, 2009, p. 272)

Furthermore, researchers have reported that lesbian and gay elderly people of color have experienced higher rates of victimization (e.g., elder abuse, neglect) than their White counterparts (Balsam & D'Augelli, 2006), further supporting the fact that individuals who hold more marginalized identities have a greater likelihood of encountering discrimination. Either way, it is evident through all of the above examples that elderly LGBT individuals experience microaggressions based on their age, their sexual orientation, and sometimes both. Again, further research would be useful in giving a voice to this community.

Finally, age microaggressions may also have a negative impact on other aging people (i.e., middle-age people) within the LGBT community. For example, Kaufman and Phua (2003) described how age plays a major role in the gay male dating scene. However, the focus on age and the standards of beauty that are normalized on the basis of age can affect both men and women. For example, one 41-year-old bisexual woman described an age microaggression that she experienced:

> I'm 41 and newly single, with two kids who I nursed for a long time, so my breasts sag. Recently I was in a hot tub with a male friend and his roommate. My female roommate was there, too. She's a lot younger than me, and her breasts don't sag. It was the first time that I picked up the feeling that aging breasts are not attractive. I am also aware that I don't think a woman would be as concerned with how my breasts look as men are . . . I realize that now I'm going to have to deal with what getting older means for my body image. (Orndorff, 1999, p. 65)

Again, although standards of beauty may also affect heterosexual and cis-gender middle-age people, having to deal with microaggressions involving both one's sexual identity and one's age can be especially stressful.

Voices of Lesbian, Gay, Bisexual, and Transgender People of Other Marginalized Groups

Finally, many groups within the LGBT community experience an array of intersectional microaggressions on the basis of their multiple oppressed identities. In this section, I describe some microaggressions that may be encountered by other populations, including LGBT youth, LGBT people of lower social classes or socioeconomic status, and LGBT people who are overweight or obese. Very few narratives in contemporary literature or examples in popular media exist, so I hope these will provide a general sense of people's experiences while also encouraging further research and literature to emerge.

LGBT youth may experience many of the same types of microaggressions that have been illustrated throughout the text. In particular, they may not only encounter bullying in their school systems and microaggressions within their families, but they may also be victimized by microaggressions because of the intersection of their age and their sexual orientation. One of the ways in which this has been documented is based on the perceptions of LGBT youth by the criminal justice system as being deviant. A documentary called *Cop Watch: A Film About Police Brutality Against LGBT Youth* indicated that LGBT youth, particularly LGBT youth of color, felt harassed by police officers for no reason (FIERCE, 2007). LGBT youth in New York City recalled incidents when police would search or arrest them for no reason other than that they were standing in a large group of other LGBT youth. Similarly, one study by the Urban Justice Center in New York City revealed a few findings about LGBT youth in the criminal justice system. First, the researchers found that the criminal justice system is generally unaware of the needs of LGBT youth (i.e., very little research has been conducted on LGBT issues within the criminal justice system). Thus, various individuals within the system are likely to not be culturally competent in working with this group. Second, they reported that gay male and transgender MTF youth were viewed as being "visible and problematic." Third, they found that LGBT youth of all genders were often stereotyped as being sex offenders and were often accused of sexually assaulting other youth (Feinstern, Greenblatt, Hass, Kohn, & Rana, 2001). Because there is a minimal academic literature that gives voice to other microaggressions toward LGBT youth (in particular, LGBT youth of color), I hope that research with this population continues.

LGBT people of lower social classes and lower socioeconomic statuses may also experience a large number of intersectional microaggressions. This may be especially prevalent for transgender people. As I mentioned in Chapter 4, transgender people have higher rates of unemployment and poverty than the general population. Such experiences can be very distressful for a transgender person who wants to undergo medical or hormonal treatment. For example, a female-to-male (FTM) participant shared that he "had no place to turn to get help in transition—and worked five jobs trying to save money for surgery that [he] never knew if [he] would be able to afford" (Singh & McKleroy, 2011, p. 38). Similarly, in one study with transgender participants, one MTF woman shared:

> For a long, long time I didn't have money and that meant no hormones. I was looking for acceptance in my relationships— but a lot of [partners] just thought they could abuse me because no one else would want to be with me. I allowed it for a minute. A friend told me about this doctor and counselor who could help me get hormones. That changed everything. I was finally looking like I felt I was [in terms of my gender identity]. I didn't have to be afraid anymore. And that made me feel like anything was possible in my life. I got a job and a good relationship. I even went back to school and was a pretty decent student. (Singh & McKleroy, 2011, p. 38)

Although this woman's story ended up having a happy ending, it is clear that not having money or resources was a big obstacle in her life.

One final subgroup that may experience intersectional micro-aggressions is LGBT people who are obese or overweight. Because of the standards of beauty that are often promoted in general American society and in the LGBT community (in particular, for gay and bisexual men and transgender MTF women), individuals who are obese or overweight may experience microaggressions from heterosexuals and from other LGBT people. The limited research that does exist regarding weight and the LGBT community has tended to focus on the body images of lesbians and gay men. For example, one meta-analysis of 27 studies revealed that gay men were more prone than heterosexual men to feel dissatisfied by their bodies, whereas there were no differences between lesbian women and heterosexual women (M. A. Morrison, Morrison, & Sager, 2004). Perhaps gay men have higher levels of body dissatisfaction than heterosexual men because of environmental microaggressions (e.g., seeing images of physically fit men in magazines, bars and clubs, and other media) and because of interpersonal microaggressions (e.g., being teased by other gay men about their bodies or their size). Perhaps sexual orientation does not predict body dissatisfaction for women because women of all sexual orientations are victims of sexual objectification. Either way, further research needs to focus on this area so we can understand the dynamics that are formed within the LGBT community due to size while also understanding the types of intergroup microaggressions that may manifest.

Case Studies

I now present and discuss three case studies that focus on and help illustrate intersectional microaggressions.

THE INTERSECTION OF CULTURE, GENDER IDENTITY, AND MORE: THE CASE OF LORENZO

Lorenzo is a 30-year-old Dominican American, transgender FTM man who grew up in a large metropolitan city on the East Coast. He is the only child of his parents, who both worked full-time and emigrated from the Dominican Republic. He had a large extended family that lived within a few miles of his home, and his family had remained in good contact with their family members back in their home country.

Although born a biological girl named Laura, Lorenzo had known that he was transgender ever since he was a little child. He rejected the gender role norms that were instilled in him by his family, who wanted him to live the life of a "normal girl." When his mother tried to make "Laura" wear dresses, Lorenzo always refused, saying that he wanted to dress like "the other boys" and wear pants. This was a common argument between Lorenzo and his mother during most of his childhood, and Lorenzo's mother eventually became more lenient and accepting of whatever "Laura" chose to wear.

As an adolescent, "Laura" lived a life that seemed somewhat typical for a teenage girl. He had several female friends, he was involved in both sports and in the arts, and he even dated boys. He did not feel like a lesbian because he was indeed attracted to boys. However, as a girl, Lorenzo felt incomplete; he felt more like a boy. Although there was an LGBT club at his high school, Lorenzo did not feel comfortable attending its meetings. He recognized that even though there was a "T" in the title of the organization, that there were not any out "T" people that were involved. He also noticed that most of the people in the organization were White. So, instead of telling anyone about how he was feeling, he began to do some research online about transgender people and identity. When he entered transgender chat rooms and read online discussion boards regarding transgender experiences, he began to gain a better understanding about himself and how he identified. In college, he made some transgender friends and met several transgender role models who were leaders in the community. It was at this point that "Laura" made some major changes. He decided that he wanted everyone to refer to him as "Lo" instead of Laura; he also started wearing more stereotypically masculine clothes, like baggy sweatshirts and jeans. While his family noticed some of the differences, they assumed that he was going through a stage and that Lo was a lesbian.

When Lo was in college, he eventually made the decision to come out to his family as a transgender man. Because Lorenzo was the only child, and because his family was Latino and Catholic, he worried that his parents would have a difficult time accepting his transgender identity. During the winter break of his sophomore year, he told his parents that he was transgender and that he was planning on physically and medically transitioning into a man. At first, his parents were shocked, stating that it was just a phase and that he would change his mind eventually. They also asked if he was sure that he wasn't "just a lesbian" and told him that being transgender "simply wasn't natural." Lo was hurt, angry, and invalidated; he told his parents that he was going to start his transition with or without their support. He returned to college, got a part-time job, and applied for more financial aid so that he could save as much money as possible to begin his transition.

After several years of hormone treatment (and no contact with his parents), Lo returned home to try to make amends with his parents. Upon arriving, he informed them that he now identifies as Lorenzo and that he would appreciate it if everyone referred to him as such. Surprisingly, Lorenzo's parents reacted differently this time around. They apologized for not being initially accepting and shared that they loved him and supported him in his decisions. Noticing his notable change in physical appearance (i.e., Lorenzo could likely "pass" as a cisgender man), they asked him incessant questions about his experiences and his medical procedures. Lorenzo shared that he had been taking hormone treatment but that he had not yet completed gender reassignment surgery. Lorenzo's mother responded by suggesting that he not continue with the surgery, stating, "This way, if you decide that you really don't want to be a man, you can always go back to being normal."

THE INTERSECTION OF SEXUALITY, ABILITY, AND MORE: THE CASE OF MARCIA

Marcia is a 22-year-old, Asian Indian bisexual woman with a disability. She is the younger of two daughters of two immigrant parents from India (both of whom are physicians) and grew up in an upper middle class family. When Marcia was 15 years old, a drunk driver hit her when she was walking home after volleyball practice. She sustained many injuries, including severe damage to her spinal cord. As a result, Marcia has used a wheelchair for mobility ever since.

Despite her disability, Marcia has been able to live a typical life. Although she wasn't able to play sports in the same way that she could when she was able-bodied, she tried to remain physically active however she could. She always had a good social network with many friends, and she maintained her interests in arts and music. In high school, she graduated with honors and was even accepted into a prestigious university. As a result of the legal battles that she and her family faced with the drunk driver, she became very interested in law. After 4 years of undergraduate studies, she graduated with a degree in political science and was accepted to law school.

During her junior year of college, Marcia started to question her sexual orientation. Although she had always had crushes on boys (even before her accident), she began to meet many lesbian and bisexual women in college with whom she found herself fascinated. Although she was still attracted to some men, she found other lesbian and bisexual women to be much more compassionate and kind than the men she was meeting at school. She also started to wonder whether a man could ever want to be in a relationship with her because of her disability, so she started to explore her sexuality by volunteering at the school's LGBT center, telling other students that she was **bi-curious**.

Throughout her last 2 years of college, Marcia made many LGBT friends, including many lesbian and bisexual women to whom she felt very attracted. One time, she started to develop romantic feelings for a female friend named Megan and decided to tell her after many weeks of spending time together. Megan replied, "Marcia, I think you're really sweet, but I really only see you as a friend." Because this was the first time that she had been rejected, Marcia felt hurt, but she was still optimistic. After the second and third such rejections, she started to feel much more pessimistic, wondering whether these women would have reacted differently if she were able-bodied.

Furthermore, Marcia struggled with telling her family that she was bi-curious. She worried that they would not accept her primarily because of their conservative Asian Indian background and the potential shame this disclosure would bring to the family. After she graduated from college, Marcia finally decided to tell someone in her family. She chose to tell her sister, Francis, who is 2 years older than she. She had known Francis to be liberal and had heard that she had at least one gay male friend; thus, she assumed her sister would be supportive. However, when Marcia finally told Francis the news, Francis replied with, "Wait, what? Why would you choose to be bisexual?" Francis continued, "Your life is already hard enough because of your disability; why would you want to add another obstacle in your life?" Marcia did not argue, and she left feeling invalidated and alone.

THE INTERSECTION OF SEXUALITY, RACE, AGE, AND MORE: THE CASE OF ADRIAN

Adrian is a 62-year-old African American man who grew up in a middle-class suburban neighborhood with a large African American population. He was the youngest of four boys, all of whom identify as heterosexual (and who eventually married and had children). Although Adrian had started to feel same-sex attractions when he was younger, he tried to block out these thoughts as much as he could. Throughout his life, he had heard many times from family members and church leaders that being gay was "an abomination," so he had tried for a long time to repress his sexual feelings, pretending to be heterosexual by dating girls and sometimes even having sex with them.

Adrian had his first encounters with other "out" gay men when he was 21. He had read about a gay male bar that was 100 miles away from where he lived, and he decided to drive there. At the bar, he noticed that the majority of the people were White and there were very few people of color present. He noticed that most of the young White men got a lot of attention from everyone, including the older White men and the other men of color. Although Adrian believed he himself was attractive and had a fit physique, he sat in the corner of the bar by himself, feeling unattractive and excluded.

Over the next 5 years or so, Adrian continued to live his life on the "**downlow,**" frequenting gay bars and bathhouses on occasion while still hiding his secret from the rest of his family. Sometimes he perused dating advertisements in gay magazines and met men secretly for casual sex. Similar to his initial perceptions about the first gay bar he attended when he was 21, he noticed that young White men received the most attention and that men of color were either nonexistent or ignored. He observed that a lot of men's profiles and advertisements included statements like "No Blacks or Asians." Every time he saw something like this, he felt almost exactly how he did when he was younger—unattractive and excluded.

When Adrian was 30, he stopped dating women altogether and decided to "stop pretending" to his family. Although he never officially came out to his family members, they eventually stopped asking him about girlfriends, which Adrian assumed meant that they knew. Meanwhile, throughout his 30s, Adrian began to feel much more comfortable identifying as a gay man and even started to date men and establish several meaningful friendships. He became involved in a few LGBT organizations and even began to volunteer his time for a group that served LGBT youth of color. When he was 40, he met James, another African American gay man, to whom he felt very attracted and connected. The two started dating and were together for 22 years; however, their relationship eventually dwindled, and the couple broke up.

Now that Adrian is 62, he has started to realize how much age affects the way that he is perceived in the LGBT community. He hardly ever frequents gay bars because he feels like he is constantly surrounded by images of young, hard-bodied gay men, which in turn reminds him of his aging body. When he does attend bars and tries to initiate conversations with younger men, many of them are rude to him or ignore him altogether. Adrian is sad that he feels excluded and unattractive no longer solely because of his race but now also because of his age.

Case Study Discussion

All three of these case studies demonstrate the complexities of intersectional identities, in particular, the impact that these identities can have on one's experiences with microaggressions. The first case study focused on Lorenzo, an FTM transgender man who is faced with several microaggressions before and after his transition. Many of these incidents match some of the gender identity microaggressions described in Chapter 4. For example, when Lorenzo's parents tell him that his gender identity is "just a phase," it could be classified as their discomfort with/disapproval of transgender experience. Similarly, when they ask him intrusive questions about his genitalia, the incident can be categorized as a denial of bodily privacy. However, perhaps the scenario is even more influenced by several other identities, in particular, his family's Dominican culture and Catholic religion. Because Latino culture may influence rigid gender roles for men and women, it may be especially difficult for his parents to understand or accept his transgender identity. Latino men tend to be expected to subscribe to *machismo* gender roles (i.e., they would be masculine, providers, and emotionally restrictive), whereas Latina women are usually expected to subscribe to *marianismo* gender roles (i.e., they would be feminine, self-sacrificing, and be most like the Virgin Mary). As a result, his immigrant parents may not comprehend how someone who was raised a girl would want to be a boy. Furthermore, because Catholicism preaches heterosexuality and procreation as the norm, it may very difficult for his family to accept anything that would go against what they are taught.

The second scenario involves Marcia, a bi-curious Asian Indian woman with a disability. Marcia also experiences microaggressions that were discussed in previous chapters. For instance, when her sister denies her bisexuality, she invalidates Marcia's experiences and identity. However, Marcia's disability seems to influence her experiences in ways that other scenarios did not describe. First, she perceives that the female friends whom she has crushes on reject her because of her disability. This type of microaggression may be similar to the experiences of desexualization described earlier in this chapter, in which people with disabilities are often perceived as asexual beings because of their disabilities. So, when Marcia's romantic interests all view her as "just as a friend," she begins to question whether this is because of her personality or physical attractiveness (which may be more typical or acceptable reasons in other scenarios) or whether it is indeed due to the fact that she is in a wheelchair. Either way, Marcia feels invalidated and hurt.

The third case study refers to Adrian, an African American male who struggles with his gay identity but who also experiences subtle discrimination within the LGBT community. Similarly, Adrian may encounter microaggressions that were described in previous chapters (e.g., he learns that being gay is an "abomination"). In this case, however, one can see how both racial microaggressions and age microaggressions can manifest within the LGBT community. Adrian experiences racial microaggressions from an early age, when he notices that gay White men are viewed as the most desirable, yet when he becomes older, he perceives that young, gay White men become the standard of beauty for the gay male community. As a result of all these perceptions, he feels excluded from the LGBT community, which exacts a toll on his mental health and self-esteem.

All three of these case studies demonstrate how some micro-aggressive incidents may appear to be much more blatant and obvious, whereas other incidents might seem well intentioned and not malicious in any way. For example, Lorenzo's initial rejection from his parents can be construed as overtly transphobic in that they are unsupportive of his gender identity and transition. However, when he returns to them, and his mother encourages him to not undergo gender reassignment surgery in case he wants to return to "normal," she may be unaware of how hurtful and invalidating her words are to her son. Similarly, in the cases of Marcia and Adrian, who perceive that other LGBT people may discriminate against them because of their disability, race, or age, the perpetrators of the microaggressions may be completely unconscious of their behaviors while also remaining oblivious to the impact these behaviors have on others. For instance, when people write "No Blacks or Asians" on their Internet dating profiles, they may not believe they are being racist or offending others. However, when Adrian (and others) read such statements, they indeed have negative reactions that can potentially harm their mental health and self-esteem.

Finally, in each of the case studies it is clear that every single identity has an impact on the individual's experiences. Even if one identity were different, the scenario could change drastically. For example, if Lorenzo were White instead of Latino, or if he were MTF instead of FTM, the scenario would be different. If Marcia were deaf or blind instead of in a wheelchair, her experiences would be different. If Adrian had a disability or was transgender, his experiences would be different. Because of this, it is important to acknowledge that when examining intersectional identities, one cannot just focus on two or three identities but must take every identity into consideration.

Discussion Questions

FOR GENERAL READERS

1. What types of intersectional microaggressions do you believe occur more often with LGBT people of color? With LGBT people of various religious groups? With LGBT people with disabilities?

2. What types of intersectional microaggressions do you notice in various institutions (e.g., your workplace or school) or systems (e.g., government, media, religion)?

3. Have you ever committed an intersectional microaggression as a perpetrator? Were you aware of your behavior? How do you feel about this today?

4. Do you feel that microaggressions that occur within the LGBT community (i.e., microaggressions toward elderly LGBT people, LGBT people of color, LGBT people with disabilities) are better or worse than those that occur in general society?

5. When you were reading each case study, what were some of the feelings that arose for you?

6. What would you do if you were in Lorenzo's situation? Marcia's situation? Adrian's situation?

7. How could systems and institutions (e.g., government, school systems, media, institutional policies) assist each character in their experiences with microaggressions? How could these systems have been helpful in the past to prevent these microaggressions altogether?

8. How would each of these scenarios be different if even one identity (e.g., sexual orientation, gender identity, race, religion, age) were different?

FOR PSYCHOLOGISTS, EDUCATORS, AND OTHER EXPERTS

1. In what ways might you improve your cultural competence in working with LGBT people of color? LGBT people with disabilities? LGBT people of religious minority backgrounds? LGBT youth? Elderly LGBT people?

2. What techniques or methods would you use in working with Lorenzo, Marcia, or Adrian?

3. What types of countertransference issues would you have in working with Lorenzo, Marcia, or Adrian?

Glossary of Key Terms

Ableism: Negative attitudes, biases, and beliefs held about people with disabilities, as well as the discrimination that occurs as a result.

Asexual: Lacking sexual attraction to others or lacking interest in sexuality altogether.

Bi-Curious: Label used to describe someone who is interested in exploring the opposite of one's sexual orientation; usually, the individual chooses this label when she or he does not want to be identified as bisexual, heterosexual, lesbian, or gay.

Conversion Therapy: A method that attempts to change one's sexual orientation from lesbian, gay, or bisexual to heterosexual; sometimes it is called *reparative therapy* or *reorientation therapy.*

Desexualization: The process of depriving or taking away one's sexuality.

Downlow: Common term used in communities of color to describe a closeted LGBT person, in particular, one who engages in same-sex sexual behaviors.

Dual Minority Status: Identity in which an individual belongs to two marginalized groups (e.g., gay and African American).

Dual Minority Stress: Psychological distress that one experiences when she or he belongs to two marginalized groups.

Transamorous: Describes one who is attracted to and seeks relationships with transgender-identified or gender nonconforming individuals.

Processes of Dealing With Microaggressions | 6

Over the past several years, I have been fortunate in having had the opportunity to speak at more than 100 colleges and universities, hospitals, community centers, conferences, and other venues where people are interested in hearing about my work on microaggressions and other areas of multicultural psychology. During the question-and-answer portion of these lectures, I am usually met with a question (or two) in which an audience member discusses an ongoing microaggression that he or she is dealing with and then asks, "What should I do?" or "What should I have done?"

When asked questions like these, I first tend to wonder whether providing a direct answer describing what I personally would have done would be particularly helpful to the person. Nevertheless, I try to gather as much as information as I can while obviously being cautious of how much the person wants to disclose, realistic about the type of setting in which we are discussing the problem, and respectful of the time constraints of the lecture. It is necessary for me to gather as much information as possible so that I am fully aware of the players involved

DOI: 10.1037/14093-007
That's So Gay! Microaggressions and the Lesbian, Gay, Bisexual, and Transgender Community, by K. L. Nadal

as well as the potential consequences. Finally, even after I feel comfortable that I have as much knowledge as is possible and appropriate, I tend to say something like, "Well, it is really is up to you, but here are a few options you could consider . . . " I have never told someone explicitly what to do, and I can't recall a scenario in which I offered only one suggestion. When I finish sharing my thoughts, I do not ask the person to decide right then and there what she or he should do; instead, I wish the individual luck, encouraging him or her to seek alternative support systems and resources if possible or available.

As I think back on these types of interactions, I realize that the dialogue that I am having in the moment (i.e., between me and the audience member) is likely an internal monologue in which she or he has already engaged. She or he has probably already thought about the details of the microaggression, the players involved, and the possible consequences. Yet I usually wonder if these are thoughts that remain internalized or if that person has ever had an opportunity to discuss those feelings with anyone else. Nonetheless, I have engaged in this type of interaction time and time again because I think it's important for individuals to verbalize these internal thoughts, to gain perspective from others, and to make decisions on their own. I also believe that participating in this dialogue in front of others can be useful in providing a model for what a loved one or ally can do when someone in her or his life comes to them after experiencing a microaggression.

In the previous five chapters of this book, I provided numerous examples and case studies of the types of microaggressions that are encountered by people within the lesbian, gay, bisexual, and transgender (LGBT) community. However, this chapter takes a different approach in that it focuses on the processes of dealing with microaggressions. What do people do when they are victims of a microaggression? How do they usually feel? What would make them feel better? I begin the chapter by reviewing three known studies that focused on the ways various groups cope with and react to microaggressions in their lives. I then share a model that hypothesizes the various ways that people can navigate microaggressions when they occur. Finally, I share three personal case vignettes from my own life, as a way of describing my own process of dealing with microaggressions, in the hope of illuminating some potential ways for people to react to such instances in their own lives.

Previous Research on Coping With Microaggressions

Three known studies have examined the psychological processes people undergo, and the coping mechanisms they use, when they experience a microaggression. These qualitative studies involved microaggressions toward lesbian, gay, and bisexual (LGB) people (Nadal, Wong, Issa, et al., 2011); women (Nadal, Hamit, Lyons, Weinberg, & Corman, in press); and African Americans (Sue, Capodilupo, & Holder, 2008). Although all of these studies focused on how individuals coped with different types of microaggressions (e.g., sexual orientation, gender, and racial micro-aggressions), there are a few themes that are common to all. Thus, it is likely that some of these can also be applied to other groups, including transgender people and LGBT people of other intersectional identities.

In Chapter 3, I described one study, conducted by me and colleagues at my research laboratory, that highlighted the ways in which LGB people cope with and react to sexual orientation microaggressions (see Nadal, Wong, Issa, et al., 2011). To review, a sample of 26 self-identified LGB participants reported the behavioral, emotional, and cognitive reactions they experienced when they were victims of microaggressions. In terms of behavioral reactions, some LGB individuals reported how they were passive, choosing not to react, and others shared how they protected themselves after microaggressions when they occurred (e.g., by avoiding certain areas where they knew they could be harassed). One gay male participant shared the following:

> I think it is more open now, but at the same time you still gotta be careful and I could just forget about it one day and then all of a sudden a situation—I'm walking down the street and someone looks at me with a group of boys and they look at me really dirty and it brings me back to reality . . . that "OK . . . I have to protect myself." (Nadal, Wong, Issa, et al., 2011, p. 29)

This example, and others, demonstrates how participants were particu-larly conscious of the potential violence that they could experience, likely because of their familiarity with the number of hate crimes that occur toward LGBT people. Protecting oneself may be similar to the "felt stigma" (Herek, 2007) that was described in Chapter 1, in which LGBT individuals may change their behavior in order to protect them-selves from danger or discomfort.

On the other hand, some participants told how they were confronta-tional when they were victims of microaggressions (e.g., overtly vocalizing their anger, assertively questioning the intentions of the microaggressor). One gay male participant recalled the following incident:

> I heard one of the kids say, "flamer," and my reaction was different—I actually walked up to the kid . . . and I said, "What did you say?" [because] I knew he'd probably back down . . . I don't think things like that should go unaddressed. (Nadal, Wong, Issa, et al., 2011, p. 29)

Furthermore, participants described four major categories of emo-tions: (a) discomfort/lack of safety, (b) anger and frustration, (c) sadness, and (d) embarrassment/shame. They also shared two opposite thought processes: (a) acceptance and conformity and (b) resilience and empowerment. One bisexual female participant described how she had accepted heterosexism to be a norm in her family: "I figure that that's just the way they are. But, you know. It happens. You have to accept the way they are, you can't do nothing about it" (Nadal, Wong, Issa, et al., 2011, p. 30). On the other hand, a lesbian participant reported actively rejecting such norms:

> I've already been there and done the whole closeted thing I am
> so over that. That was miserable for me, I'm never going back to
> that and if people can't accept me that's their problem as far as
> I'm concerned and not mine. (Nadal, Wong, Issa, et al., 2011, p. 30)

So although there were times where participants accepted that heterosexism was a reality and they conformed to such norms, some participants shared that the source of their resilience was their empowerment as LGB people.

My research team also conducted a study that focused on the processes that women underwent when they were the victims of gender microaggressions (see Nadal, Hamit, et al., in press). Ten female participants in various focus groups described their behavioral reactions, emotional reactions, and cognitive reactions when they were victims of microaggressions. Behavioral reactions ranged from passivity (i.e., not responding to the microaggressions at all) to confrontation (i.e., vocalizing their frustration directly when a microaggression occurred). An example of passivity includes the following anecdote shared by one participant:

> My friends [and I] would . . . either laugh it off or put our heads
> down . . . Or like somebody would throw up the middle finger.
> I don't know. What could we do? What were we supposed to say?
> (Nadal, Hamit, et al., in press)

Meanwhile, an example of a confrontation includes one female participant who described how she reacts to a man who catcalls her: "Basically, I just go tell him to screw off. [Laughter] The guy, the guy always is like, 'Oh yeah, whatever then I didn't need to know your number anyway.' [Then], he just walks away, just like that" (Nadal, Hamit, et al., in press).

Similarly to those in Nadal, Wong, and Issa's (2011) study, the female participants in Nadal, Hamit, et al.'s (in press) study also were concerned for their safety. They tended to be avoidant at times (e.g., avoiding potential environments where microaggressions may occur) and self-protective (e.g., calling someone on their cell phone or walking in groups with male friends to avoid being catcalled). One female participant related how she often feels when she is in a potentially unsafe environment with a man:

> After awhile it's like, okay, am I comfortable with the guy or
> not? What's the escape plan? What do you do now? How are

you going to protect yourself? So I think when you go through those experiences you never you never feel safe 100% even if you know the person or not.

The female participants felt emotional reactions to microaggressions, such as feelings of humiliation, discomfort, anger, fear, and guilt. Sometimes these women would be more vocal about their feelings and externalize them to others; at other times these feelings were internalized and repressed. Finally, the women vocalized similar types of cognitive reactions as those in the LGB study: Some accepted gender microaggressions as a regular part of life, whereas others said that overcoming such experiences made them feel more resilient.

Finally, in a qualitative study with 13 self-identified African American participants, four major themes were reported when individuals described their reactions to microaggressions (Sue, Capodilupo, & Holder, 2008). First, participants described a "healthy paranoia" that they felt. Simply stated, they shared how they often questioned whether race was involved in certain situations that made them feel uncomfortable. Participants viewed this as being "healthy" because they knew, not only from their own personal histories but also from the perspectives of their African American family members and friends, that many interactions were influenced by race. Second, participants shared a "sanity check" in which they would indeed turn to loved ones and allies when they experienced subtle discrimination. Getting this social support was necessary to validate the person's experience and to counter the paranoia that she or he felt. For example, one participant shared these feelings:

> As opposed to being paranoid—I have people in my sphere of influence that I can call up and share my authentic feelings with, so that there's sort of this healing, there's just this healing circle that I have around myself, and these are people who I don't have to be rational with if I'm battling racism. (Sue, Capodilupo, et al., 2008, p. 332)

A third theme involved empowering and validating one's self; participants reported a process in which they would soothe themselves after they were victims of microaggressions, often reminding themselves that they were not at fault. For example, one woman stated, "I find that is keeping your voice. . . . If I decide I want to do an intervention, I'm not necessarily doing it for them. I'm doing it for me" (Sue, Capodilupo, et al., 2008, p. 332). The final theme was "rescuing offenders," which is a thought process that occurred when participants considered the aggressor's feelings over their own. Many participants reported that because they were aware of the stereotypes people have of African Americans, they made sure that their body language communicated nonthreatening behavior. This cognition could be considered a protective factor in that these individuals were taking measures to prevent certain negative outcomes from occurring (e.g., arguments, perpetuation of stereotypes).

In all three of these studies, it is evident that members of various marginalized groups may cope with microaggressions in a number of ways. All three groups of participants were able to illustrate the behavioral reactions, emotional reactions, and cognitive reactions they experienced when a microaggression occurred. Behaviorally, it seemed that some individuals were passive and did nothing at all, whereas others were more confrontational toward the microaggressor. The emotional reactions ranged from sadness to anger to humiliation and guilt. Finally, cognitively, some participants learned to just accept things the way that they were, and others learned to be resilient and to empower themselves whenever a microaggression occurred.

In all three groups it was evident that when people experienced microaggressions, they never walked away feeling good about themselves. Although some say that they have become resilient, and others claim they have learned to be accepting or tolerant of others' prejudice or microaggressive behavior, in reality they may have learned to rationalize as a means of alleviating negative feelings. Some might consider such a coping mechanism a positive one in that the person is not dwelling on negative emotions. On the other hand, others may consider rationalizing a negative coping mechanism in that people who rationalize are repressing or avoiding their emotion altogether. Regardless, it is up to the individual to decide which coping mechanism would be most psychologically healthy and beneficial for him or her. Perhaps, however, it may be helpful for people to be cognizant of which type of coping mechanism they tend to use most often, as well as which one seems to be the most effective in different types of situations.

A Model for Dealing With Microaggressions

In the *American Psychologist* article in which racial microaggressions was reintroduced to the literature, Sue and colleagues (2007) illustrated the "Catch 22" that people of color experience when they are witnesses or recipients of racial microaggressions. In other words, victims of microaggressions may question whether they should respond or react to the microaggression because of the many potential negative consequences. Because microaggressions are so often ambiguous, seemingly innocuous, and covert, they may wonder if they are just being paranoid of whether the instance really did occur. They may even question whether the perpetrator was aware of her or his actions, whether she or he intended to be offensive or hurtful, or both.

Microaggressions and the uncertainty of whether and how to respond may cause people significant distress, as they must consider the context, the players involved, the environment they are in, and the amount of time they have to react. In this brief moment in time, they may have to instantaneously weigh their options, knowing that whatever course of action they opt to take could have unfavorable consequences. If they do choose to say something, an argument may ensue, which may then lead to psychological discomfort (and potentially even physical safety issues). If they choose not to say something, they may feel regretful and perseverate on their lack of response.

In one book chapter that I wrote (Nadal, 2010b), I described a model that involved several internal questions that an individual may ask her- or himself in the few seconds after experiencing a microaggression:

- Did this microaggression really occur?
- Should I respond to this microaggression?
- How should I respond to this microaggression?

In Table 6.1, I break down these three steps to show specific thought processes and actions an individual might use to help deal with a micro-aggression in the moment it occurs. Let's now review each of these questions.

DID THIS MICROAGGRESSION REALLY OCCUR?

Sometimes microaggressions may be so glaringly apparent that a person can identify them easily. For example, in Chapter 3, when I described the case of Daniel, the 14-year-old Mexican American boy who was constantly bullied by his classmates, the majority of the microaggression incidents were very obvious (e.g., his classmates calling him a "sissy" or a "fairy" and saying that he "played sports like a girl"). His classmates were intentionally trying to insult Daniel, and it was clear that their word choices were all homophobic or genderist. However, there are many incidents when individuals may question whether a microaggression really was indeed a microaggression. For example, in the case of Marcia, the bi-curious Asian Indian woman with a disability, it is unclear whether her romantic crushes did not feel similarly about her because she was in a wheelchair (see Chapter 5). Similarly, Adrian, the gay 62-year-old African American man in Chapter 5 who feels subtle racial discrimination at gay bars may have difficulty "proving" that his perceptions are correct. Finally, Sid, the 41-year-old female-to-male transgender man in Chapter 4 who overheard his coworker Liz use the word *trannies,* may have initially wondered whether he had heard her correctly or if she said something completely different. These are the types of incidents in which the LGBT individual may need more information or support in order to decide whether something was truly microaggressive.

TABLE 6.1

Processes of Reacting to, and Coping With, Microaggressions

Question step	Internal monologue	Action steps
Step 1: Did this microaggression really occur?	Did I hear/see what I really thought I heard/saw? Did the person act that way because of my sexual orientation or gender identity?	An individual may look to witnesses (e.g., passersby, coworkers, etc.) for reactions. She or he may directly ask for feedback or may rely on body language or facial expressions. If the person is alone, she or he may call a loved one to describe the incident and to receive validation.
Step 2: Should I respond to this microaggression?	What will happen if I confront this person? How will this affect my relationship with her or him? Will my physical or psychological safety be compromised if I say something? If I don't confront the person, how will I feel, and how will it affect me in the future?	An individual starts to internally weigh the costs and benefits of confronting the perpetrator, taking into particular consideration the (a) environment and (b) perceived threat. She or he may again turn to others for support, may ask witnesses for feedback immediately or some time later, and/or seek advice/validation from a loved one who is not present.
Step 3: How should I respond to this microaggression?	If I assertively confront this person, what will happen? If I respond in a passive–aggressive manner, or with humor, what will happen?	An individual begins to weigh out the costs and benefits of each type of response. She or he chooses to act in one of three ways: (a) aggressively, (b) passive–aggressively, or (c) assertively.

When microaggressions are experienced when other friends and allies are present, it could be much easier to ask someone else if he or she heard, saw, or experienced the same incident. For instance, if Sid's coworker, Liz, did make the transphobic comment in front of other people at the office, Sid might ask a coworker if she or he heard the word that Liz used. However, when an individual is alone and experiences a microaggression, she or he may be confused or even feel paranoid about whether something really happened. In this case, it may be helpful to trust one's instincts, ask someone (e.g., bystanders, passersby) if the potential microaggression really occurred, or seek support from others for validation (Nadal, 2010b). For example, perhaps Marcia just needs to trust her instincts that she does experience a lot of ableist microaggressions because of her disability; because it happens so often (to her and to other people with disabilities), perhaps she can learn to feel confident that she is not just being paranoid. If she does want or need more external validation, maybe she can seek support from another friend with a disability or an ally who can validate her experiences or serve as a reality check if there is indeed another factor that may be involved.

Similarly, Adrian may need to trust his instincts as well, in particular, because his experience is one that is shared by so many other people of color in the LGBT community and because he has similar experiences regularly. However, if he wants extra external validation, he can ask other passersby or loved ones. Let's say that Adrian noticed a specific incident in which an African American man was treated as a second-class citizen at a gay bar; perhaps he could scan the room to see if anyone (e.g., another person of color, a White ally) saw the same thing that he did. At that point, he may directly ask the other person if she or he had the same perception. Sometimes even a confirming facial expression from a stranger or passerby can be enough validation that someone needs to identify something as a microaggression.

SHOULD I RESPOND TO THIS MICROAGGRESSION?

If the individual is confident (or at least somewhat confident) that the incident was indeed a microaggression, there are two more questions to consider: (a) If she or he responds, what are the potential risks and/or consequences? (b) If she or he does not respond, what are the risks and/or possible consequences? (Nadal, 2010b).

There are a few factors that one might think about at this point. First, there is the issue of safety. If there is a potential for one's physical safety to be harmed, the individual may wonder whether confronting the person would be worth it. Thus, perhaps the individual can consider two more factors: (a) the immediate environment (e.g., a public setting with others around, or a deserted area) and (b) the perceptions of the perpetrator's physical threat (e.g., the physical size and stature of the perpetrator, the number of perpetrators present, and the aggression level or personality style of the perpetrator; Nadal, 2010b). For example, Daniel, the high school student who is being bullied, may not want to confront the microaggressors at all because he may indeed worry about his safety. However, there are probably places and situations in which he especially would not want to confront his bullies; he likely would never want to confront them in a place where there are no authority figures, nor would he likely want to confront them when there are several boys there at the same time (particularly if they appear violent or aggressive). This same type of thought process may occur for an adult LGBT person who overhears someone use a disparaging term like *faggot* or *tranny* or *she-male*. If the LGBT person is walking alone home at night and overhears the slur(s), confronting the individual may not be worth it; however, if the word is used jokingly in a workplace or university environment, perhaps the person may feel safer in confronting the microaggressor directly and instantaneously.

In addition to physical safety, one should consider the psychological consequences that may occur when responding to microaggressions. Because it is likely that the microaggressor could become defensive, angry, and argumentative, the individual may wonder whether getting in an argument would be worth it at all. Does she or he even have the time or energy to engage in an argument with this microaggressor? Could this microaggression lead to another microaggression? If a microaggression takes place in public (e.g., an individual overhears someone on the subway or at a grocery store say something transphobic), confronting the person (who is a stranger) may consume significant time and energy. If a microaggression occurs in a school setting (e.g., a professor makes a heterosexist comment), a student may hesitate to confront the individual because she or he may worry about her or his grade. If a microaggression occurs in a workplace setting (e.g., a coworker says something like, "That's so gay"), responding may not only cause tension in the individual's working relationship with the microaggressor but also may damage one's potential for promotion opportunities or even threaten one's job security. Finally, confronting a microaggression might actually be more distressful than the microaggression itself; thus, a victim might just walk away from a microaggression because she or he views it as the least distressful consequence.

Despite all of this, *not* confronting a microaggressor can have negative consequences. As mentioned earlier, the individual may feel regret for not saying anything and may ruminate about the scenario and about what she or he should have or could have said. For example, let's consider the example just given, in which an LGBT individual overhears a transphobic comment on the subway. If the individual walks away without saying anything to confront the perpetrator, she or he may feel disappointed or guilty, perhaps even worrying that the perpetrator may continue using such discriminatory language in the future. In fact, many LGBT people and others may feel compelled to confront microaggressors because they feel it is their responsibility to educate others about what is unacceptable and discriminatory, in order to prevent such behavior from continuing. Because of this, some LGBT people might prefer to confront microaggressions, even in the slightest ways, in order to avoid feeling responsible for not doing anything at all.

HOW SHOULD I RESPOND TO THIS MICROAGGRESSION?

Once individuals decide to respond to a perpetrator, they must consider *how* to do so. An aggressive or confrontational approach may have consequences that are not constructive. For example, angrily yelling at someone who makes a homophobic remark may lead to a potentially destructive or exhausting argument (which may even compromise one's safety or one's mental health). When a victim of a microaggression turns around and insults a perpetrator in reaction to feeling hurt or offended, the action may actually be counterproductive because now the perpetrator has a reason to be upset with the victim. For instance, if a lesbian who is being teased by her sister for being a "dyke" counteracts by teasing her sister about her weight or her intelligence, her sister may now be unable to hear how she was originally at fault for using homophobic language.

At the same time, it might be understandable when LGBT people (and other people of marginalized groups) do become confrontational toward perpetrators. When individuals experience many micro-aggressions throughout their lifetime, it might be only human for them to react intensely to some. For example, an LGBT young person who is bullied daily might finally fight back after years of being harassed. Furthermore, sometimes victims of microaggressions may be intention-ally aggressive in responding to their perpetrators, in order to prove that they are strong and resilient (e.g., because Asian American women are often stereotyped as being meek and submissive, an Asian American lesbian might vocalize her anger in order to prove the stereotype wrong).

Sometimes, individuals may be passive-aggressive in confronting perpetrators of microaggressions. Using humor is one way of commu-nicating annoyance or disgust and might be easier to do. For instance, if a coworker makes a heterosexist joke, it might feel less threatening for an LGBT person to use sarcasm to convey disapproval. Body language (e.g., eye rolling, disapproving facial expressions) or scoffing can show that one is upset or frustrated with another's behavior. Sometimes being passive-aggressive is useful when a victim wants to communicate something without having to engage in a confrontation or become psycho-logically involved or distressed. However, passive-aggressive behavior might also be ineffective because perpetrators might not understand that what they said or did was hurtful. As a result, they might attribute another person's passive-aggressive behavior to something else.

When a person is victimized by a microaggression, another approach might be to use an assertive approach by engaging in a composed and deliberate dialogue with the perpetrator. This may involve the victim calmly approaching the perpetrator, asking about her or his intention, and directly divulging how the microaggression made the individual feel. Perhaps this type of technique may be easier in some settings than in others. For instance, if a microaggression is committed by someone with whom the victim already has an existing relationship, it might not be difficult to directly point out the hurtful statement or behavior to this person. If the perpetrator has a history of being open minded, reflective, and nondefensive, then perhaps the task of assertively confronting her or him might cause little distress. However, if the perpetrator is a stranger, and/or if the perpetrator is known to have been defensive, less reflective, or closed minded in the past, having a rational conversation about the topic might be challenging.

One technique that might be helpful if one does decide to confront a microaggressor is to attack the behavior, not the person. A common tool in conflict management in general, this method involves

- pointing out the behaviors of the microaggressor(s),
- using "I" statements, and
- emphasizing that you are not judging the individual's personality or morality.

First, pointing out behaviors (or statements) involves identifying exactly what transpired. Using facts to describe the series of events is helpful in engaging in a rational and sound dialogue. Next, using "I" statements means that the victim will accentuate how she or he felt in reaction to the behaviors or statements. Finally, emphasizing that you are focusing only on the individual's behavior and not questioning her or his personality or morality is useful because people in general believe they are good, moral people. Thus, when someone challenges them, they may become defensive. When people are guarded in this way, they may not actually listen to any feedback or criticism; instead, they may just start to think about the ways they can retort or justify their actions and behaviors.

Another element that is helpful in engaging in dialogue about sensitive issues like discrimination is to ensure that both parties are actively listening. One tip that I have found to be very helpful is to paraphrase what someone said immediately after she or he is done speaking, as a way of clarifying that I understand her or his perspective. I then ask the individual to do the same after I speak my opinion or share my feelings, because I want to make sure that she or he knows exactly where I am coming from. Using this method can be helpful because both parties must actively listen to the other's opinion instead of already formulating arguments in their head.

I must emphasize that although these are two ways of attempting to confront a microaggression, these techniques may not always be successful. The ways in which conflicts are dealt with in general are contingent on a number of factors, namely, the parties involved, the history and relationship between the parties, the communication styles that are used, the environment that the conflict takes place, and the emotions that are involved. Thus, other factors may also complicate microaggression confrontations, including the relationship between the two individuals prior to the microaggression and the emotions and communication styles of both parties. Accordingly, it may be necessary for victims of microaggressions to take all of these factors into consideration when confronting an individual, to prepare for any potential stress that may emerge from the dispute.

Finally, regardless of how victims handle microaggressions, it may be necessary for them to find support and resources that may help them not only practically but also psychologically. In terms of practical support, it may be important for people to familiarize themselves with different places, groups, and institutions that can be helpful in addressing micro-aggressions. For example, if a person experiences microaggressions in a workplace, perhaps she or he may turn to the human resources department and become acquainted with the company's policies with issues of discrimination and harassment. Furthermore, LGBT people who experience microaggressions in workplaces, school systems, and other institutions may want to be connected to local LGBT community or legal organizations that can assist in advocating for them if necessary (e.g., if they do decide to pursue legal action if microaggressions or overt discrimination has negatively affected their work experiences).

At the same time, victims of microaggressions may also need social support that can be beneficial in ensuring that their mental health needs are met. Ideally, most LGBT individuals have family, friends, and allies in their social support network to whom they can turn when they are victims of microaggressions. However, when they are shunned by their families and friends, it would be especially beneficial for them to seek social support from the LGBT community. In many major cities across the United States, there are LGBT community centers with an array of programs for many sectors within the community (e.g., counseling services, substance abuse treatment, support groups for older people). There are many national LGBT hotlines people can call when they need support, and there are also many websites and community organizations that can provide resources and validation to LGBT people in need. Finally, perhaps it would be especially helpful for members and allies of the LGBT community to be more vocal and visible in their neighborhoods, work-places, churches, and school systems so that isolated LGBT people know that there are indeed others who care about their well-being.

My Personal Process in Responding to Microaggressions

Throughout this book, I have provided several case studies that have demonstrated the types of microaggressions that may be commonly experienced by various members of the LGBT community. Because this section involves the processes of dealing with and coping with micro-aggressions, I thought it would be most beneficial to describe personal microaggressions that have occurred in my own life as a way of illus-trating how someone initially reacts to a microaggression, feels when a microaggression occurs, and decides whether to respond or confront the perpetrator. As I mentioned earlier in this chapter, people must take several things into consideration. They must first confirm that the microaggression did indeed occur and was indeed a microaggression.

They must carefully consider whether they should respond, given the environment, the parties involved, and the potential consequences. If they do choose to confront the perpetrator, they should be strategic in their approach. Sometimes confronting microaggressions can be successful; at other times the individual may walk away from the situation feeling much more distressed than he or she did after the actual microaggression itself. Thus, I share these examples to demonstrate that there is no "right" answer of how to respond to microaggressions. In any circumstance, there are potential negative consequences. However, it is up to the individual to make the decision that would be best for them.

I am choosing to share my personal reactions to microaggressions for many reasons. First, I want to provide you all with the internal psychological process that any victim of a microaggression may experience. Because the case studies in previous chapters are written from a third-person perspective, you may not have had a complete picture of what the microaggression victim was going through. In hearing my first-person narrative, I hope you will be able to understand the conflicting emotions, the decision-making process, and the psychological consequences that result from microaggressions. Furthermore, I share three different types of incidents to highlight the fact that sometimes you may not confront someone who commits a microaggression, sometimes you may respond to microaggressions and it might not be successful, and sometimes you choose to respond and it results in a meaningful and effective dialogue.

Before I begin, I must share a bit about who I am as a way of providing some context for these situations. I am a self-identified gay, Filipino American, cisgender, able-bodied man. I am in my mid-30s, I have an average-to-athletic build, and a bald/clean-shaven head. As a Filipino American, I am typically mistaken for several racial and ethnic groups, including Filipino, Latino, Asian, Pacific Islander, Middle Eastern, and multiracial/African American. I do identify as gender conforming, but I am told that I have both masculine and feminine behaviors, traits, and styles of speech. I am out of the closet to anyone who matters (i.e., I have been out to all of my family and friends since my mid-20s), but I know that I sometimes pass (mostly to strangers who may assume that everyone is heterosexual). I have a doctoral degree in counseling psychology, and I currently identify as middle- to upper middle class, even though my family has working- to middle-class roots. I have lived in New York City, in the heart of Manhattan, for over 10 years, but I spent my whole childhood and adolescence in California. I tend to get along well with people, and I've been told that I am outspoken and outgoing; however, I also admit that I tend to be complacent and timid in certain situations.

The following three vignettes are based on actual situations that have occurred in my life. I have changed many details and identifying characteristics of people and locations to protect people's privacy.

Pseudonyms are used throughout. All of these scenarios occurred in the past 3 years.

VIGNETTE NO. 1: THE INVALIDATING HANDSHAKE

Not too long ago, I was asked to speak at an LGBT conference about experiences of LGBT people of color. The lecture itself went very well, and I was happy to be able to connect with the various LGBT leaders whom I met and engaged with. I was also excited because I noticed two colleagues in the audience whom I had known from a professional organization for years: Yvonne (a heterosexual, cisgender, White American woman in her early 30s) and George (a heterosexual, cisgender, White American man in his mid-to-late 40s). After the lecture, I first went to greet Yvonne with a big hug and kiss on the cheek, because we hadn't seen each other in quite some time and were indeed very good friends. Yvonne, who also knew George, called him over to where we were standing. He came over immediately and greeted her with a big hug. Thinking it was my turn next, I approached him too, but instead, he stuck his hand out, gesturing that he was only going to give me a handshake. Confused and taken aback, I said, still smiling, "What's with the handshake, George?" He replied, "Come on, Kevin. I'm a dude."

Many things ran through my mind at this point. Why was he so willing to give a hug to Yvonne and not to me? Was it just based on gender? Did he just not hug men in general? Was it based on my sexual orientation? Was there any chance it could also be based on race? For a few seconds, thoughts flew around in my mind. He does know that I am gay, right? I know I've definitely talked about my relationships and other LGBT-related experiences in front of him at some point. But I also don't know if he ever really talked about it with me or actually told me that he was "okay" with gay people. Why wouldn't he want to hug me? Did he think that I was going to molest him or something? He's not even cute. I could totally do better!

My thought process continued. Should I say something? He knows that I study microaggressions, right? Does he know he's committing a microaggression right now? He's an educated person and is in a helping profession. He needs to know that this is not okay. I have nothing to lose.

I finally laughingly replied, "Forget the handshake. Give me a hug!"

George then proceeded to give me a hug, but did one of those "masculine" hugs where there is brief touching only in the upper body and ends with two pats to the back. Meanwhile, my thoughts continued. Should I say anything else? I did.

"George, so is there a reason why you didn't want to give me a hug? Is it because I'm gay?" I asked, in a consciously nonthreatening way.

He said, "No, no, no. It's because I don't hug men."

"Are you sure?" I replied. "Well, how come you don't hug men?"

"I just don't," he affirmed.

"Okay. I'll let this go, but know that when you do that to a gay man, it can be construed that you are scared that we are going to molest you or something."

We continued to chat about nonsense for an obligatory 3 minutes or so before Yvonne signaled that we should probably just walk away. After we said our goodbyes to George, I turned to Yvonne and asked, "What was that all about?" She validated me, and we discussed what had happened for a few more minutes, before moving onto another topic. We both agreed that it was good that I said something, but we both were unclear whether George was telling the truth.

VIGNETTE NO. 2: AN INTERVIEW WITH A NEWS REPORTER

A couple of years ago, I was touring around the country with my book, *Filipino American Psychology: A Handbook of Theory, Research, and Clinical Practice* (Nadal, 2011a). I was lucky enough to travel to places in various regions in the United States—some with large Filipino American populations and others with much smaller Filipino American populations. Depending on the size of the community, the number of events or stops in a given city would differ. When I was in one particular city, I had about four different stops in the course of 2 or 3 days. Two stops were at college campuses, one was at a community center, and one was at a press event where I would have the opportunity to talk to several local Filipino American media outlets.

The first night I arrived, I lectured at one of the colleges, and the next afternoon I spoke at a community center. So, by early evening, I was exhausted. Yet, I knew I had to attend this press event and another college lecture later that night, so I drank my coffee and put on my smiling face. If I recall correctly, there were at least three interviews to complete. The first was with a radio station, the second with a television news reporter, and the third with an online magazine. I was told that each would last about 15 to 20 minutes. I eagerly wanted to get started so that I could be finished, rest (maybe even nap!), and go to my next lecture.

The first interview went smoothly. I was happy it was on the radio, so I didn't have to worry about what I looked like. But because the second one was a videotaped interview, I made sure that my tie was straightened and that I had nothing in my teeth. The interviewer was a Filipina American woman who was around 35 years old. I hypothesized, based on the mild strength of her Filipino accent, that she was likely someone who had immigrated within the past 10 years. She provided me with a list of questions to review, and then we started the interview.

She asked questions directly from her sheet: "Why did you decide to write this book?" "What do you think is important for Filipinos to take away from this book?" and so on. We engaged in a dialogue about issues such as colonization, ethnic identity, and family dynamics. We had a good rapport, and she seemed to understand everything that I was trying to convey. And then she went off-script.

"So Kevin, our viewers want to know. Are you married?"

"Um," I replied, shocked and startled because I wasn't prepared to answer anything about my personal life. I also think that she definitely was assuming that I was heterosexual because I definitely cannot get married in this state (or my own state at the time).

"Well, do you have a girlfriend?" she jokingly asked next.

"Um," I hesitantly replied, as I started to think about what I should say. For a few seconds, my mind raced. Why does she think I'm heterosexual? Didn't she read my biography before interviewing me? Does she assume that everyone is heterosexual? How could she not know that I'm gay? "No, I don't have a girlfriend," I replied.

My thoughts were all over the place: Should I come out to her right now? Why do LGBT people always have to announce their sexuality? It isn't fair. Heterosexual people never have to announce that they are straight. Then I start to think if maybe I am embarrassed to say that I'm gay. Why would I be embarrassed? I am out to everyone in my life, and I speak about LGBT issues all over the country. Maybe it's because this reporter is Filipino and grew up Catholic and maybe I think she's going to judge me. But still, I don't think it's fair that I have to out myself when it's not even a relevant part of the conversation.

"Well, are you looking for a girlfriend?" she inquired.

My mind wandered more. I started to realize that this woman is probably just trying to be friendly and is asking a question that she probably asks anyone. However, why couldn't she ask me a gender-neutral question like "Are you dating anyone?" or even "Do you have a boyfriend?" I would have gladly answered her then—I think. Either way, I knew that I wanted to stay true to myself. I didn't want to lie to her. So I decided to answer everything she asks me truthfully.

"No, I am *definitely* not looking for a girlfriend," I said, smiling, hinting, I hope, at my gay identity. She smiled, changed the subject, and we ended the interview. The next interviewer set up immediately, and I was never in contact with the previous news reporter ever again.

VIGNETTE NO. 3: A CONVERSATION WITH FAMILY MEMBERS

I was sitting in the living room of my apartment with three of my cousins (who are siblings), watching television. Romeo and Aubrey are cisgender teenage boys (likely heterosexual), whom I don't see as often as I would like; Kathleen is a cisgender, heterosexual female cousin who is currently a college student with whom I have a good relationship. The boys were teasing each other, in the way that a lot of teenage boys do. Just then, I heard Romeo say to Aubrey, "Stop being so gay!"

I immediately reacted: "What did you say?" I couldn't believe my ears. I thought that my own family members would know what is acceptable and unacceptable to say. Didn't he know that comment would be offensive to his gay older cousin sitting 5 feet away?

Romeo replied, embarrassed, "Nothing."

"Did you call him 'gay'?" I calmly asked.

"Yeah, but I didn't mean it like that."

"Well, what did you mean then?" I started to notice that he was visibly uncomfortable, which made me realize that he did feel remorseful for saying what he said. But then I started to think that if he said it now, he probably said it in his everyday life with his friends. Perhaps he just knew to be politically correct and not to say it in front of his gay older cousin, but he didn't realize how offensive the term is.

Romeo then continued to tell me that he and his friends did say things like "That's so gay," but that it had "nothing to do with gay people." He shared, "We mean it to mean things that are bad or dumb . . . If someone was actually gay I would never call him that." Aubrey, my other male cousin, agreed with him, sharing similar sentiments and behaviors of his own friends.

"Okay, I understand," I said. "And I know you probably aren't intending to hurt a gay person's feelings when you use the word like that. But when you say things like that, you allow people to continue to think that gay people *are* bad or dumb or weird. And worse yet, if you say that in front of someone who may be gay but in the closet, you're basically telling them that you think it's okay to make fun of gay people. And maybe that person won't come out of the closet to you because they think you'll be homophobic, when I know that you are not."

Kathleen, the only female in the room, chimed in and shared how she stopped saying "gay" in a negative context when she entered college. She said that she made some LGBT friends in her dorm and that she learned how hurtful saying "That's so gay" is. I asked her to tell me about all of the things that she had learned. I smiled as she told me that she knows words like *transgender* and *pansexual* and *queer,* and I smiled even more as her brothers listened to her. The boys and I continued to talk about the term, and they promised me that they wouldn't use it in a derogatory manner anymore. They also promised me that they would try to correct their friends, too. We changed the subject and continued watching TV comfortably for the rest of the night.

Vignette Discussion

In all three of these vignettes, I attempted to illustrate the types of microaggressions that may occur, as well as the internal thought processes that can accompany them. In each scenario, you can notice each step. First, I had to decide whether the microaggression did indeed happen. Did my heterosexual male colleague really refuse to give me a hug? Did the news reporter really assume that I was heterosexual? Did my cousin really use *gay* in a negative context? Next, I had to question whether heterosexism or other bias was involved. Was George being heterosexist in not wanting to hug me? Was the news reporter demonstrating heteronormative bias in asking if I was married? Was my cousin's derogatory use of *gay* reflective of his heterosexist bias?

When I did recognize that the incident was a microaggression, I had to decide whether I wanted to reply. For the first scenario, I thought to myself, "I have nothing to lose" because we weren't in a situation where George had any real power over me. So, even if he became very defensive, I would not have to deal with him on a regular basis after that. If we were in the same work environment and I saw him on a daily basis, perhaps I would not have said anything, in order to avoid any potential tension. Perhaps I also realized that he might be willing to engage in a conversation with me because I knew that he is an educated person in a helping profession, which I would hope means that he would have good communication skills, good self-awareness, or both. Perhaps I also felt safe because my friend Yvonne was present and I trusted that she would come to my aid if the conversation needed another perspective. Given all of these factors, I decided to say something. However, it is important to acknowledge that if the circumstance were even slightly different, perhaps I would not have said anything at all.

In the second scenario, I chose to barely do or say anything at all. Sure, I answered the reporter's questions in a way that I felt comfortable with, yet I did not address her heteronormative biases at all, which means that she may continue to act on those biases with others in her life (and maybe even with other LGBT people). Perhaps I chose not to say anything because I realized that it wasn't worth it. I did not want to have any type of intense discussion on camera, particularly because I knew I had a full night ahead of me. Perhaps I also thought that a brief conversation about heteronormativity would not have made a difference in her life, and maybe she would have to learn about it another time. Finally, perhaps the cultural dynamics negatively influenced my ability to openly talk about being gay. Because Filipino American culture tends not to talk about LGBT issues (and sexuality in general), my internalized homophobia and remnants of Catholic guilt prevented me from being able to be open about my sexual orientation.

In the final scenario, I decided to confront the microaggression directly and immediately for a few reasons. First, it involved members of my family, whom I genuinely care about and whom I want to be aware about LGBT issues and power and privilege issues in general. Second, because I was the oldest person in the room (with the most education and the most material wealth), and because it was my home, I had the most power in the room, which likely meant that I felt comfortable leading a conversation about the topic. If the situation had involved an older person in my family, more educated than me, or with more material wealth than me, or if the conversation had taken place in someone else's home, then perhaps I would not have been as forthright with initiating the conversation.

In all three vignettes, I also illustrated different ways of handling certain situations. Although I did directly confront my colleague in the first scenario, I consciously tried to be as nonthreatening as possible (Yvonne or George can attest to whether they perceived it that way). Nonetheless, I did not raise my voice; in fact, I attempted to keep a lighthearted attitude, by keeping my demeanor just as it was before the interaction occurred. I imagine that if I became aggressive in any way, George could have used that as an excuse to dismiss my point. I also realize, as a person of color, that he may have viewed any aggression as being potentially threatening. So, I simply asked him directly about his intention and his behavior. Regardless of whether George was being honest with me about his intention, I walked away feeling satisfied that I assertively confronted him.

As described earlier, I did not take much action at all in the second scenario. But what I did try to do was maintain a level of humor by alluding to the fact that I was *definitely* not looking for a girlfriend. Sometimes, being able to laugh at certain difficult situations can be a healthy way of dealing with them. Although certain microaggressions have consequences that might not be funny at all, there are times when people use humor as a way to overcome some of the nonsense that they have to deal with. For example, I have told my friends about this scenario, and we all jokingly described what we could have said to shock the news reporter on camera (e.g., I could have said, "I don't have a girlfriend, but I do have lots of GIRRRL-friends!" or "I'm not married, but I am looking for a husband. Do you have a brother?"). I also know that my friends and I laugh about the horrible race-based pickup lines that men use to try to pick us up at the bar. For instance, when someone is curious about my race or ethnicity and asks, "So, what are you?" I tend to reply, "I'm a Taurus!" Sometimes, using humor can be a way of bonding with others who encounter similar microaggressions while validating individuals when they discover that they are not the only ones who experience those types of incidents.

Finally, the way in which I chose to handle the third scenario was again to remain calm and collected. I did not want to shame my little cousin, so I did not want to raise my voice, and I did not want to seem that I was punishing him. I tried to validate him by telling him that I didn't think that he was homophobic but that his behavior might be perceived that way. I also wanted him to hear my perspective, while also repeating what he was saying so that he knew that I understood his. Either way, I am happy that I was able to have a good conversation with him, and I only hope that he is able to have similar conversations with his friends who might say "That's so gay!" in the future.

Discussion Questions

FOR GENERAL READERS

1. What goes through your mind when you are the victim of a microaggression?
2. Do you tend to turn to others for support when you are the victim of a microaggression? If so, whom?
3. Do you tend to confront microaggressions when they occur?
4. Are there certain people that you avoid confronting? Are there certain people that you have an easier time confronting? How come?
5. What were your reactions to each vignette? What would you have done differently?
6. Have you experienced similar types of microaggressions in your life? How did you handle these experiences? Were you happy about how you handled these experiences?
7. Do you think that humor could be a beneficial way to deal with microaggressions?

FOR PSYCHOLOGISTS, EDUCATORS, AND OTHER EXPERTS

1. How would you handle a situation in which a client, student, or other disclosed to you that she or he has been a victim of a microaggression?
2. How would you handle a situation in which a client, student, or other accused of you being microaggressive?
3. How would you handle a situation in which a client, student, or other was microaggressive toward you?

Conclusion: What Can You Do?

7

t has often been said that academics and researchers, particularly those in the social sciences, "preach to the choir" because we conduct our studies and publish our findings for the rest of the academic community to see and read, without the rest of society ever really discovering what we have found. I have been guilty of this myself. While I know that I have published a good amount of academic literature regarding multicultural issues in psychology, my guess is that most of the people who read my work are other professors, other researchers, graduate students, and maybe a few other practitioners (e.g., teachers, nonprofit directors, student services personnel). Because of this, I sometimes wonder whether the community members that might be most influenced by our work know that we are even doing the work, or whether the work we are doing actually affects them. For example, do the young lesbian, gay, bisexual, and transgender (LGBT) kids who are bullied every day know that there are so many people who care about their physical

DOI: 10.1037/14093-008
That's So Gay! Microaggressions and the Lesbian, Gay, Bisexual, and Transgender Community, by K. L. Nadal

and psychological safety and are trying their best to advocate for their needs? Does the transgender person of color who is being discriminated against every day because of her or his race and gender identity know that there are people out there who are writing about intersectional identities and the psychological distress that comes from having dual minority status? Does the person who constantly hears phrases like "That's so gay!" at her or his workplace or school know that this is called a *microaggression*, that microaggressions are real and common experiences for LGBT people and others of marginalized status, and that microaggressions can have a negative impact on their mental health? I presume that most of these individuals have never heard terms like *intersectional identities* or *microaggressions* and perhaps never will.

Because it can be so easy for academic literature to remain stuck in the PsycINFO and ERIC databases, it is important for academics and researchers to make our work more accessible to the people who might actually benefit from it in the larger world. We cannot just write in academic jargon any longer and reserve our words of wisdom for academic conferences and college-level classes. We cannot just be happy when we get another manuscript accepted into a peer-reviewed journal, even if we know that it will help us with our tenure or promotion. We cannot simply encourage our graduate students to think critically about multicultural or social justice issues and hope for the best. If we are truly passionate about our work (as I know most of us claim to be), we have to make sure that our work somehow gets translated for and applied to the rest of society.

At the same time, whenever there is a social issue or problem that is introduced to the general society, it can be easy for people to simply think, "Well, what can I really do about that?" It can be easy to feel apathetic and to believe that there is not one thing that one individual can do to make a real change in the world. What really can I do to help homelessness? What really can I do to help cure AIDS? What really can I do to solve world poverty? Yes, these are huge issues that may be difficult to tackle alone as one individual. However, I am a firm believer that if every single person did her or his part, change would come. If every single person did one thing, big or small, perhaps we as a collective could make a difference and instill change. And even if that change comes slowly, or not at all, I am confident that we still need to be active however we can, because then at least we would be trying to do something, instead of doing nothing.

This chapter focuses on what *you* can do to help combat microaggressions. Some of these recommendations may seem too big to tackle, maybe because you might not have the power or resources to carry them out. However, some of these recommendations are not difficult at all. Sure, they may take some courage, and you may need to overcome a bit of discomfort. But if you know that you can take some action to make even a little bit of change in the world, wouldn't you want to take it? If you knew that you could make even a little difference to help an LGBT person to avoid a lifetime of psychological distress, wouldn't you want to make that difference?

Recommendations for Families

Families are where children first learn about their values and where they initially start to develop their personalities. Families are also where they receive their first messages about anything that is different (e.g., race, religion, gender, sexual orientation), and these messages may in turn have an impact on their values and personalities. Thus, parents who openly discuss issues of diversity and difference with their children from a very early age help their children to see the reality of power, oppression, and fairness in the world, and in doing so may prevent microaggressions before they happen (Nadal, Hamit, & Issa, 2010). When parents have dialogues with their children about discrimination, prejudice, and diversity from an early age, they can start with elementary lessons (e.g., how hateful words and behaviors can hurt others). They can also initially discuss diversity of all sorts—gender, sexual orientation, race, ethnicity, religion, ability, social class, and size—so that their children develop familiarity with other groups at an early age.

Some of the studies on race among Black and White children (and how they have been taught about race) are telling about the ways that race negatively influences the biased thoughts and behaviors of children and adolescents. Studies have found that African American children are likely to learn about race and racism from their parents at a very early age; furthermore, when African American children have more awareness of race, they have been found to attain better grades in school, have fewer behavioral problems, and develop healthier racial identities (see Hughes, Bigler, & Levy, 2007, for a review). On the other hand, White students who learn about historical racism in the United States during elementary and middle school are more likely to have less biased attitudes toward African Americans than those who do not (Hughes et al., 2007). Thus, it is clear that learning about discrimination from an early age can have its advantages for both those in the dominant group and in a target group.

Applying this knowledge to teaching about the acceptance of LGBT people and experiences can be helpful for children in two ways. First, if an individual is heterosexual, teaching her or him (as a child) to be accepting of all people regardless of sexual orientation or gender identity can help to reduce the biases he or she will have as an adult. Similar to the White children who learn about racism from an early age, heterosexual adults who were taught as children to accept LGBT people may be more empathetic, compassionate, and socially conscious. In turn, as adults, they may be less likely to commit sexual orientation and gender identity microaggressions altogether, less defensive and more open to admitting fault if they do commit microaggressions, and more capable of standing up against microaggressions when they witness them.

On the other hand, if a child is indeed LGBT or questioning, normalizing LGBT experiences can be validating and may lead to a healthier sense of self and a positive psychological outcome for the child. Similar to the African Americans who were taught about race from an early age, LGBT children who are taught to love themselves may develop good self-esteem, have a healthier sense of self, and perhaps even perform better in school. LGBT children who are taught that people who discriminate are the ones that are at fault may perhaps be alleviated of any shame and guilt that they may have acquired if they were taught that being LGBT was wrong or immoral. Thus, when they encounter a microaggression, they may be able to identify the event as being heterosexist or transphobic, be able to externalize fault instead of holding themselves responsible for the event, and have the coping mechanisms and strength to deal with the microaggression. Because LGBT youth are more likely than their heterosexual counterparts to feel isolated or lonely (Martin & D'Augelli, 2003), for their healthy development it is necessary for families to provide environments where they can feel accepted.

Parents and other family members must also recognize their own biases and how those biases may unintentionally affect those around them. For example, because many people tend to have assumptions about gender role norms and what is considered acceptable for boys or girls, they may act (or react), consciously or unconsciously, when another family member, particularly a child, engages in gender nonconforming behaviors. If a young boy wants to wear a dress and someone tells him, "Dresses are only for girls!" or "Be a man!" a message is sent that gender roles are rigid and that there is only one way for boys to be. Such a message can have a negative impact whether or not the child is transgender. But if the child is indeed transgender, the accumulation of messages like these can take a negative toll on the child's self-esteem, perhaps even affecting development and mental health. If the child is not transgender, hearing statements like these can reinforce the stereotypes that boys are supposed to be masculine and emotionally restricted. As a result, perhaps this child will not be able to express healthy emotions during adolescence or adulthood because he believes it would make him less of a man. So, instead of dealing with problems in healthy ways, he may turn to anger, violence, or substance abuse.

It is also important for parents and other family members to set a tone for what is acceptable language and behavior in the home. If a child calls another person a "fag" or a "dyke" as a synonym for "bad" or "weird," and a parent does not object, the child is unconsciously learning that such language and behavior is accepted not just in the home but in any environment. Because of this, addressing microaggressions like these in direct and straightforward ways can help to extinguish negative behaviors. Engaging in nonpunitive conversations when directly confronting microaggressions would be ideal, so that children can actually understand *why* they should not be using homophobic or transphobic language, instead of just stopping to be politically correct. For example, in Chapter 6, I shared the story of a conversation that I had with a younger teenage family member about his use of the term *gay*. While I easily could have punished him and told him to stop, I instead engaged him in a conversation so that he could understand my perspective and why use of the term was hurtful.

Dealing with microaggressions in families does not consist only of promoting safe and accepting environments for children, it also means confronting microaggressions by other adults in the family. Sometimes I hear people say things like, "Well, she's my grandma and she's 80 years old, so there's no use even trying to talk to her about it" or "Well, my uncle is really religious, so I just don't listen to him when he says homophobic things." While each family is different, with a huge spectrum of dynamics involved, allowing anyone in the family (regardless of age, generation, religion, or life experience) to make offensive microaggressive comments can create a hostile environment. If "grandma" or "uncle" or someone else makes these upsetting comments, perhaps you personally have the emotional strength to dismiss them, but what about the young LGBT teenager in the room who is struggling with her or his identity? If you do not say anything, that teenager may assume that you agree with the speaker, or that you at least are tolerant of her or his views. While you may not be able to change that person's mind, you can at least vocalize something like, "I know that this is your opinion, but I don't agree with what you are saying, and I'd appreciate if you didn't say things like this around the family." In doing so, you become an ally in the room, but you also create a safer environment where you minimize the potential for further microaggressions.

One last recommendation for families is to normalize the experiences of LGBT people. Instead of treating them as an outside group, perhaps getting to know more about LGBT history, LGBT communities, and LGBT experiences can help someone to feel more comfortable with LGBT people instead of viewing them as the "other." One study found that the more educated heterosexual people were and the more exposure they had to LGBT people (e.g., having friends who are gay and lesbian), the more likely they were to be allies (Fingerhut, 2011). With that being said, perhaps it might be beneficial to become more educated about LGBT people by attending LGBT community events, watching LGBT films, and reading LGBT literature. If your town or community offers it, take your child to a performance of the gay men's chorus or to a spoken word night at an LGBT poetry space. If such activities aren't available, rent a movie like *Boys Don't Cry*, *TransAmerica*, or *Camp*, watch it with your family, and discuss some of their reactions to the transphobia in the films. For religious families, a documentary like *For the Bible Tells Me So* (http://www.forthebibletellsmeso.org/indexd.htm) can be useful in helping to resolve conflicting messages about sexuality and religion. Educating family members about LGBT people and normalizing their experiences can be one way to increase nonbiased attitudes, which would in turn minimize their capacity to be microaggressors.

Getting to know LGBT people can be another way of increasing familiarity with the group, which in turn can minimize your own biases and the biases held by other family members. Introducing LGBT people to your family can foster their acceptance of LGBT people in general while also decreasing microaggressions that may occur within your home and your loved ones' lives outside of the family. By no means am I urging you to go out and make a token gay/lesbian/bisexual/transgender friend. Rather, I am suggesting that you foster friendships with LGBT people organically, which includes making a genuine effort to learn about their life experiences. Exposure to people or things that are different can be the best way to eliminate fear or trepidation.

Recommendations for Schools

Similar to families, school systems are among the first places that children learn about issues of diversity and difference. To foster optimal levels of acceptance while minimizing the potential for microaggressions toward students, teachers and other educational leaders may need special training to gain cultural competence in this area. Many systemic and institutional obstacles may need to be addressed. Does the school have an antidiscrimination policy, an antibullying policy, or both? Are these policies effective and conducive to creating a safe environment for their students? If the answer is yes, then perhaps more of the focus needs to be on enforcing these policies. If the answer is no, then perhaps the school community needs to revisit their present policies to ensure that they have the best interests of the children at heart. For example, if a school does not have an antibullying policy, then perhaps the Parent–Teacher Association needs to organize and advocate for it. As I mentioned in Chapter 1, nearly nine out of 10 LGBT students experience harassment at school, and nearly two thirds feel unsafe because of their sexual orientation. As a result, nearly a third of these LGBT students skipped at least one day of school in the past month, and those who were harassed regularly had lower grade point averages than those who were less harassed (Gay, Lesbian, and Straight Education Network, 2010). If children do not feel safe in their own schools, how can we expect them to learn and perform well? And if these policies do not exist or are not enforced, who is going to advocate for them if parents and teachers do not?

Most educational systems operate on a heteronormative structure and pedagogy, which then isolates LGBT students who are struggling with their identities. For instance, the federal education campaign "Abstinence Only Until Marriage" is one program that can be very isolating for LGBT students and that also enables the heterosexist bullying and harassment that occurs in hallways and classrooms (Fine & McClelland, 2006). Because children and adolescents are taught that sexuality is acceptable only in the context of heterosexual marriage, students may view heterosexuality and gender conformity as the norm, resulting in heterosexual and cisgender students feeling normalized while LGBT students learn that they are different or inferior. Thus, it is important for educators at all levels to recognize that if they want their LGBT students to feel included, they need to revisit the programs and pedagogies they are teaching and promoting.

Teachers can take many steps to create a safe environment to promote diversity and minimize microaggressions. I came across a website called *Understanding Prejudice,* which provided a very helpful list called "Tips for Elementary School Teachers" (http://www.understanding prejudice.org/teach/elemtips.htm). Their recommendations included the following:

1. Creating an inclusive environment (e.g., ensuring that classroom posters, pictures, books, music, toys, dolls, and other materials are diverse in terms of race, ethnicity, gender, age, family situations, disabilities, and so on);
2. integrating children's own experiences (e.g., avoiding a "tourist approach" to multiculturalism that limits diversity to holidays, special events, and history months);
3. addressing children's questions and concerns (e.g., directly answering diversity-related questions rather than side-stepping the question or changing the topic); and
4. dealing with discriminatory behavior (e.g., explicitly stating that you will not tolerate racial, ethnic, religious, sexual, or

other offensive jokes, slurs, or behaviors, and explain why. (Understanding Prejudice, 2011)

I appreciate this list because it offers practical techniques for teachers to use. I also believe that the list can be applied to all levels of instruction—middle school, high school, and even college and graduate school. Let me explain a bit more about why I chose these four specific tips. First, creating an inclusive classroom is important for children as a way of combatting the power and privilege that can be taught in classroom settings. Peggy McIntosh (2003) wrote about "White privilege" and how one of the privileges associated with being White is that one sees images of oneself everywhere (e.g., in magazines, television, picture books), which in turn allows one to feel normalized and perhaps unconsciously superior. Thus, it might be helpful for children to be exposed to literature that depicts LGBT people in a positive light so that (a) heterosexual children learn to be inclusive of LGBT experiences and (b) LGBT children do not feel excluded, which then may negatively influence their learning. When reading books to children about families, it might be useful to integrate books with same-sex parents or divorced parents or grandparents as the primary guardians, so that children who belong to these types of families can feel accepted and those who do not can become more educated that all types of families are common and equally as good as their own.

Second, I appreciated that the list included "avoiding a tourist approach." When diversity becomes an afterthought that is discussed only on special occasions, teachers may inadvertently communicate that it is not as important as topics that get integrated regularly. For example, teaching children about discipline is not something that is reserved for special occasions; it is something that is integrated into everyday curricula. Sometimes it may not be planned, and it may be something that the teacher must suddenly integrate into the lesson plan for the day. Sometimes teaching discipline may be inconvenient and something that teachers do not want to do. However, at the end of the day, teachers know that it is a crucial part of students' learning and development. Diversity should be taught the same way. LGBT examples can be introduced into all school subjects, including everything from math problems to reading samples to learning about social studies. Again, if LGBT people (and other groups) are taught about in this way, they become normalized, which in turn may reduce students' biases and prevent future microaggressions.

Furthermore, my thoughts about addressing children's questions and concerns directly and dealing with discriminatory behaviors are similar to how I feel they should be treated in the family. First, students should not be punished when they commit a microaggression; rather, it is important that they understand why it is hurtful for others when they make some comments. Second, being direct and vocal when a microaggression occurs is necessary because silence can convey acceptance, agreement, or tolerance. If a teacher hears a homophobic or transphobic slur being used, even by another teacher (Kosciw & Diaz, 2006), it is necessary that she or he address it right away to communicate that such language is not viewed as acceptable.

My final thoughts about how to decrease microaggressions in school systems are directed toward other students, particularly those who consider themselves allies to the LGBT community. When a child is being bullied, particularly for being LGBT, it can be extremely devastating for her or him to report such incidents to a teacher or principal for many reasons, including (a) the fear that bullies may retaliate and (b) the fact that she or he may have to admit to being LGBT. When a fellow student is being harassed or victimized by any other type of microaggression, a response by peers is meaningful for two main reasons. First, the peer is actually doing her or his part to create a safer school environment for everyone (and especially the victim). Second, the peer is demonstrating to the victim of this bullying that she or he is an ally who does not condone any type of victimizing behavior.

Recommendations for Workplaces

Workplaces are sites where microaggressions occur frequently. One of the difficulties here is that many factors may influence the ways in which microaggressions manifest and the ways in which people react. First, because of the power dynamics between employers and employees and coworkers, it may be difficult to confront microaggressions because one might be concerned about the security of one's employment, as well as other potential tension that may transpire. Second, because microaggressions are so subtle and innocuous, it can be difficult for an individual to "prove" that they were exposed to a microaggression, particularly if they want to report the incident to human resources personnel.

Thus, there are a few things that employers can do to promote comfortable and culturally competent work environments, while also preventing microaggressions from occurring. Perhaps the most important thing is to integrate education about microaggressions into multicultural competence training models in all workplace settings and other institutions (Nadal, Griffin, et al., 2010). Many organizations require newly hired employees to attend diversity training, which many individuals do grudgingly because they may believe that racism and other forms of discrimination no longer exist. Because of this, it may be more important for individuals to learn about microaggressions (i.e., subtle discrimination) and how their unconscious and unintentional biases and behaviors may negatively influence their professional relationships. Because microaggressions are likely to be much more commonplace than overt interpersonal discrimination, employees may be more open to this sort of discussion. Moreover, because diversity trainings tend to focus on race and often do not include issues related to sexual orientation or gender identity (Green, Callands, Radcliffe, Luebbe, & Klonoff, 2009), employers must ensure that LGBT people (and other marginalized groups) are included.

Employers and supervisors can cultivate awareness of microaggressions and the ways in which such instances can affect workplace dynamics, with the goal of preventing them and responding appropriately when they occur. For example, they can model appropriate workplace language and behavior. For instance, using terms like *partners* instead of *husbands and wives* can be beneficial in promoting an LGBT-friendly environment. Second, when microaggressions do occur, supervisors and other workplace leaders should learn to enact and model effective interpersonal skills in coping with them (e.g., responding in a nondefensive manner when confronted by an employee or coworker on microaggressive behaviors). Using some of the techniques that I discussed in Chapter 6 (e.g., using "I" statements, active listening) can be helpful in making sure employees feel heard and validated.

Creating an open environment in which it would be comfortable and safe to discuss microaggressions promotes an accepting work environment. For instance, when multicultural issues (e.g., issues of race, gender, sexual orientation) are integrated into staff meetings and other work interactions, employees may feel safe addressing microaggressions when they do occur. Perhaps open dialogue can be facilitated in which coworkers can voice their opinions about diversity issues. Either way, discussing microaggressions can be helpful both in promoting safe environments and preventing future microaggressions.

Finally, depending on the type of workplace, it may be possible for policies regarding microaggressions to be developed. While there are many laws and policies that protect against sexual harassment and overt discrimination (e.g., Title VII of the Civil Rights Act of 1964, which prohibits workplace discrimination on the basis of sex, race, color, religion, and national origin), many of these laws do not directly cover sexual orientation or gender identity and thus do not protect the rights of LGBT people (Berkley & Watt, 2006). Until such legislation is passed, it may be necessary for workplaces and other institutions to develop their own policies to prevent any type of discrimination against LGBT people. However, in terms of microaggressions, perhaps procedures and protocol can be created for dealing with incidents involving the more subtle forms of discrimination. If companies themselves do not want to implement these policies, perhaps unions or other employee organizations can advocate for these policies in order to protect LGBT employees in the workplace.

Recommendations for Neighborhoods and Communities

When I refer to *neighborhoods and communities,* I am speaking about any environment outside of the home, school, or workplace. These environments include public spaces (e.g., shopping malls, restaurants, public parks), religious institutions (e.g., mosques, temples, churches), and other organizations (e.g., sports leagues, community centers). Many of the microaggressions that occur in these settings may be those types of incidents that are spontaneous and that people do not know how to react to immediately. This is contrary to family, school, and workplace settings, where individuals may have time to react or at least have opportunities to deal with the microaggression at a later time.

In addition to all of the other techniques I have shared regarding families, schools, and workplaces (e.g., address the microaggression directly, create a safe environment), I offer two further thoughts about how to deal with microaggressions in your community. The first is one way to deal with microaggressions when you witness them. In this type of situation, it can be very helpful to be a support system or resource when others are victims to microaggressions. Validate their experience by telling them that you noticed it and that you believe it was motivated by bias. Allow them to share their thoughts and feelings about the incident, being a sounding board because they may or may not have someone in their own network to serve this purpose and because you were present and can attest firsthand to what they experienced. If the microaggressor is still present and you feel compelled to say something to her or him, you (as an ally, bystander, or third party) may be very beneficial in assisting the person to understand their behavior.

My second thought about microaggressions in the community is to prevent them from occurring. One way that you can do this is by educating others about microaggressions (Nadal, Hamit, & Issa, 2010). Because members of the general society, particularly those who are not familiar with social justice issues, may not recognize subtle forms of discrimination, they will also be unable to recognize the harm that microaggressions may have on people's mental health. Perhaps providing a definition of *microaggressions* and emphasizing how they are often unconscious and unintentional may be met with less resistance or defensiveness. Perhaps labeling something as a *potential microaggression* instead of as *racist, sexist,* or *homophobic* may be an easier way to start a dialogue about discrimination and prejudice (Nadal, Hamit, et al., 2010). If everyone educated everyone else about microaggressions, perhaps the word would spread and people would be better positioned to avoid engaging in them.

Recommendations for Government

My final set of recommendations is for changes in government and policies. Although it would be ideal for governmental officials and policymakers to promote social justice and instill changes themselves, it is important for constituents to advocate for these changes. Thus, this section provides recommendations for talking points that citizens can use when meeting with or writing letters to their elected officials.

EMPHASIZE COMMON GROUND

While politicians may have competing political ideas and stances, it is likely that most elected officials would believe in ensuring that the laws of the land are reflective of the best interests of all of the people. If all people, including those in the LGBT community, are to be treated as first-class citizens of this country, then all laws need to reflect that. If the civil rights of all people are to be protected, then this must include the civil rights of LGBT people too. Emphasize values like freedom, hard work, and right to an education, and describe how LGBT people share these common values. Discuss how the LGBT movement is similar to the fight that our American forefathers and foremothers had when they fled to this country in pursuit of freedom from religious persecution. Share how LGBT people are asking for the same access to life, liberty, and the pursuit of happiness as any other individual has in the history of the United States.

DESCRIBE CONCRETE HARMS

Throughout the book, many examples (both empirically based and anecdotal) describe how discrimination may have a negative impact on the lives of LGBT people. For instance, some of the research has described how LGBT persons are at higher risk for committing suicide (Waldo, Hesson-McInnis, & D'Augelli, 1998), as well as for developing an array of mental and physical health problems (Almeida, Johnson, Corliss, Molnar, & Azrael, 2009; Cochran, 2001; Cochran, Mays, Alegria, Ortega, & Takeuchi, 2007; I. H. Meyer, 2003; I. H. Meyer & Northridge, 2007). In previous chapters, I also described how LGBT people are not protected under the law (e.g., how it is still legal in 29 states to be fired for being lesbian, gay, or bisexual; how it is still legal in 35 states to be fired for being transgender or gender nonconforming). Furthermore, I shared how transgender people have a higher number of disparities than cisgender people, including higher rates of unemployment, poverty, and homelessness. Use statistics like these as a way of supporting your argument that discrimination on interpersonal, institutional, and systemic levels negatively affects LGBT people. Cite research articles, particularly those that utilize large sample sizes, to provide the empirical evidence that LGBT people have needs that are remaining unmet.

TELL YOUR PERSONAL STORIES

Personal anecdotes can be used to illustrate the many ways in which people are affected by oppression. Describe how biased and micro-aggressive legislation has had a negative impact on your life or the lives of your loved ones. For instance, express how being treated unfairly in the workplace has taken a toll on your mental or physical health. Discuss how not having the same right to marry the partner of your choice makes you feel like a second-class citizen. Articulate how being denied the opportunity to adopt a child makes you feel like your government is stereotyping you as immoral or deviant. And describe how you feel when public officials and policymakers do not stand up against biased laws and how their silence communicates acceptance, agreement, or tolerance of these laws.

Storytelling can also dispel any misconceptions that elected officials may have of the LGBT community. If political leaders believe that bullying is not any different than it was 20 years ago or that bullying does not affect LGBT kids more than it does heterosexual kids, then they may not see a need for antibullying legislation. However, if they hear a personal story about a child who has been bullied and the torment that she or he experienced, perhaps they would have different perceptions of the problem. Similarly, if government leaders believe that workplace discrimination does not exist or that LGBT people aren't profiled by police officers, then they likely will not feel passionately about endorsing laws or policies to prevent these injustices. However, perhaps a letter to your congressperson with a personal recollection of a time that a person was fired for being LGBT would help in passing legislation to prohibit workplace discrimination on the basis of sexual orientation or gender identity in all 50 states. Further, perhaps telling an elected official about the time you were stopped and frisked by a police officer for no reason could assist in elucidating the reality for many LGBT people.

PROVIDE A HISTORICAL CONTEXT

Educating elected officials about the history of the civil rights movement can be a helpful talking point. For example, when Proposition 8 was passed in California in November 2008 and banned same-sex marriage throughout the state, many government officials believed that it was the "will of the people" because the majority voted. However, when the majority holds an opinion that is not in the best interests of the minority, do they really have the right to make a decision for them? If the majority made every decision throughout the history of the United States, we would likely still have slavery, women and people of color would not be able to vote or own property, and interracial couples would not be able to get married. The majority of people did not want any of those things to happen, but because of wise judicial leaders who believed in civil rights for all, all of those laws were overturned.

Perhaps you might explain how we live in a country in which interracial marriage was once illegal. Talk about the *Loving v. Virginia* (1967) case, which stated that antimiscegenation laws (which prohibited marriage between people of two different races) were in violation of the 14th Amendment of the U.S. Constitution (http://www.ameasite. org/loving.asp). Providing this historical context can be useful in demonstrating that although some citizens may be unhappy about government decisions due to personal or religious reasons, sometimes it is the responsibility of government leaders to make decisions that will benefit all of society. Furthermore, point out how contemporary society may not even be able to imagine a world in which interracial marriage is illegal, and describe how a similar sentiment may be shared for future generations about same-sex marriage.

A Personal Message to the LGBT Community

To conclude this text, I send my personal message to my LGBT and queer sisters, brothers, and friends. I wrote this book in hopes that heterosexual and cisgender people will be more cognizant of the ways that hate hurts and negatively impacts our lives. I also wrote this book to honor all of you and your experiences. I hope that you can relate to some of the incidents that I describe throughout the text, and I hope that reading about some of these microaggressions will validate that you were not paranoid or irrational for feeling or reacting the way that you did.

As a community, we have gone through so much. In some parts of the world, it is still illegal to be us. Sadly, in other parts of the world, we could even be killed for just existing. Regardless of all of the hardships that all of us have had to endure, I hope that you have learned that there is nothing wrong with you. You are not evil or immoral. You are not an abomination. You are not psychologically disordered or deficient. In fact, you are perfect. You're amazing just the way you are. You are a firework. You are beautiful. You were born this way. I hope that you can accept that, and I hope that you can help me to teach this to all of those who are still struggling with knowing that.

With all of this being said, I think it is important for us to acknowledge two major things. First, there are some major divides in our LGBT community, which we sometimes do not want to talk about. There is discrimination between the men and the women, the cisgender and the transgender, the monosexuals and the bisexuals, the White people and the people of color, the able-bodied and people with disabilities, the older and the younger, and the list goes on. If you are part of the group with power or privilege in any of these combinations, I hope that you can recognize that you too, despite your own oppression and marginalization, can be an oppressor and microaggressor. I hope that you can be open to hearing when others point out your weaknesses, in the same way that you would want people to hear you when you are victimized. We can no longer deny that there are power structures (and struggles) in our LGBT community. We have to do our parts to address these issues if we really want to mobilize and advocate for our needs. This may require recognizing our own biases and stereotypes and engaging in difficult and tense dialogues. But I believe that these actions are necessary if we want to move in the right direction. And I believe that since we all know what it is like to be marginalized in the greater society, we genuinely want what is best for the entire community.

The second issue that needs to be addressed is the need for more activism and change in our community. As I have learned more about elderly LGBT people, I am deeply saddened to know that the very people who fought so hard for our rights and risked their lives for what they believed was right are the same people who are being overlooked, abandoned, and dismissed today. Perhaps the reason for this lack of honor and respect for elderly LGBT people is because the youth today have taken for granted all that the LGBT trailblazers of the past have done for us.

Because we now live in a world in which many of us have much more privilege and equality and in which many of us feel safe going out

at night and loving whomever we choose, it can be easy to be complacent. It can be easy to be apolitical and turn a blind eye to all of the real
issues that are negatively affecting the rest of our community. There are
still thousands of LGBT people in this country who may feel unable to
come out of the closet or who struggle with even identifying as LGBT.
Many of these people live in parts of the country where the closest LGBT
bar or organization is hundreds of miles away. Many of them are part
of families, ethnic groups, or religious communities that may disown
them (or potentially hurt them) if they admitted to who they really are.
There are also thousands of LGBT children who are being kicked out
of their homes on a regular basis. They sometimes run away to cities like
New York or San Francisco, where they think they will be accepted; but
because they don't have a job or education, they often end up homeless
on the streets or turn to drugs or sex work as a means of coping or survival. There are still LGBT people living in poverty, LGBT children who
are being bullied, and elderly LGBT people who are being abused. There
are LGBT immigrants who cannot get their documentation because
same-sex marriage isn't recognized by U.S. Immigration and Customs
Enforcement. There are still thousands of LGBT people who are addicted
to drugs and other substances. And yes, there are still thousands of LGBT
people who are getting infected with HIV/AIDS and other STDs on a daily
basis. Sure, we cannot get married or adopt children in most states, but
some of us are still struggling to even be alive.

I write all of this to you because I know that for me, it is very easy to
sit at my favorite bars in Chelsea or Hell's Kitchen, watch an entertaining
drag show, and then leave holding my boyfriend's hand as I walk down
the street. But I do know that there is so much more work to be done.
I know that I have to channel the spirits and convictions of the LGBT
pioneers and other civil rights leaders that came before us. If I indeed
want to "make it better" for future generations of LGBT people, then
I have to do more. And I hope you realize that you do, too.

In Solidarity,
Kevin Leo Yabut Nadal, PhD

References

Abbott, D., & Howarth, J. (2007). Still off-limits? Staff views on supporting gay, lesbian and bisexual people with intellectual disabilities to develop sexual and intimate relationships. *Journal of Applied Research in Intellectual Disabilities, 20,* 116–126. doi:10.1111/j.1468-3148.2006.00312.x

Ablow, K. (2011, September 21). *Don't let your kids watch Chaz Bono on "Dancing With the Stars."* FoxNews.com. Retrieved from http://www.foxnews.com/opinion/2011/09/02/dont-let-your-kids-watch-chaz-bono-on-dancing-with-stars/

Adams, E. M. (2005). Moving from random acts of inclusion toward LGB-affirmative institutions. In J. M. Croteau, J. S. Lark, M. A. Lidderdale, & Y. B. Chung (Eds.), *Deconstructing heterosexism in the counseling professions: A narrative approach* (pp. 21–28). Thousand Oaks, CA: Sage. doi:10.4135/9781452204529.n2

Adelman, M., Gurevitch, J., de Vries, B., & Blando, J. (2006). Openhouse: Community building and research in the LGBT aging population. In D. Kimmel, T. Rose, & S. David (Eds.), *Lesbian, gay, bisexual, and transgender aging: Research and clinical perspectives* (pp. 247–264). New York, NY: Columbia University Press.

Aggrawal, A. (2008). *Forensic and medico-legal aspects of sexual crimes and unusual sexual practices.* Boca Raton, FL: CRC Press/Taylor and Francis Group. doi:10.1201/9781420043099

Akerlund, M., & Chung, M. (2000). Teaching beyond the deficit model: Gay and lesbian issues among African Americans, Latinos, and Asian Americans. *Journal of Social Work Education, 36,* 279–292.

Alexander, B. (2010, October 2). The bullying of Seth Walsh: Requiem for a small-town boy. *Time Magazine.* Retrieved from http://www.time.com/time/nation/article/0,8599,2023083,00.html#ixzz21CKSNuJO

Alizadeh, M., & Johnson, C. A. (2011, November 28). UN to Iran: There are no excuses for denying LGBT people their human rights. *Huffington Post.* Retrieved from http://www.huffingtonpost.com/hossein-alizadeh/iran-gay-rights_b_1116837.html

Allen, C. (2011, October 11). *Actor Chad Allen's coming out story—In his own words.* Retrieved from http://dot429.com/articles/2010/10/11/actor-chad-allen-s-coming-out-story-his-own-words

Alliance for Board Diversity. (2008). *Women and minorities on Fortune 100 boards.* Retrieved from http://theabd.org/Women%20and%20Minorities%20on%20F100%20Boards_2008.pdf

Almeida, J., Johnson, R. M., Corliss, H. L., Molnar, B. E., & Azrael, D. (2009). Emotional distress among LGBT youth: The influence of perceived discrimination based on sexual orientation. *Journal of Youth and Adolescence, 38,* 1001–1014. doi:10.1007/s10964-009-9397-9

American Psychiatric Association. (1952). *Mental disorders: Diagnostic and statistical manual.* Washington, DC: Author.

American Psychological Association. (2009). *Report of the Task Force on Appropriate Therapeutic Responses to Sexual Orientation.* Washington, DC: Author.

Anti-Defamation League. (2001). *Hate crime laws.* Retrieved from http://www.adl.org/99hatecrime/provisions.asp

Anzaldúa, G. (1999). *Borderlands/La Frontera: The new mestiza* (2nd ed.). San Francisco, CA: Aunt Lute Books.

Aterovis, J. (2006). It ain't easy being green. *Edge Magazine.* Retrieved from http://www.edgeptown.com/index.php?ch=columnists&sc=Josh%20Aterovis&id=49396

Baker, J. G., & Fishbein, H. D. (1998). The development of prejudice towards gays and lesbians by adolescents. *Journal of Homosexuality, 36,* 89–100. doi:10.1300/J082v36n01_06

Balsam, K., & D'Augelli, A. (2006). The victimization of older LGBT adults. In D. Kimmel, T. Rose, & S. David (Eds.), *Lesbian, gay, bisexual, and transgender aging* (pp. 110–130). New York, NY: Columbia University Press.

Balsam, K. F., Molina, Y., Beadnell, B., Simoni, J., & Walters, K. (2011). Measuring multiple minority stress: The LGBT People of Color Microaggressions Scale. *Cultural Diversity and Ethnic Minority Psychology, 17,* 163–174. doi:10.1037/a0023244

Barr, D. A. (2008). *Health disparities in the United States: Social class, race, ethnicity, and health.* Baltimore, MD: Johns Hopkins University Press.

Beckstead, A. L., & Morrow, S. L. (2004). Mormon clients' experiences of conversion therapy: The need for a new treatment approach. *The Counseling Psychologist, 32,* 651–690. doi:10.1177/0011000004267555

Bell, M. D., & Vila, R. I. (1996). Homicide and homosexual victims: A study of 67 cases from Broward County Florida Medical Examiner's office (1982–1992) with special emphasis on "overkill." *The American Journal of Forensic Medicine and Pathology, 17,* 65–69. doi:10.1097/00000433-199603000-00012

Berkley, R. A., & Watt, A. H. (2006). Impact of same-sex harassment and gender-role stereotypes on Title VII protection for gay, lesbian, and bisexual employees. *Employee Responsibilities and Rights Journal, 18,* 3–19. doi:10.1007/s10672-005-9001-8

Bernstein, M., & Kostelac, C. (2002). Lavender and blue: Attitudes about homosexuality and behavior toward lesbians and gay men among police officers. *Journal of Contemporary Criminal Justice, 18,* 302–328.

Berrill, K. T. (1992). Anti-gay violence and victimization in the United States: An overview. In G. M. Herek & K. T. Berrill (Eds.), *Hate crimes: Confronting violence against lesbians and gay men* (pp. 19–45). Newbury Park, CA: Sage.

Bicks, J. (Writer), & Thomas, P. (Director). (2000). Boy, girl, boy, girl [Television series episode]. In D. Star (Executive producer), *Sex and the city.* New York, NY: HBO.

Bith-Melander, P., Sheroran, B., Sheth, L., Bermudez, C., Drone, J., Wood, W., & Schroeder, K. (2010). Understanding sociocultural and psychological factors affecting transgender people of color in San Francisco. *Journal of the Association of Nurses in AIDS Care, 21,* 207–220. doi:10.1016/j.jana.2010.01.008

Bjork, D. (2004). Disclosure and the development of trust in the therapeutic setting. In J. M. Glassgold & S. Iasenza (Eds.), *Lesbians, feminism, and psychoanalysis: The second Wave* (pp. 95–105). Binghamton, NY: Harrington Park Press.

Bordador, N. E. (2010). From exile to homecoming. In K. L. Nadal (Ed.), *Filipino American psychology: A collection of personal narratives* (pp. 193–199). Bloomington, IN: Author House.

Boswell, J. (1994). *Same-sex unions in premodern Europe.* New York, NY: Vintage Books.

Brady, S., & Busse, W. J. (1994). The Gay Identity Questionnaire: A brief measure of homosexual identity formation. *Journal of Homosexuality, 26,* 1–22.

Brice, A., & Sebazco, N. (2009). *Demonstrators demand justice in Puerto Rico gay teen's slaying.* Retrieved from http://www.cnn.com/2009/CRIME/11/19/puerto.rico.gay.slaying/index.html

Bronsky, M. (2011). *A queer history of the United States (revisioning American history).* Boston, MA: Beacon Press.

Broverman, A. (2009). *This Ability #39: Gay and disabled in Canada? Back in the closet for you.* Retrieved from http://this.org/blog/2009/11/03/gay-lesbian-disability/

Bruyère, S. M., von Schrader, S., Coduti, W., & Bjelland, M. (2010). United States employment disability discrimination charges: Implications for disability management practice. *The International Journal of Disability Management Research, 5,* 48–58. doi:10.1375/jdmr.5.2.48

Buhl, L. (2008, May 15). Stepping out of the shadows: GLBT seniors raise their voices. *Gay and Lesbian Times,* Issue 1064. Retrieved from http://www.gaylesbiantimes.com/?id=12208

Bulokhov, A. S. (2009). Claiming marginal sexual identity within mainstream religious culture: Soulforce Q Equality Ride Case Study. In A. M. Zuccarini & C. Zuccarini (Eds.), *Persons and sexuality: Interdisciplinary reflections* (pp. 45–52). Oxford, England: Inter-Disciplinary Press.

Bumiller, E. (2011, July 22). Obama Ends "Don't Ask, Don't Tell" Policy. *The New York Times.* Retrieved from http://www.nytimes.com/2011/07/23/us/23military.html

Burn, S. M. (2000). Heterosexuals' use of "fag" and "queer" to deride one another: A contributor to heterosexism and stigma. *Journal of Homosexuality, 40,* 1–11. doi:10.1300/J082v40n02_01

Burn, S. M., Kadlec, K., & Rexer, R. (2005). Effects of subtle heterosexism on gays, lesbians, and bisexuals. *Journal of Homosexuality, 49,* 23–38. doi:10.1300/J082v49n02_02

Capodilupo, C. M., Nadal, K. L., Corman, L., Hamit, S., Lyons, O., & Weinberg, A. (2010). The manifestation of gender microaggressions. In D. W. Sue (Ed.), *Microaggressions and marginality: Manifestation, dynamics, and impact* (pp. 193–216). New York, NY: Wiley.

Carrubba, M. D. (2005). Invisibility, alienation, and misperceptions: The experience of being bisexual. In J. M. Croteau, J. S. Lark, M. A. Lidderdale, & Y. B. Chung (Eds.), *Deconstructing heterosexism in the counseling professions: A narrative approach* (pp. 41–45). Thousand Oaks, CA: Sage.

Catalyst (2011a). *Women CEOs of the Fortune 1000.* Retrieved from http://www.catalyst.org/publication/322/women-ceos-of-the-fortune-1000

Catalyst (2011b). *Women's earnings and income.* Retrieved from http://www.catalyst.org/publication/217/womens-earnings-and-income

Cerny, J. A., & Polyson, J. (1984). Changing homonegative attitudes. *Journal of Social and Clinical Psychology, 2,* 366–371. doi:10.1521/jscp.1984.2.4.366

Chan, C. (1989). Issues of identity development among Asian-American lesbians and gay men. *Journal of Counseling & Development, 68,* 16–20. doi:10.1002/j.1556-6676.1989.tb02485.x

Chan, C. (1992). Cultural considerations in counseling Asian American lesbians and gay men. In S. Dworkin & F. Gutierrez (Eds.), *Counseling gay men and lesbians* (pp. 115–124). Alexandria, VA: American Association for Counseling and Development.

Chauncey, G. (1995). *Gay New York: Gender, urban culture, and the making of the gay male world, 1890–1940.* New York, NY: Basic Books.

Cheng, Z. (2004). Hate crimes, posttraumatic stress disorder and implications for counseling lesbians and gay men. *Journal of Applied Rehabilitation Counseling, 35,* 8–16.

Chernin, J. N., & Johnson, M. R. (2003). *Affirmative psychotherapy and counseling for lesbians and gay men.* Thousand Oaks, CA: Sage.

Chung, Y. B., & Szymanski, D. M. (2006). Racial and sexual identities of Asian American gay men. *Journal of LGBT Issues in Counseling, 1,* 67–93. doi:10.1300/J462v01n02_05

Church of Jesus Christ of Latter-Day Saints. (1990). *For the strength of youth* [Brochure]. Salt Lake City, UT: Author.

Cicotello, L. (2000). She'll always be my daddy. In N. Howey & E. Samuels (Eds.), *Out of the ordinary: Essays on growing up with gay, lesbian, and transgender parents* (pp. 131–142). New York, NY: Stonewall Inn.

Civil Rights Act of 1964, Pub. L. 88-352, 42 U.S.C., 78 Stat. 241.

Cochran, S. D. (2001). Emerging issues in research on lesbians' and gay men's mental health: Does sexual orientation really matter? *American Psychologist, 56,* 931–947. doi:10.1037/0003-066X.56.11.931

Cochran, S. D., Mays, V. M., Alegria, M., Ortega, A. N., & Takeuchi, D. (2007). Mental health and substance use disorders among Latina/o and Asian American lesbian, gay, and bisexual adults. *Journal of Consulting and Clinical Psychology, 75,* 785–794.

Comstock, G. D. (1991). *Violence against lesbians and gay men.* New York, NY: Columbia University Press.

Conerly, G. (1996). The politics of Black lesbian, gay, and bisexual identity. In B. Beemyn & M. Eliason (Eds.), *A lesbian, gay, bisexual, and transgender anthology* (pp. 133–145). New York, NY: New York University Press.

Cook-Daniels, L. (2003). *Lesbian, gay male, bisexual, and transgendered elders: Elder abuse and neglect issues.* Portland, OR: The Survivor Project. Retrieved from http://www.survivorproject.org/elderabuse.html

Corpus, M. J. H. (2010). I am a tomboy. In K. L. Nadal (Ed.), *Filipino American psychology: A collection of personal narratives* (pp. 187–192). Bloomington, IN: Author House.

Cowan, G., Heiple, B., Marquez, C., Khatchadourian, D., & McNevin, M. (2005). Heterosexuals' attitudes toward hate crimes and hate speech against gays and lesbians: Old-fashioned and modern heterosexism. *Journal of Homosexuality, 49,* 67–82. doi:10.1300/J082v49n02_04

Cox, L. (2009, April 17). *"Smear the queer": Gay students tell their stories.* ABC News Online. Retrieved from http://abcnews.go.com/Health/Mind MoodNews/story?id=7352070&page=1

D'Augelli, A. R. (1992). Lesbian and gay male undergraduates' experiences of harassment and fear on campus. *Journal of Interpersonal Violence, 7,* 383–395. doi:10.1177/088626092007003007

D'Emilio, J. (1983). *Sexual politics, sexual communities.* Chicago, IL: The University of Chicago Press.

DeJesus-Torres, M. (2000). Microaggressions in the criminal justice system at discretionary stages and its impact on Latino(a)/Hispanics. *The Justice Professional, 13,* 69–89. doi:10.1080/1478601X.2000.9959574

de la Luz Montes, A. (2003). Tortilleras on the prairie: Latina lesbians writing in the Midwest. *Journal of Lesbian Studies, 7*(3), 29–46. doi:10.1300/J155v07n03_03

de Vries, B. (2009). Aspects of life and death, grief and loss in lesbian, gay, bisexual, and transgender communities. In K. Doka & A. S. Tucci (Eds.), *Living with grief: Diversity and end-of-life care* (pp. 243–257). Washington, DC: Hospice Foundation of America.

Diaz, R. M., Bein, E., & Ayala, G. (2006). Homophobia, poverty, and racism: Triple oppression and mental health outcomes in Latino gay men. In A. M. Omoto & H. S. Kurtzman (Eds.), *Sexual orientation and mental health: Examining identity and development in lesbian, gay, and bisexual people* (pp. 207–224). Washington, DC: American Psychological Association.

Dixon, E., Frazer, S., Mitchell-Brody, M., Mirzayi, C., & Slopen, M. (2010). *Hate violence against lesbian, gay, bisexual, transgender, queer and HIV-affected communities in the United States in 2010: A report from the National Coalition of Anti-Violence Programs.* New York, NY: National Coalition of Anti-Violence Programs.

Don't Ask, Don't Tell Repeal Act of 2010, Pub. L. 11-321 H.R. 2965, § 4023.

Dover, K. (1978). *Greek homosexuality.* Cambridge, MA: Harvard University Press.

Dovidio, J. F., Gaertner, S. L., Kawakami, K., & Hodson, G. (2002). Why can't we all just get along? Interpersonal biases and interracial distrust. *Cultural Diversity and Ethnic Minority Psychology, 8,* 88–102. doi:10.1037/1099-9809.8.2.88

Dowson, T. A. (2006). Archaeologists, feminists, and queers: Sexual politics in the construction of the past. In P. L. Geller & M. K. Stockett (Eds.), *Feminist anthropology: Past, present, and future* (pp. 96–98). Philadelphia: University of Pennsylvania Press.

Dunbar, E. (2006). Race, gender, and sexual orientation in hate crime victimization: identity politics or identity risk? *Violence and Victims, 21,* 323–337.

Dworkin, S. H. (2005). Jewish, bisexual, feminist in a Christian hetero-sexist world: Oy vey! In J. M. Croteau, J. S. Lark, M. A. Lidderdale, & Y. B. Chung (Eds.), *Deconstructing heterosexism in the counseling professions: A narrative approach* (pp. 65–70). Thousand Oaks, CA: Sage. doi:10.4135/9781452204529.n9

Eskridge, W. N. (2008). *Dishonorable passions: sodomy laws in America, 1861–2003.* New York, NY: Penguin Group.

Federal Bureau of Investigation. (2008). *Hate crime statistics, 2007.* Washington, DC: U.S. Department of Justice.

Feinstern, R., Greenblatt, A., Hass, L., Kohn, S., & Rana, J. (2001). *Justice for all? A report on lesbian, gay, bisexual and transgendered youth in the New York Juvenile Justice System.* New York, NY: Urban Justice Center.

Field, J. (1993). Coming out of two closets. *Canadian Woman Studies, 13*(4), 18–19.

FIERCE. (2007). Cop watch: A film about police brutality against LGBT youth [Motion picture]. New York, NY: Author.

Fine, M., & McClelland, S. I. (2006). Sexuality education and desire: Still missing after all these years. *Harvard Educational Review, 76,* 297–338.

Fingerhut, A. W. (2011). Straight allies: What predicts heterosexuals' alliance with the LGBT community? *Journal of Applied Social Psychology, 41,* 2230–2248. doi:10.1111/j.1559-1816.2011.00807.x

Fitzgerald, L. F., Gelfand, M. J., & Drasgow, F. (1995). Measuring sexual harassment: Theoretical and psychometric advances. *Basic and Applied Social Psychology, 17,* 425–445.

Funders for Lesbian and Gay Issues. (2004). *Aging in equity: LGBT elders in America.* New York, NY: Author.

Garnets, L., Herek, G. M., & Levy, B. (1990). Violence and victimization of lesbians and gay men: Mental health consequences. *Journal of Interpersonal Violence, 5,* 366–383. doi:10.1177/088626090005003010

Gay and Lesbian Alliance Against Defamation. (2011). *Where we are on TV report: 2010–2011 season.* New York, NY: Author. Retrieved from http://www.glaad.org/publications/tvreport10

Gay, Lesbian and Straight Education Network. (2004).*The 2003 National School Climate Survey: The school related experiences of our nation's lesbian, gay, bisexual and transgender youth.* New York, NY: Author.

Gay, Lesbian and Straight Education Network. (2010). *The 2009 National School Climate Survey: The experiences of lesbian, gay, bisexual and trans-gender youth in our nation's schools.* New York, NY: Author.

Gilley, B. J. (2006). *Becoming Two-Spirit: Gay identity and social acceptance in Indian country.* Lincoln: University of Nebraska Press.

Glasgow, K., & Murphy, S. (1999). Success stories of a fat, biracial/Black, Jewish, lesbian assistant principal. In W. J. Letts & J. T. Sears (Eds.), *Queering elementary education: Advancing the dialogue about sexualities and schooling* (pp. 217–224). Lanham, MD: Rowman & Littlefield.

Glick, P., & Fiske, S. T. (2001). An ambivalent alliance: Hostile and benevolent sexism as complementary justifications for gender inequality. *American Psychologist, 56,* 109–118. doi:10.1037/0003-066X.56.2.109

Goodwill, K. A. (2000). Religion and the spiritual needs of gay Mormon men. *Journal of Gay & Lesbian Social Services: Issues in Practice, Policy & Research, 11*(4), 23–37.

Gosine, K., & Pon, G. (2011). On the front lines: The voices and experiences of racialized child welfare workers in Toronto, Canada. *Journal of Progressive Human Services, 22,* 135–159. doi:10.1080/10428232.2011.599280

Grant, J. M. (2009). *Outing age 2010.* Washington, DC: National Gay and Lesbian Task Force Policy Institute.

Green, D., Callands, T. A., Radcliffe, A. M., Luebbe, A. M., & Klonoff, E. A. (2009). Clinical psychology students' perceptions of diversity training: A study of exposure and satisfaction. *Journal of Clinical Psychology, 65,* 1056–1070. doi:10.1002/jclp.20605

Greene, B. (1994). Ethnic minority lesbians and gay men: Mental health and treatment issues. *Journal of Consulting and Clinical Psychology, 62,* 243–251. doi:10.1037/0022-006X.62.2.243

Griffin, K. E. (2010). *Empathy levels for victims of hate crimes versus non-hate crimes: The effects of victim, participant, and hate crime characteristics* (Unpublished master's thesis). John Jay College of Criminal Justice, City University of New York.

Guter, B., & Killacky, J. (2004). *Queer crips: Disabled gay men and their stories.* New York, NY: Harrington Park Press.

Haber, D. (2009). Gay aging. *Gerontology & Geriatrics Education, 30,* 267–280. doi:10.1080/02701960903133554

Hackell, S. (2011). Teachers tell bullied kids: Don't be so gay. *Halstead Gazette.* Retrieved from http://www.halsteadgazette.co.uk/news/south_essex_news/9337363.Teachers_tell_bullied_kids__Don_t_be_so_gay/

Hall, J. M., & Fields, B. (2012). Race and microaggression in nursing knowledge development. *Advances in Nursing Science, 35,* 25–38.

Han, C. (2007). They don't want to cruise your type: Gay men of color and the racial politics of exclusion. *Social Identities, 13,* 51–67. doi:10.1080/13504630601163379

Han, C. (2009). Chopsticks don't make it culturally competent: Addressing larger issues for HIV prevention among gay, bisexual, and queer Asian Pacific Islander men. *Health & Social Work, 34,* 273–281. doi:10.1093/hsw/34.4.273

Hankin, K. (2002). *The girls in the back room: Looking at the lesbian bar.* Minneapolis: University of Minnesota Press.

Harper, G. W., Jernewall, N., & Zea, M. C. (2004). Giving voice to emerging science and theory for lesbian, gay, and bisexual people of color. *Cultural Diversity and Ethnic Minority Psychology, 10,* 187–199. doi:10.1037/1099-9809.10.3.187

Hatzenbuehler, M. L., McLaughlin, K. A., Keyes, K. M., & Hasin, D. S. (2010). The impact of institutional discrimination on psychiatric disorders in lesbian, gay, and bisexual populations: A prospective study. *American Journal of Public Health, 100,* 452–459.

Herek, G. M. (2000). The psychology of sexual prejudice. *Current Directions in Psychological Science, 9,* 19–22. doi:10.1111/1467-8721.00051

Herek, G. M. (2007). Confronting sexual stigma and prejudice: Theory and practice. *Journal of Social Issues, 63,* 905–925. doi:10.1111/j.1540-4560.2007.00544.x

Herek, G. M. (2008). Hate crimes and stigma-related experiences among sexual minority adults in the United States: Prevalence estimates from a national probability sample. *Journal of Interpersonal Violence, 24,* 54–74. doi:10.1177/0886260508316477

Herek, G. M., & Capitanio, J. P. (1999). Sex differences in how heterosexuals think about lesbians and gay men: Evidence from survey context effects. *Journal of Sex Research, 36,* 348–360.

Herek, G. M., Cogan, S. C., & Gillis, J. R. (2002). Victim experiences of hate crimes based on sexual orientation. *Journal of Social Issues, 58,* 319–339. doi:10.1111/1540-4560.00263

Herek, G. M., & Garnets, L. D. (2007). Sexual orientation and mental health. *Annual Review of Clinical Psychology, 3,* 353–375. doi:10.1146/annurev.clinpsy.3.022806.091510

Herek, G. M., Gillis, J. R., & Cogan, J. C. (1999). Psychological sequelae of hate crime victimization among lesbian, gay, and bisexual adults. *Journal of Consulting and Clinical Psychology, 67,* 945–951. doi:10.1037/0022-006X.67.6.945

Hill, D. B., & Willoughby, B. L. B. (2005). The development and validation of the Genderism and Transphobia Scale. *Sex Roles, 53,* 531–544. doi:10.1007/s11199-005-7140-x

Hill, J. S., Kim, S., & Williams, C. D. (2010). The context of racial microaggressions against indigenous peoples: Same old racism or something new? In D. W. Sue (Ed.), *Microaggressions and marginality: Manifestation, dynamics, and impact* (pp. 105–122). New York, NY: Wiley.

Huebner, D. M., & Davis, M. C. (2007). Perceived antigay discrimination and physical health outcomes. *Health Psychology, 26,* 627–634. doi:10.1037/0278-6133.26.5.627

Hughes, J. M., Bigler, R. S., & Levy, S. R. (2007). Consequences of learning about historical racism among European American and African American children. *Child Development, 78,* 1689–1705. doi:10.1111/j.1467-8624.2007.01096.x

Hunt, B., Matthews, C., Milsom, A., & Lammel, J. A. (2006). Lesbians with physical disabilities: A qualitative study of their experiences with counseling. *Journal of Counseling & Development, 84,* 163–173. doi:10.1002/j.1556-6678.2006.tb00392.x

Hunt, B., Milsom, A., & Matthews, C. R. (2009). Partner-related rehabilitation experiences of lesbians with physical disabilities. *Rehabilitation Counseling Bulletin, 52*, 167–178. doi:10.1177/0034355208320933

Ibañez, G. E., Van Oss Marin, B., Flores, S. A., Millett, G., & Diaz, R. M. (2009). General and gay-related racism experienced by Latino gay men. *Cultural Diversity and Ethnic Minority Psychology, 15*, 215–222. doi:10.1037/a0014613

Institute of Medicine. (2011). *The health of lesbian, gay, bisexual, and transgender people: Building a foundation for better understanding.* Washington, DC: National Academies Press.

International Transgender Day of Remembrance. (2009). Retrieved from http://www.transgenderdor.org/

Johnston, M. P., & Nadal, K. L. (2010). Multiracial microaggressions: Exposing monoracism in everyday life and clinical practice. In D. W. Sue (Ed.), *Microaggressions and marginality: Manifestation, dynamics, and impact* (pp. 123–144). New York, NY: Wiley.

Jones, B. E. (2001). Is having the luck of growing old in the gay, lesbian, bisexual, transgender community good or bad luck? *Journal of Gay & Lesbian Social Services: Issues in Practice, Policy & Research, 13*(4), 13–14.

Jonsen, A. R., & Stryker, J. (1993). *The social impact of AIDS in the United States.* Washington, DC: National Academy Press.

Kane, M. (2011, August 31). Chelsea Lately resorts to transphobic humor to mock Chaz Bono. *Gay and Lesbian Alliance Against Defamation.* Retrieved from http://www.glaad.org/2011/08/31/chelsea-lately-resorts-to-transphobic-humor-to-mock-chaz-bono

Kaufman, G., & Phua, V. C. (2003). Is ageism alive in date selection among men? Age requests among gay and straight men in internet personals ads. *The Journal of Men's Studies, 11*, 225–235. doi:10.3149/jms.1102.225

Keller, R. M., & Galgay, C. E. (2010). Microaggressive experiences of people with disabilities. In D. W. Sue (Ed.), *Microaggressions and marginality: Manifestation, dynamics, and impact* (pp. 241–267). New York, NY: Wiley.

Koken, J. A., Bimbi, D. S., & Parsons, J. T. (2009). Experiences of familial acceptance–rejection among transwomen of color. *Journal of Family Psychology, 23*, 853–860. doi:10.1037/a0017198

Kort, M. (2005, September 13). Portia heart & soul. *The Advocate,* 40–46. Retrieved from http://www.advocate.com/politics/commentary/2005/08/29/portia-heart-amp-soul

Kosciw, J. G., & Diaz, E. M. (2006). The 2005 National School Climate Survey: The experiences of lesbian, gay, bisexual and transgender youth in our nation's schools. New York, NY: Gay, Lesbian and Straight Education Network.

Kotsopoulos, A., & Mills, J. (1994). *The Crying Game:* Gender, genre and "postfeminism." *Jump Cut: A Review of Contemporary Media, 39.* Retrieved from http://www.ejumpcut.org/archive/onlinessays/JC39folder/CryingGameK-M.html

Kozee, H. B., Tylka, T. L., Augustus-Horvath, C. L., & Denchik, A. (2007). Development of psychometric evaluation of the Interpersonal Sexual Objectification Scale. *Psychology of Women Quarterly, 31,* 176–189. doi:10.1111/j.1471-6402.2007.00351.x

Levitt, H. M., Ovrebo, E., Anderson-Cleveland, M. B., Leone, C., Jeong, J. Y., Arm, J. R., . . . Horne, S. G. (2009). Balancing dangers: GLBT experience in a time of anti-GLBT legislation. *Journal of Counseling Psychology, 56,* 67–81. doi:10.1037/a0012988

Lewis, J. A. (2010, August). *Gendered racial microaggressions among Black women: Construction and validation of an initial scale.* Paper presented at the 118th Annual Convention of the American Psychological Association, Washington, DC.

Lewis, R. J., Derlega, V. J., Brown, D., Rose, S., & Henson, J. M. (2009). Sexual minority stress, depressive symptoms, and sexual orientation conflict: Focus on the experiences of bisexuals. *Journal of Social and Clinical Psychology, 28,* 971–992.

Loiacano, D. K. (1989). Gay identity issues among Black Americans: Racism, homophobia, and the need for validation. *Journal of Counseling & Development, 68,* 21–25. doi:10.1002/j.1556-6676.1989.tb02486.x

Lombardi, E. L., Wilchins, R., Priesing, D., & Malouf, D. (2001). Gender violence: Transgender experiences with violence and discrimination. *Journal of Homosexuality, 42,* 89–101.

Loving v. Virginia 388 U.S. 1 (1967).

Lyons, C. J. (2006). Stigma or sympathy? Attributions of fault to hate crime victims and offenders. *Social Psychology Quarterly, 69,* 39–59.

Manalansan, M. F. (2003). *Global divas: Filipino gay men in the diaspora.* Durham, NC: Duke University Press.

Martin, J. I., & D'Augelli, A. R. (2003). How lonely are gay and lesbian youth? *Psychological Reports, 93,* 486.

Matthew Shepard and James Byrd, Jr., Hate Crimes Prevention Act of 2009, Pub. L. 111-84, 18 U.S.C. § 249

Mays, V. M., & Cochran, S. D. (2001). Mental health correlates of perceived discrimination among lesbian, gay, and bisexual adults in the United States. *American Journal of Public Health, 91,* 1869–1876. doi:10.2105/AJPH.91.11.1869

Mays, V. M., Cochran, S. D., & Rhue, S. (1993). The impact of perceived discrimination on the intimate relationships of Black lesbians. *Journal of Homosexuality, 25,* 1–14. doi:10.1300/J082v25n04_01

McConahay, J. B. (1986). Modern racism, ambivalence, and the Modern Racism Scale. In J. F. Dovidio & S. L. Gaertner (Eds.), *Prejudice, discrimination and racism* (pp. 91–125). Orlando, FL: Academic Press.

McDevitt, J., Balboni, J., Garcia, L., & Gu, J. (2001). Consequences for victims: A comparison of bias- and non-bias-motivated assaults. *American Behavioral Scientist, 45,* 697–713.

McIntosh, P. (2003). White privilege: Unpacking the invisible knapsack. In S. Plous (Ed.), *Understanding prejudice and discrimination* (pp. 191–196). New York, NY: McGraw-Hill.

McKeown, E., Nelson, S., Anderson, J., Low, N., & Elford, J. (2010). Disclosure, discrimination and desire: Experiences of Black and South Asian gay men in Britain. *Culture, Health & Sexuality, 12,* 843–856. doi: 10.1080/13691058.2010.499963

McLaughlin, K. A., Hatzenbuehler, M. L, & Keyes K. M. (2010). Responses to discrimination and psychiatric disorders among Black, Hispanic, female, and lesbian, gay, and bisexual individuals. *American Journal of Public Health, 100,* 1477–1484.

Meezan, W., & Martin, J. I. (Eds.). (2003). *Research methods with gay, lesbian, bisexual, and transgender populations.* Binghamton, NY: Haworth Press.

Meiner, J. C. (2000). Memoirs of a gay fraternity brother. In M. Adams, W. J. Blumenfeld, R. Cataneda, H. W. Hackman, M. L. Peters, & X. Zuniga (Eds.), *Readings for diversity and social justice: An anthology on racism, anti-Semitism, sexism, heterosexism, ableism, and classism* (pp. 299–301). New York, NY: Routledge.

Meyer, D. (2010, October). Evaluating the severity of hate-motivated violence: Intersectional differences among LGBT hate crime victims. *Sociology, 44,* 980–995. doi:10.1177/0038038510375737

Meyer, I. H. (1995). Minority stress and mental health in gay men. *Journal of Health and Social Behavior, 36,* 38–56. Retrieved from http://www.jstor.org/stable/2137286 doi:10.2307/2137286

Meyer, I. H. (2003). Prejudice, social stress, and mental health in lesbian, gay, and bisexual populations: Conceptual issues and research evidence. *Psychological Bulletin, 129,* 674–697. doi:10.1037/0033-2909.129.5.674

Meyer, I. H., & Northridge, M. E. (Eds.). (2007). *The health of sexual minorities: Public health perspectives on lesbian, gay, bisexual, and transgender populations.* New York, NY: Springer.

Minwalla, O., Rosser, B. R. S., Feldman, J., & Varga, C. (2005). Identity experience among progressive gay Muslims in North America: A qualitative study within Al-Fatiha. *Culture, Health & Sexuality, 7,* 113–128. doi:10.1080/13691050412331321294

Mobley, M., & Pearson, S. M. (2005). Blessed be the ties that bind. In J. M. Croteau, J. S. Lark, M. A. Lidderdale, & Y. B. Chung (Eds.), *Deconstructing heterosexism in the counseling professions: A narrative approach* (pp. 89–96). Thousand Oaks, CA: Sage. doi:10.4135/9781452204529.n13

Morrison, M. A., & Morrison, T. G. (2002). Development and validation of a scale measuring modern prejudice toward gay men and lesbian women. *Journal of Homosexuality, 43,* 15–37. doi:10.1300/J082v43n02_02

Morrison, M. A., Morrison, T. G., & Sager, C. L. (2004). Does body satisfaction differ between gay men and lesbian women and heterosexual men and women? A meta-analytic review. *Body Image, 1,* 127–138. doi:10.1016/j.bodyim.2004.01.002

Morrison, T. G., Parriag, A. V., & Morrison, M. A. (1999). The psychometric properties of the Homonegativity Scale. *Journal of Homosexuality, 37,* 111–126. doi:10.1300/J082v37n04_07

Mulcahy, R. (Director). (2009). *Prayers for Bobby* [Motion picture]. Beverly Hills, CA: Daniel Sladek Entertainment.

Murphy, R. (Writer/Director), Falchuk, B. (Writer), & Brennan, I. (Writer). (2010). Theatricality [Television series episode]. In R. Murphy (Producer), *Glee.* Los Angeles, CA: Ryan Murphy Productions.

Nadal, K. L. (2008). Preventing racial, ethnic, gender, sexual minority, disability, and religious microaggressions: Recommendations for promoting positive mental health. *Prevention in Counseling Psychology: Theory, Research, Practice and Training, 2,* 22–27.

Nadal, K. L. (2010a). Gender microaggressions and women: Implications for mental health. In M. A. Paludi (Ed.), *Feminism and women's rights worldwide: Vol. 2. Mental and physical health* (pp. 155–175). Santa Barbara, CA: Praeger.

Nadal, K. L. (2010b). Responding to racial, gender, and sexual orientation microaggressions in the workplace. In M. Paludi, E. DeSouza, & C. Paludi Jr. (Eds.), *The Praeger handbook on understanding and preventing workplace discrimination: Legal, management, and social science perspectives* (pp. 23–32). Santa Barbara, CA: Praeger.

Nadal, K. L. (2011a). *Filipino American psychology: A handbook of theory, research, and clinical practice.* New York, NY: Wiley.

Nadal, K. L. (2011b). The Racial and Ethnic Microaggressions Scale (REMS): Construction, reliability, and validity. *Journal of Counseling Psychology, 58,* 470–480. doi:10.1037/a0025193

Nadal, K. L., & Corpus, M. J. H. (2012). "Tomboys" and "baklas": Experiences of lesbian and gay Filipino Americans. *Asian American Journal of Psychology.* Advanced online publication. doi:10.1037/a0030168

Nadal, K. L., Davidoff, K., Davis, L., Wong, Y., Marshall, D., & McKenzie, V. (2012). *Intersectional identities and microaggressions: Influences of race, gender, sexual orientation, and religion.* Manuscript submitted for publication.

Nadal, K. L., Escobar, K. M., Prado, G., David, E. J. R., & Haynes, K. (2012). Racial microaggressions and the Filipino American experience: Recommendations for counseling and development. *Journal of Multicultural Counseling and Development, 40,* 156–173.

Nadal, K. L., Griffin, K., Vargas, V., Issa, M., Lyons, O., & Tobio, M. (2010). Processes and struggles with racial microaggressions from the White American perspective: Recommendations for workplace settings.

In M. Paludi, E. DeSouza, & C. Paludi Jr. (Eds.), *The Praeger handbook on understanding and preventing workplace discrimination: Legal, management, and social science perspectives* (pp. 155–180). Santa Barbara, CA: Praeger.

Nadal, K. L., & Griffin, K. E. (2011). Microaggressions: A root of bullying, violence, and victimization toward lesbian, gay, bisexual, and transgender youth. In M. A. Paludi (Ed.), *The psychology of teen violence and victimization* (pp. 3–21). Santa Barbara, CA: Praeger.

Nadal, K. L., Griffin, K. E., Hamit, S., Leon, J., Tobio, M., & Rivera, D. P. (2012). Subtle and overt forms of Islamophobia: Microaggressions toward Muslim Americans. *Journal of Muslim Mental Health, 6,* 16–37.

Nadal, K. L., Hamit, S., & Issa, M. A. (2010). Overcoming gender and sexual orientation microaggressions. In M. Paludi & F. Denmark (Eds.), *Victims of sexual assault and abuse: Resources and responses for individuals and families* (pp. 21–43). Santa Barbara, CA: Praeger.

Nadal, K. L., Hamit, S., Lyons, O., Weinberg, A., & Corman, L. (in press). Gender microaggressions: Perceptions, processes, and coping mechanisms of women. In M. A. Paludi (Ed.), *The psychology of business success.* Santa Barbara, CA: Praeger.

Nadal, K. L., Issa, M., Leon, J., Meterko, V., Wideman, M., & Wong, Y. (2011). Sexual orientation microaggressions: "Death by a thousand cuts" for lesbian, gay, and bisexual youth. *Journal of LGBT Youth, 8,* 234–259. doi:10.1080/19361653.2011.584204

Nadal, K. L., Issa, M.-A., Griffin, K., Hamit, S., & Lyons, O. (2010). Religious microaggressions in the United States: Mental health implications for religious minority groups. In D. W. Sue (Ed.), *Microaggressions and marginality: Manifestation, dynamics, and impact* (pp. 287–310). New York, NY: Wiley.

Nadal, K. L., Rivera, D. P., & Corpus, M. J. H. (2010). Sexual orientation and transgender microaggressions in everyday life: Experiences of lesbians, gays, bisexuals, and transgender individuals. In D. W. Sue (Ed.), *Microaggressions and marginality: Manifestation, dynamics, and impact* (pp. 217–240). New York, NY: Wiley.

Nadal, K. L., Skolnik, A., & Wong, Y. (2012). Interpersonal and systemic microaggressions toward transgender people: Implications for counseling. *Journal of LGBT Issues in Counseling, 6,* 55–82.

Nadal, K. L., Vargas, V., Meterko, V., Hamit, S., & McLean, K. (2012). Transgender female sex workers: Personal perspectives, gender identity development, and psychological processes. In M. A. Paludi (Ed.), *Managing diversity in today's workplace* (pp. 123–153). Santa Barbara, CA: Praeger.

Nadal, K. L., Wong, Y., Griffin, K., Sriken, J., Vargas, V., Wideman, M., & Kolawole, A. (2011). Microaggressions and the multiracial experience. *International Journal of Humanities and Social Sciences, 1,* 36–44.

Nadal, K. L., Wong, Y., Issa, M., Meterko, V., Leon, J., & Wideman, M. (2011). Sexual orientation microaggressions: Processes and coping mechanisms for lesbian, gay, and bisexual individuals. *Journal of LGBT Issues in Counseling, 5,* 21–46. doi:10.1080/15538605.2011.554606

National Center for Transgender Equality & the National Gay and Lesbian Task Force. (2009). *National Transgender Discrimination Survey: Preliminary results.* Retrieved from http://transequality.org/Resources/Trans_Discrim_Survey.pdf

National Gay and Lesbian Task Force. (2011). *Challenges facing LGBT elders.* Retrieved from http://thetaskforce.org/issues/aging/challenges

Noelle, M. (2002). The ripple effect on the Matthew Shepard murder: Impact on the assumptive worlds of members of the targeted group. *American Behavioral Scientist, 46,* 27–50. doi:10.1177/0002764202046001004

O'Brien, J. M. (2005). Sexual orientation, shame, and silence: Reflections on graduate training. In J. M. Croteau, J. S. Lark, M. A. Lidderdale, & Y. B. Chung (Eds.), *Deconstructing heterosexism in the counseling professions: A narrative approach* (pp. 97–102). Thousand Oaks, CA: Sage. doi:10.4135/9781452204529.n14

Orfield, G., Marin, P., & Horn, C. L. (Eds.). (2005). *Higher education and the color line: College access, racial equity, and social change.* Cambridge, MA: Harvard University Press.

Orndorff, K. (1999). *Bi lives: Bisexual women tell their stories.* Tucson, AZ: See Sharp Press.

Peel, F. (1999). Violence against lesbians and gay men: Decision-making in reporting and not reporting crime. *Feminism & Psychology, 9,* 161–167.

Peterson, B. W. (Writer), & Babbit, J. (Director). (1999). But I'm a cheerleader [Motion picture]. Santa Monica, CA: Lionsgate.

Phillips, J. C. (2005). Being bisexual in the counseling professions: Deconstructing heterosexism. In J. M. Croteau, J. S. Lark, M. A. Lidderdale, & Y. B. Chung (Eds.), *Deconstructing heterosexism in the counseling professions: A narrative approach* (pp. 115–120). Thousand Oaks, CA: Sage. doi:10.4135/978145 2204529.n17

Phua, V. C., & Kaufman, G. (2003). The crossroads of race and sexuality: Date Selection among men in internet "personals" ads. *Journal of Family Issues, 24,* 981–994. doi:10.1177/0192513X03256607

Pierce, C., Carew, J., Pierce-Gonzalez, D., & Willis, D. (1978). An experiment in racism: TV commercials. In C. Pierce (Ed.), *Television and education* (pp. 62–88). Beverly Hills, CA: Sage.

Pledger, C. (2003). Discourse on disability and rehabilitation issues: Opportunities for psychology. *American Psychologist, 58,* 279–284. doi:10.1037/0003-066X.58.4.279

Pope, A. M., & Tarlov, A. R. (Eds.). (1991). *Disability in America: Toward a national agenda for prevention.* Washington, DC: National Academy Press.

Rayburn, N. R., & Davison, G. C. (2002). Articulated thoughts about antigay hate crimes. *Cognitive Therapy and Research, 26,* 431–447.

Read, M. (2010, October). *Vince Vaughn defends gay joke in* Dilemma. Retrieved from http://gawker.com/5664522/vince-vaughn-defends-gay-joke-in-dilemma

Rivera, D. P., Forquer, E. E., & Rangel, R. (2010). Microaggressions and the life experience of Latina/o Americans. In D. W. Sue (Ed.), *Microaggressions and marginality: Manifestation, dynamics, and impact* (pp. 59–83). New York, NY: Wiley.

Rose, S. M., & Mechanic, M. B. (2002). Psychological distress, crime features, and help-seeking behaviors related to homophobic bias incidents. *American Behavioral Scientist, 46,* 14–26. doi:10.1177/0002764 2020 46001003

Rosenfeld, D. (1999). Identity work among lesbian and gay elderly. *Journal of Aging Studies, 13,* 121–144. doi:10.1016/S0890-4065(99)80047-4

Rostosky, S. S., Riggle, E. D. B., Gray, B. E., & Hatton, R. L. (2007). Minority stress experiences in committed same-sex couple relationships. *Professional Psychology: Research and Practice, 38,* 392–400. doi:10.1037/0735-7028.38.4.392

Rostosky, S. S., Riggle, E. D. B., Horne, S. G., & Miller, A. D. (2009). Marriage amendments and psychological distress in lesbian, gay and bisexual (LGB) adults. *Journal of Counseling Psychology, 56,* 56–66. doi:10.1037/a0013609

Rothman, E. F., Exner, D., & Baughman, A. L. (2011). The prevalence of sexual assault against people who identify as gay, lesbian, or bisexual in the United States: A systematic review. *Trauma, Violence, & Abuse, 12,* 55–66. doi:10.1177/1524838010390707

Schlitter, R. (2008, November). Gay officials who blazed trails. *Washington Post.* Retrieved October 5, 2011 from http://www.washington post.com/wpyn/content/article/2008/11/28/AR2008112802576.html

Schwartz, J. (2010, October 2). Bullying, suicide, punishment. *The New York Times.* Retrieved from http://www.nytimes.com/2010/10/03/weekinreview/03schwartz.html

Sears, D. O. (1988). Symbolic racism. In P. A. Katz & D. A. Taylor (Eds.), *Eliminating racism: Profiles in controversy* (pp. 53–84). New York, NY: Plenum Press.

Serano, J. (2007). *Whipping girl: A transsexual woman on sexism and the scapegoating of femininity.* Berkeley, CA: Seal Press.

Shelton, K., & Delgado-Romero, E. A. (2011). Sexual orientation microaggressions: The experiences of lesbian, gay, bisexual, and queer clients in psychotherapy. *Journal of Counseling Psychology, 58,* 210–221. doi:10.1037/a0022251

Silverschanz, P., Cortina, L. M., Konik, J., & Magley, V. J. (2008). Slurs, snubs, and queer jokes: Incidence and impact of heterosexist harassment in academia. *Sex Roles, 58,* 179–191. doi:10.1007/s11199-007-9329-7

Sinecka, J. (2008). "I am bodied." "I am sexual." "I am human." Experiencing deafness and gayness: A story of a young man. *Disability & Society, 23*, 475–484. doi:10.1080/09687590802177049

Singh, A. A., & McKleroy, V. S. (2011). "Just getting out of bed is a revolutionary act": The resilience of transgender people of color who have survived traumatic life events. *Traumatology, 17*, 34–44. doi:10.1177/1534765610369261

Smith, L. C., Shin, R. Q., & Officer, L. M. (2012). Moving counseling forward on LGB and transgender issues: Speaking queerly on discourses and microaggressions. *The Counseling Psychologist, 40*, 385–408. doi:10.1177/0011000011403165

Smith, S. D. (2004). Sexually underrepresented youth: Understanding gay, lesbian, bisexual, transgendered, and questioning (GLBT-Q) youth. In J. L. Chin (Ed.), *Psychology of prejudice and discrimination: Bias based on gender and sexual orientation* (Vol. 3, pp. 151–199). Westport, CT: Praeger/Greenwood.

Sohng, S., & Icard, L. (1996). Korean gay men in the United States: Toward a cultural context for social service practice. *Journal of Gay & Lesbian Social Services, 5*, 115–138. doi:10.1300/J041v05n02_06

Solorzano, D., Ceja, M., & Yosso, T. (2000). Critical race theory, racial microaggressions, and campus racial climate: The experiences of African American college students. *Journal of Negro Education, 69*, 60–73.

Stein, G. L., Beckerman, N. L., & Sherman, P. A. (2010). Lesbian and gay elders and long-term care: Identifying the unique psychosocial perspectives and challenges. *Journal of Gerontological Social Work, 53*, 421–435. doi:10.1080/01634372.2010.496478

Stern, K. (2009). *Queers in history: The comprehensive encyclopedia of historical gays, lesbians and bisexuals.* Dallas, TX: BenBella Books.

Stotzer, R. L. (2008). Gender identity and hate crimes: Violence against transgender people in Los Angeles County. *Sexuality Research and Social Policy, 5*, 43–52.

Sue, D. W. (Ed.). (2010). *Microaggressions and marginality: Manifestation, dynamics, and impact.* New York, NY: Wiley.

Sue, D. W., Bucceri, J. M., Lin, A. I., Nadal, K. L., & Torino, G. C. (2009). Racial microaggressions and the Asian American experience. *Asian American Journal of Psychology, S*(1), 88–101. doi: 10.1037/1948-1985.S.1.88

Sue, D. W., & Capodilupo, C. M. (2008). Racial, gender, and sexual orientation microaggressions: Implications for counseling and psychotherapy. In D. W. Sue & D. Sue (Eds.), *Counseling the culturally diverse: Theory and practice* (5th ed., pp. 105–130). New York, NY: Wiley.

Sue, D. W., Capodilupo, C. M., & Holder, A. M. B. (2008). Racial microaggressions in the life experience of Black Americans. *Professional Psychology: Research and Practice, 39*, 329–336. doi:10.1037/0735-7028.39.3.329

Sue, D. W., Capodilupo, C. M., Torino, G. C., Bucceri, J. M., Holder, A. M., Nadal, K. L., . . . Esquilin, M. E. (2007). Racial microaggressions in everyday life: Implications for counseling. *American Psychologist, 62,* 271–286. doi:10.1037/0003-066X.62.4.271

Sue, D. W., Lin, A. I., Torino, G. C., Capodilupo, C. M., & Rivera, D. P. (2009). Racial microaggressions in the classroom. *Cultural Diversity and Ethnic Minority Psychology, 15,* 183–190. doi:10.1037/a0014191

Sue, D. W., Nadal, K. L., Capodilupo, C. M., Lin, A. I., Rivera, D. P., & Torino, G. C. (2008). Racial microaggressions against Black Americans: Implications for counseling. *Journal of Counseling & Development, 86,* 330–338. doi:10.1002/j.1556-6678.2008.tb00517.x

Swim, J. K., & Cohen, L. L. (1997). Overt, covert, and subtle sexism: A comparison between the attitudes toward women and modern sexism scales. *Psychology of Women Quarterly, 21,* 103–118. doi:10.1111/j.1471-6402.1997.tb00103.x

Swim, J. K., Hyers, L. L., Cohen, L. L., & Ferguson, M. J. (2001). Everyday sexism: Evidence for its incidence, nature, and psychological impact from three daily diary studies. *Journal of Social Issues, 57,* 31–53. doi:10.1111/0022-4537.00200

Swim, J. K., Mallett, R., & Stangor, C. (2004). Understanding subtle sexism: Detection and use of sexist language. *Sex Roles, 51,* 117–128. doi:10.1023/B:SERS.0000037757.73192.06

Takahashi, R. (2007). Reflections on meanings and applications of social justice. *Journal of Ethnic & Cultural Diversity in Social Work, 16,* 179–188.

Trujillo, C. (1991). (Ed.). *Chicana lesbians: The girls our mothers warned us about.* Berkeley, CA: Third Woman Press.

Understanding Prejudice. (2011). *Tips for elementary school teachers.* Retrieved from http://www.understandingprejudice.org/teach/elemtips.htm

U.S. Census Bureau. (2007). *Current Population Survey, Table PINC-01: Selected characteristics of people, by total money income in 2006, work experience in 2006, race, Hispanic origin, and sex.* Retrieved from http://pubdb3.census.gov/macro/032007/perinc/new01_001.htm

Waldo, C. R., Hesson-McInnis, M. S., & D'Augelli, A. R. (1998). Antecedents and consequences of victimization of lesbian, gay, and bisexual young people: A structural model comparing rural university and urban samples. *American Journal of Community Psychology, 26,* 307–334. doi:10.1023/A:1022184704174

Walloch, G. (2004). Two performance pieces. In B. Guter & J. R. Killacky (Eds.), *Queer crips: Disabled gay men and their stories* (pp. 1–5). Binghamton, NY: Harrington Park Press.

Walls, N. E. (2008). Toward a multidimensional understanding of heterosexism: The changing nature of prejudice. *Journal of Homosexuality, 55,* 20–70. doi:10.1080/00918360802129287

Ward, J. (2008). White normativity: The cultural dimensions of Whiteness in a racially diverse LGBT organization. *Sociological Perspectives, 51*, 563–586. doi:10.1525/sop.2008.51.3.563

Watkins, N. L., LaBarrie, T. L., & Appio, L. M. (2010). Black undergraduates' experience with perceived racial microaggressions in predominantly White colleges and universities. In D. W. Sue (Ed.), *Microaggressions and marginality: Manifestation, dynamics, and impact* (pp. 25–58). New York, NY: Wiley.

Weiner, R. (2009, October). Hate crimes bill signed into law 11 years after Matthew Shepard's death. *The Huffington Post.* Retrieved from http://www.huffingtonpost.com/2009/10/28/hate-crimes-bill-to-be-si_n_336883.html

Wicke, T., & Cohen, R. (2009). A community responds to collective trauma: An ecological analysis of the James Byrd murder in Jasper, Texas. *American Journal of Community Psychology, 44*, 233–248. doi:10.1007/s10464-009-9262-8

Wiebold, J. (2005). Fluidity in the disclosure and salience of my identities. In J. M. Croteau, J. S. Lark, M. A. Lidderdale, & Y. B. Chung (Eds.), *Deconstructing heterosexism in the counseling professions: A narrative approach* (pp. 129–134). Thousand Oaks, CA: Sage. doi:10.4135/9781452204529.n19

Wilhelm, J. J. (1995). *Gay and lesbian poetry: An anthology from Sappho to Michelangelo.* New York, NY: Garland.

Willis, D. G. (2004). Hate crimes against gay males: An overview. *Issues in Mental Health Nursing, 25*, 115–132. doi:10.1080/01612840490268090

Willis, D. G. (2008). Meanings in adult male victims' experiences of hate crime and its aftermath. *Issues in Mental Health Nursing, 29*, 567–584. doi:10.1080/01612840802048733

Wilpers, B. (2010). *The trials of Oscar Wilde.* Munich, Germany: Grin Verlag.

Wilson, P. A., Valera, P., Ventuneac, A., Balan, I., Rowe, M., & Carballo-Dieguez, A. (2009). Race-based sexual stereotyping and sexual partnering among men who use the Internet to identify other men for bareback sex. *Journal of Sex Research, 46*, 399–413. doi:10.1080/00224490902846479

Wright, J. A., & Wegner, R. T. (2012). Homonegative microaggressions and their impact on LGB individuals: A measure validity study. *Journal of LGBT Issues in Counseling, 6*, 34–54. doi:10.1080/15538605.2012.648578

Yosso, T. J., Smith, W. A., Ceja, M., & Solorzano, D. G. (2009). Critical race theory, racial microaggressions, and campus racial climate for Latina/o undergraduates. *Harvard Educational Review, 79*, 659–690.

Index

About the Author

Kevin L. Nadal, PhD, is a professor, psychologist, performer, activist, and author who received his doctorate in counseling psychology from Columbia University in New York City. He earned bachelor's degrees in psychology and political science from the University of California, Irvine, and a master's degree in counseling from Michigan State University. He is currently an associate professor of psychology at John Jay College of Criminal Justice of the City University of New York, where he also serves as the deputy director of the forensic mental health counseling program.

Dr. Nadal's research focuses primarily on multicultural issues in psychology, in particular, those involving sexual orientation, race, ethnicity, gender, and gender identity. He is one of the leading researchers on the psychological impacts of *microaggressions*, or subtle forms of discrimination, toward people of color; lesbian, gay, bisexual, and transgender (LGBT) people; and women. He is the author of *Filipino American Psychology: A Handbook of Theory, Research, and Clinical Practice* (2011) and the coeditor of *Women and Mental Disorders* (2011). His work has been published in numerous journals, including *American Psychologist*, the *Journal of Counseling Psychology*, the *Journal of Multicultural Counseling and Development*, the *Journal of College Student Development*, and the *Journal of LGBT Issues in Counseling*.

Dr. Nadal was a board member of the American Psychological Association's Committee on LGBT Concerns, as well as a fellow of the Robert Wood Johnson Foundation. He is an executive board member of the Asian American Psychological Association (AAPA) and was the recipient of the AAPA Early Contributions to Excellence Award in 2011. He is a national trustee of the Filipino American National Historical Society (FANHS) and the current president of the metropolitan New York chapter of FANHS.

Dr. Nadal has been a keynote speaker for many colleges, universities, and organizations across the country and abroad. He facilitates diversity and mental health trainings with the New York Police Department and other nonprofit and corporate organizations. He is also a stand-up comedian and spoken-word artist who has performed across the United States since 2000.

Dr. Nadal enjoys spending his free time with his family and friends as well as traveling all over the world and meeting new people. His hobbies include singing karaoke, exercising, practicing Bikram yoga, watching Broadway shows, and walking the streets of New York City with his 7-lb black-and-tan Chihuahua, Christiano Tomas.